Tools for Improving Principals' Work

This book is part of the Peter Lang Education list.
Every volume is peer reviewed and meets
the highest quality standards for content and production.

PETER LANG
New York • Washington, D.C./Baltimore • Bern
Frankfurt • Berlin • Brussels • Vienna • Oxford

Tools for Improving Principals' Work

EDITED BY
JIANPING SHEN

PETER LANG
New York • Washington, D.C./Baltimore • Bern
Frankfurt • Berlin • Brussels • Vienna • Oxford

Library of Congress Cataloging-in-Publication Data

Tools for improving principals' work / Edited by Jianping Shen.
   pages cm
   Includes bibliographical references and index.
   1. School principals. 2. School management and organization.
3. Educational leadership. I. Shen, Jianping, 1965– editor of compilation.
   LB2831.9.T67   371.2—dc23   2012016212
   ISBN 978-1-4331-1574-5 (hardcover)
   ISBN 978-1-4331-1573-8 (paperback)
   ISBN 978-1-4539-0862-4 (e-book)

Bibliographic information published by **Die Deutsche Nationalbibliothek.**
Die Deutsche Nationalbibliothek lists this publication in the "Deutsche
Nationalbibliografie"; detailed bibliographic data is available
on the Internet at http://dnb.d-nb.de/.

The paper in this book meets the guidelines for permanence and durability
of the Committee on Production Guidelines for Book Longevity
of the Council of Library Resources.

© 2012 Peter Lang Publishing, Inc., New York
29 Broadway, 18th floor, New York, NY 10006
www.peterlang.com

All rights reserved.
Reprint or reproduction, even partially, in all forms such as microfilm,
xerography, microfiche, microcard, and offset strictly prohibited.

Printed in the United States of America

Contents

1. The Need for Tools to Improve Principalship: An Introduction   1
   Jianping Shen

2. Vanderbilt Assessment of Leadership in Education: 13
   A New Tool for Principal Evaluation and Professional Growth
   Andrew C. Porter, Joseph Murphy, Ellen Goldring, Stephen N. Elliott, & Xiu Chen Cravens

3. A Data-Driven Approach to Assess and Develop Instructional   47
   Leadership with the PIMRS
   Philip Hallinger

4. Identifying Leadership and Organizational Processes Related   71
   to School Outcomes and Improvement: Validating an Instrument
   Ronald H. Heck & George A. Marcoulides

5. Data-Informed Decision-Making on High-Impact Strategies: 107
   An Instrument for Improving Principalship
   Jianping Shen, Van E. Cooley, Xin Ma, Patricia L. Reeves, Walter L. Burt, J. Mark Rainey, & Wenhui Yuan

6. Data-Informed Decision-Making: A Guidebook for Data Points 137
   and Analyses for School Improvement
   Jianping Shen, Van E. Cooley, Gary Marx, Elizabeth Kirby,
   & David E. Whale

7. The Leadership Performance Planning Worksheet (LPPW): 169
   A Development Tool for Early Career School Leaders
   Lynn M. Scott

8. The SAM Process: Changing Principals and Their Relationships 201
   with Teachers via Time/Task Analysis™ and TimeTrack™
   Mark Shellinger

9. SREB's *High Schools That Work* School Improvement Model 211
   James E. Bottoms & Paula E. Egelson

   Index 235

• 1 •

The Need FOR Tools TO Improve Principalship

An Introduction

JIANPING SHEN

Researchers have documented the importance of principalship in improving school in general and in enhancing student achievement in particular (e.g., Bossert, Dwyer, Rowan, & Lee, 1982; Hallinger & Heck, 1996; Louis, Leithwood, Wahlstrom, & Anderson, 2010; Marzano, Waters, & McNulty, 2005; Waters & Kingston, 2005). Given the emphasis on the importance of principalship, there is a need for tools to improve principalship, particularly those tools emphasizing principalship dimensions associated with student achievement. Given the accountability movement with a particular focus on student achievement and the advent of the evaluation era (including evaluation of principals), the need for tools for improving principalship is even more urgent. In this edited volume, authors present tools with a particular focus on improving learning-centered principalship.

The Importance of Principalship

According to Louis et al. (2010), leadership is found to be second only to classroom instruction among school-related factors that affect student learning. In the literature, there have been efforts to quantify the association between principal leadership, on one hand, and student achievement and other school outcomes, on the other. As to the association between principal leadership and student achievement, Marzano et al. (2005) conducted a meta-analysis of 70 empirical studies published in the prior 25 years and found that the simple bivariate correlation between principal leadership and student achievement at the school level, corrected for attenuation, is .25. In other words, principal leadership accounts for about 6.25% of the variance in student achievement at the school level. Still some other studies took the mediated model by which school principalship is associated with school process, which is, in turn, associated with student outcome. For example, Newmann, Rutter, and Smith (1989) found that measures of principal behaviors can have standardized regression coefficients up to 0.38 on teachers' sense of efficacy, community and expectation, indicating small but significant effects of principal behaviors on the school process. Researchers found that school organizational factors, many of which are reflections of principal leadership, account for about 10% to 38% of the total variance in teacher efficacy, community and expectation (Newmann, Rutter, & Smith, 1989). Later, Barnett, McCormick and Conners (2000) suggested that teacher-related outcomes show an intra-class correlation up to 25%.

The studies by Newmann et al. (1989) and Barnett et al. (2000), with a focus on the association between principal behavior and teacher efficacy, community and expectation, modeled the first path in the mediated model with the assumption that these school process variables will impact student achievement. The chapter by Heck and Marcoulides in this book goes a step further to model simultaneously not only how principal leadership impacts school process, but also how school process, in turn, impacts school performance. They found that leadership is indirectly associated with school performance via school climate and teacher attitudes. The standardized path coefficients were .71 from leadership to school climate, .33 from school climate to teacher attitudes, and .34 from teacher attitudes to school performance, with an indirect effect of .08 from leadership to school performance. Various effect sizes in the literature indicate a significant role for principals in improving schools, in general, and student achievement, in particular.

The literature not only indicates *the extent* to which principals impact the school process and student outcome, but also reveals *how* principal leadership impacts student achievement and other school outcomes. For example, Hallinger and Heck (1996) concluded, based on a large scale of literature review, that "principal leadership that makes a difference is aimed toward influencing internal school processes that are directly linked to student learning" (p. 38). Wahlstrom, Louise, Leithwood, & Anderson (2010), in their most recent comprehensive study of school leadership, concluded that the common core of basic leadership practices includes "setting directions," "developing people," "redesigning the organization," and "managing the instructional program." Through empirical research, we know much about the principalship (Shen & Associates, 2005), particularly the dimensions of principals' work that affect student learning. The knowledge on both the effect size of principalship and how principalship impacts school process and student achievement is the foundation for developing tools to improve principalship.

The Need for Tools for Improving Principalship

When the Wallace Foundation launched its national initiative on educational leadership, the Foundation and its grantees realized that there was a need for evidence-based tools for improving principalship. Therefore, among its funding priorities, the Foundation funded the development and validation of some of the tools collected in this book, including Vanderbilt Assessment of Leadership in Education (VAL-ED) that focuses on the intersection of 6 processes and 6 core competence areas, the Leadership Performance Planning Worksheet (LPPW) that emphasizes leadership behaviors for new principals, and SAM that tracks and helps analyze how principals spend their time. The two instruments on data-informed decision-making in this book were also developed as part of the initiative in Michigan funded by the Wallace Foundation. Although funded by the Foundation, all possible errors associated with the tools are the sole responsibility of the authors'. Other tools not funded by Wallace Foundation are also included in this book.

A Preview of the Tools Included in the Book

Vanderbilt Assessment of Leadership in Education (VAL-ED)

VAL-ED is a principal evaluation tool developed by Porter and his colleagues. The underlying framework for VAL-ED is illustrated in Table 1 (Goldring, Cravens, Murphy, Porter, Elliott, & Carson, 2009). It consists of six core components and six key processes, resulting in a combination of 36 cells. Porter and his colleagues detailed in Chapter 2 (a) the rigorous process of how they have developed this particular tool and (b) the alignment of VAL-ED with Interstate School Leaders Licensure Consortium (ISLLC) standards. The tool has sound psychometric properties in terms of construct validity and internal consistency validity, among others.

As Porter and his colleagues summarized in Chapter 2, the following statements captured the characteristics of VAL-Ed:

> First, the VAL-ED uses *360-degree feedback*, from teachers, principals, and supervisors. Second, the content of the proposed assessment is *learning-centered* leadership behaviors, behaviors that are related to increases in student achievement. Third, the assessment

TABLE 1. The VAL-ED's Framework of Core Components and Key Processes

Core Components	Key Processes					
	Planning	Implementing	Supporting	Advocating	Communicating	Monitoring
High Standards for Student Learning						
Rigorous Curriculum (content)						
Quality Instruction (pedagogy)						
Culture of Learning & Professional Behavior						
Connections to External Communities						
Performance Accountability						

*From Goldring et al. (2009), p. 23.

is of leadership *behaviors*, not knowledge, dispositions, or personal characteristics of leaders. Fourth, the VAL-ED requires respondents to identify *evidence* on which they are basing their assessment of principal behaviors. Fifth, the *psychometric properties* are clearly documented and the authors have an ongoing program of research that will continue to yield evidence concerning the reliability and validity of VAL-ED scores.

Principal Instructional Management Rating Scale (PIMRS)

Hallinger's Principal Instructional Management Rating Scale (PIMRS) is among the first to measure principals' instructional leadership and it has been widely used over the years. As a matter of fact, the author just reviewed how the instrument was used in dissertation over three decades (Hallinger, 2011). As the author argued in Chapter 3, among various leadership approaches such as teacher leadership and distributed leadership, instructional leadership has shown the most significant impact on student learning. The underlying conceptual framework for PIMRS is as in Table 2, including three dimensions and 10 subscales.

Over the years, validation studies have been conducted to support the instrument's reliability, face validity, content validity and discriminant validity. Based on many years of using the tool, the author discussed barriers to instructional leadership,

TABLE 2. Dimensions and Subscales of PIMRS

Dimension	Subscale
Defining the school mission	Frames the school's goals Communicates the school's goals
Managing the instructional program	Coordinates the curriculum Supervises and evaluates instruction Monitors student progress
Developing the school learning climate program	Protects instructional time Provides incentives for teachers Provides incentives for learning Promotes professional development Maintains high visibility

*Adapted from Hallinger's Chapter 3 in this book.

including (a) the assumption that principals have expertise in curriculum and instruction, (b) the professional norm that instruction is in the teacher's domain of influence, (c) the system's expectation for principals that emphasize responsibilities other than instructional leadership, and (d) the many roles that principals play that make it very difficult for their instructional leadership. The author illustrated how to use the instrument, and makes the distinction among the purposes of using the tool for self-assessment, professional development, and evaluation.

Organization of the School and Teacher Satisfaction with Their Work Environment (OSTSWE)

As part of a line of research on how leadership and organizational process influence school outcomes, Heck and Marcoulides developed an instrument entitled Organization of the School and Teacher Satisfaction with Their Work Environment (OSTSWE), shown as an appendix in Chapter 4. Figure 1 illustrates the conceptual framework underlying their instrument as the authors illustrated:

Through testing using various samples, Heck and Marcoulides reported in Chapter 4 that, among others, leadership has an indirect effect on school outcome via school climate and teacher attitudes and behaviors. Their findings have implications, among others, for assessing leadership, school climate, and teacher attitudes, as these are directly or indirectly related to school outcomes. Therefore, subscales and items related to leadership, organizational climate, and teacher attitudes and behaviors could be used to collect data for improving the principalship. The following subscales and items are particularly useful for the purpose of improving the principalship: (a) *leadership processes* including three subscales—use of available resources

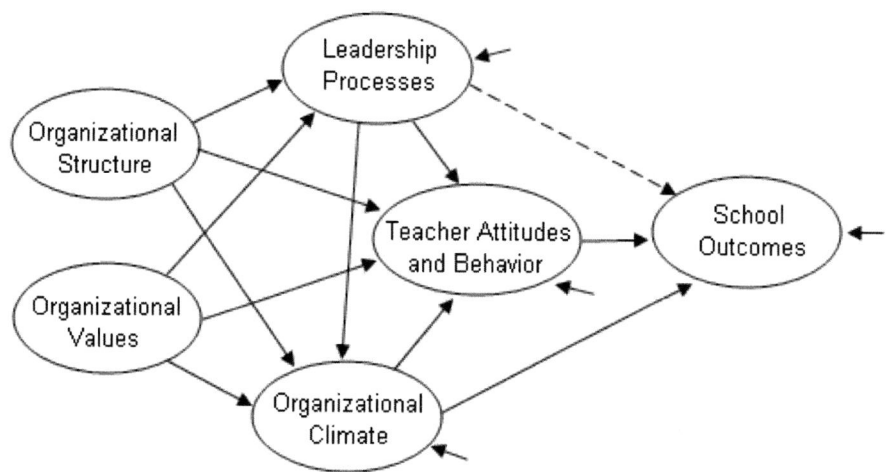

FIGURE 1. Proposed model of variables affecting school outcomes.
*Adapted from Heck's Chapter 4 in this book.

(items 6, 7 and 46, alpha = .70), principal responsiveness (items 11–14, alpha = .86), and leadership (items 24–30, alpha = .79); (b) *organizational climate* including three subscales—social relationships (items 40–45, alpha = .75), communication processes (items 8–10, alpha = .77), and teacher collegiality (items 20–23, alpha = .79); and (c) *teacher attitudes and behaviors* including two subscales—teachers' perceptions of student needs and skills (items 35, 36, 47, alpha = .73) and perceptions about parent support and involvement (items 31, 38, 39, alpha = .77).

Data-Informed Decision-Making on High-Impact Strategies: An Instrument for Principals

In Chapter 5 Shen and his colleagues connected three streams of literature to develop an instrument for measuring the degree to which principals engage in data-informed decision-making on high-impact strategies that are empirically associated with higher student achievement. The three literature streams are (a) the importance of data-informed decision-making, (b) the role of principals in school effectiveness, and (c) high-impact strategies for raising student achievement. They used Marzano's (2003) 11 high-impact strategies as a framework to develop items. Therefore, the instrument measures the extent to which principals engage in data-informed decision-making for the 11 high-impact strategies in Table 3 that are associated with higher student achievement.

TABLE 3. Marzano's Framework as a Foundation for Instrument Development

School-level Factor
    1. Guaranteed and viable curriculum (Items 1–4)
    2. Challenging goals and effective feedback (Items 5–8)
    3. Parent and community involvement (Items 9–12)
    4. Safe and orderly environment (Items 13–16)
    5. Collegiality and professionalism (Items 17–20)

Teacher-level Factor
    6. Instructional strategies (Items 21–23)
    7. Classroom management (Items 24–26)
    8. Classroom curriculum design (Items 27–30)

Student-level Factor
    9. Home environment (Items 31–34)
    10. Learned intelligence (Items 35–38)
    11. Student motivation (Items 39–42)

*From Marzano (2003).

Shen and his colleagues collected data from principals and teachers to validate the instrument. In terms of the reliability (internal consistency measured by Cronbach's alpha), the reliability indices range from 0.90 to 0.96 for the subscales and 0.98 for the whole instrument based on data collected from principals, and vary from 0.83 to 0.91 for the subscales and 0.98 for the whole instrument based on data collected from teachers. Therefore, the instrument's reliability was validated by data collected from both principals and teachers. In terms of validity as measured by factorial validity, based on the data collected from principals, the comparative fit index (CFI) is 0.91 and standardized root mean square residual (SRMR) is 0.05; based on data collected from teachers, the CFI is 0.93 and SRMR is 0.05. Generally speaking, CFI greater than 0.90 and SRMR less than 0.08 are considered a good fit between the data and the model. Thus, the instrument's factorial validity is supported by the data.

Therefore, the instrument is validated for use by both principals themselves and their teachers. The instrument could be used for principals' self-assessment and improvement. Principals could look at the data to identify their strengths and weaknesses, compare the ratings from themselves and their teachers to identify the consistency and discrepancy, and track the growth over time.

Data-Informed Decision-Making: A Guidebook for Data Points and Analyses for School Improvement

Along with the accountability system, large amounts of data have been generated for student achievement, school process, and student background data, among others. Data-informed decision-making has also been promoted as a mechanism for school renewal. However, the issue of "data literacy"—i.e., how to use data for data-informed decision-making and school improvement—has been a challenge for the field. Both the teacher education program and the educational leadership program have much room for improvement in terms of developing "data literacy."

As part of a project working with 16 principals, Shen and his colleagues developed, in a partnership between university personnel and practitioners, the data-informed decision-making guidebook for school improvement teams. The guidebook was based on Michigan Department of Education's (2005) Michigan School Improvement Framework, which focuses on the strands and standards in Table 4.

TABLE 4. Michigan School Improvement Framework at a Glance

Strand	Standard
1. Teaching for Learning	1.1. Curriculum 1.2. Instruction 1.3. Assessment
2. Leadership	2.1. Instructional Leadership 2.2. Shared Leadership 2.3. Operational and Resource Management
3. Personnel and Professional Development	3.1. Personnel Qualifications 3.2. Professional Development
4. School and Community Relations	4.1. Parent/Family Involvement 4.2. Community Involvement
5. Data and Information Management	5.1. Data Management 5.2. Information Management

*Adapted from Michigan Department of Education (2005).

The Michigan framework has benchmarks under each standard with a total of five strands, 12 standards, and 26 benchmarks. The guidebook provides two illustrations for each of the benchmarks in the Michigan School Improvement Framework in terms of (a) what data to use and (b) how to analyze the data to inform decisions for school improvement. The guidebook has the following four main characteristics: (a) more summative than formative, (b) decision-oriented,

(c) need-based, and (d) catering to a wide range of audience. The literature review of Chapter 5 indicates that other states have school improvement frameworks similar to Michigan's. Therefore, the guidebook could be used by practitioners across the states.

The Leadership Performance Planning Worksheet (LPPW): A Development Tool for Early Career Leaders

The purpose of the LPPW is to develop and strengthen critical leadership skills and behaviors in early-career school leaders, particularly *new* principals. LPPW, developed as part of the Wallace Foundation's national initiative on educational leadership, was piloted in New City Leadership Academy and several initiatives in other states. Table 5 illustrates the framework underlying LPPW.

TABLE 5. Conceptual Framework of LPPW

Dimension and Focus	Number of Behavior Indicators
1.0 Personal Behavior: addressing the principals' code of conduct and how they exemplify themselves in their leadership role	5 behaviors
2.0 Resilience: responding to detractors from their leadership style	5 behaviors
3.0 Communication: Focusing on the breadth and quality of a principal's communication	5 behaviors
4.0 Student Performance: Emphasizing primarily instructional leadership including goal setting and instructional strategies	8 behaviors
5.0 Situational Problem Solving is the comprehensiveness and agility of a principal's problem solving techniques	4 behaviors
6.0 Learning: facilitating and modeling a learning culture in the school	4 behaviors
7.0 Supervision of Staff: exemplifying direct leadership including working with staff	4 behaviors
8.0 Management: exemplifying organizational leadership including setting priorities and allocating resources	4 behaviors

*Adapted from Scott's Chapter 7 in this book.

LPPW is intended to be used by a new principal and his or her mentor/coach. For each of the behavioral indicators, the worksheet rating scale has two categories: (a) approaching the standard and (b) meeting the standard. The mentor/coach could observe, interview, and discuss with the new principal to arrive at a rating for each behavioral indicator, list the areas of strength and weakness, develop strategies to improve, and document progress in areas identified for improvement earlier. In the chapter Scott, the author, provided rich data from piloting the tool as well as testimonials from the users.

SAM: A tool to Increase Principal Time on Instructional Leadership

In Chapter 8, Shellinger presented tools to help principals to reduce their time on administrative duties and increase time devoted to instructional leadership. An objective observer uses the tool TimeTrack™, which has 25 management and instructional leadership descriptors, to collect data on how a principal spends his or her time, and the tool Time/Task Analysis™ condenses the descriptors into three major categories: (a) primarily *instructional*, (b) primarily *managerial*, and (c) primarily *personal*. Use of the term "primarily" allows for categorization of activities that may overlap or be connected. Current and longitudinal data use could be displayed, with a purpose to improve the principal's practice to increase the time devoted to instructional leadership.

How we use our time impacts our productivity. We have learned much from, for example, Taylor's time analysis as part of the scientific management (Taylor, 1911) and "time-on-task" for student learning in education (Stalling, 1980). Shellinger mentions in Chapter 8 that the average US principal spends less than 32% of the day on teaching and learning. Independent evaluation of principals who were involved in using the tools indicated that the average gain by the end of the first year in instructional leadership time for participating principals was five hours and 57 more minutes every week, amounting to 27 extra days each year. By the end of the second year, the gain increased to eight hours and 30 more minutes every week, equivalent to 38 extra days each year. By the end of the third year of participation the gain in instructional leadership time continued to increase to 12 hours and 20 more minutes every week, about 55 extra days each year.

High Schools That Work

Developed by the Southern Regional Education Board over a course of more than 25 years, High Schools That Work (HSTW) is a large-scale high school reform model that focuses on getting secondary school students educated and prepared for careers or college. The model has 10 principles such as high expectations, work-based learning, students actively engaged, and culture of continuous improvement. Embedded in HSTW reform effort are tools useful for principals—*Using the HSTW Assessment to Improve Student Achievement and Readiness for College and Careers: A Guide and Workbook for HSTW Sites*, a workbook, and *Establishing*

Benchmarks for New and Maturing HSTW Sites, a framework. Samples of these two tools can be found at the conclusion of the chapter. Principals and their staff could use the tools to set student achievement goals and benchmark instructional activities and student support.

Coda: The Use of Tools for Both Practice and Research

Authors of various tools presented the information on how these tools should be used. It is important to point out that the tools could be used for improving both practice and research. As far as improving practice is concerned, the tools could be used for self-assessment by principals, assessment by others, professional development, and in some cases evaluation. Principals and others could use these tools to improve principalship. As far as research is concerned, the tools presented in the book could also be used as instruments to collect data on various aspects of the principalship, which could be used to study the association between principalship and other factors, investigate the effect of various interventions to improve principalship, and validate other tools.

References

Barnett, K., McCormick, J., & Conners, R. (2000, December). *Leadership behaviour of secondary school principals, teacher outcomes and school culture.* Paper presented at the annual conference of the Australian Association for Research in Education, Sydney, Australia.

Bossert, S., Dwyer, D., Rowan, B., & Lee, G. (1982). The instructional management role of the principal. *Educational Administration Quarterly, 18*(3), 34–64.

CCSSO. (2008). *Educational leadership policy standards: ISLLC 2008.* Washington, DC: Council of Chief State School Officers.

Goldring, E., Cravens, X., Murphy, J., Porter, A., Elliott, S. N., & Carson, B. (2009). The evaluation of principals: What and how do states and urban districts assess leadership. *The Elementary School Journal, 110,* 19–39.

Hallinger, P. (2011). A review of three decades of doctoral studies using the Principal Instructional Management Rating Scale: A lens on methodological progress in educational leadership. *Educational Administration Quarterly, 47*(2), 271–306.

Hallinger, P., Bickman, L., & Davis, K. (1996). School context, principal leadership, and student reading achievement. *The Elementary School Journal, 96,* 527–549.

Hallinger, P., & Heck, R. H. (1996). Reassessing the principal's role in school effectiveness: A review of empirical research, 1980–1995. *Educational Administration Quarterly, 32*(1), 5–44.

Heck, R. H., & Hallinger, P. (2009). Assessing the contribution of distributed leadership to school improvement and growth in math achievement. *American Educational Research Journal, 46,* 626–658.

Louis, K. S., Leithwood, K., Wahlstrom, K. L., Anderson, S., et al. (2010). *Investigating the links to improved student learning*. University of Minnesota: Center for Applied Research and Educational Improvement.

Marzano, R. (2003). *What works in schools: Translating research into action*. Alexandria, VA: ASCD.

Marzano, R. J., Waters, T., & McNulty, B. A. (2005). *School leadership that works*. Alexandria, VA: Association for Supervision and Curriculum Development.

Michigan Department of Education. (2005). *Michigan School Improvement Framework*. Retrieved from http://www.michigan.gov/documents/SIF_4-01-05_130701_7.pdf

Newmann, F. M., Rutter, R. A., & Smith, M. S. (1989). Organizational factors that affect school sense of efficacy, community, and expectations. *Sociology of Education, 62,* 221–238.

Shen, J., & Associates. (2005). *School principals*. New York: Peter Lang.

Stalling, J. (1980). Allocated academic learning time revisited, or beyond time on task. *Educational Researcher, 9*(11), 11-16.

Taylor, F. W. (1911). *The principles of scientific management*. New York: Harper & Brothers.

Wahlstrom, K. L., Louise, K. S., Leithwood, K., & Anderson, S. E. (2010). *Investigating the links to improved student learning: Executive summary of research findings*. Minneapolis, MN: Center for Applied Research and Educational Improvement, University of Minnesota.

Waters, T., & Kingston, S. (2005). The standards we need: A comparative analysis of performance standards shows us what is essential for principals to know and be able to do to improve achievement. *Leadership, 35*(1), 14–17.

Vanderbilt Assessment OF Leadership IN Education

A New Tool for Principal Evaluation and Professional Growth

ANDREW C. PORTER, JOSEPH MURPHY, ELLEN GOLDRING,
STEPHEN N. ELLIOTT, & XIU CHEN CRAVENS

Introduction

Leadership is a central ingredient in school success defined in terms of value added to student achievement (Leithwood, Louis, Anderson, & Wahlstrom, 2004; Marzano, Waters, & McNulty, 2005; Murphy & Hallinger, 1985). A number of recent efforts have been undertaken to improve the quality of principal leadership, including the establishment of the Interstate School Leadership Licensure Consortium (ISLLC) standards (Council of Chief State School Officers [CCSSO], 1996, 2008); growth in principal professional development, coaching, and mentoring; and training program accreditation (the National Council for Accreditation of Teacher Education process). However, there has been relatively little focus in research and practice on the assessment of principal leadership effectiveness. When there has been movement toward leadership assessment, it has been in the form of assessment for certification (e.g., Education Testing Service's pre-service assessments for principals), or it has been with instruments with few, if any, documented psychometric properties and little research support (Goldring, Porter, Murphy, Elliott & Cravens, 2009).

Against this backdrop, a team of researchers from Vanderbilt University, the University of Pennsylvania, and Arizona State University began development and validation of the Vanderbilt Assessment of Leadership in Education™ (VAL-ED), a multirater, evidence-based assessment of principals' instructional leadership. The process began with the establishment of a theoretical framework (Porter, Goldring, Murphy, Elliott, & Cravens, 2006) that connects with research on effective leadership and professional standards (Goldring et al., 2009). Next, a series of qualitative and quantitative development and pilot studies were conducted (Porter et al., 2010a). Following the pilot studies, teachers, principals, and supervisors were engaged in a national field trial of the VAL-ED. More than 270 schools—elementary, middle, and high; suburban, urban, and rural; and from all four regions of the country—participated (Porter et al., 2010b).

As of the spring of 2011, the VAL-ED was being used by more than 280 school districts with about 2000 schools nationwide for principal evaluation purposes. Studies that collect further psychometric evidence for validity and reliability are ongoing and supported by the U.S. Department of Education.

This chapter introduces the VAL-ED as a principal evaluation tool that is markedly different from current instruments employed by states and districts throughout the United States. First, the VAL-ED uses *360-degree feedback*, from teachers, principals, and supervisors. Second, the content of the proposed assessment is *learning-centered* leadership behaviors, behaviors that are related to increases in student achievement. Third, the assessment is of leadership *behaviors*, not knowledge, dispositions, or personal characteristics of leaders. Fourth, the VAL-ED requires respondents to identify *evidence* on which they are basing their assessment of principal behaviors. Fifth, the *psychometric properties* are clearly documented and the authors have an ongoing program of research that will continue to yield evidence concerning the reliability and validity of VAL-ED scores. In short, the VAL-ED is conceptually and theoretically grounded and the resulting scores are reliable and valid for purposes of evaluating learning-centered leadership.

When completed as designed by a representative and large portion of eligible respondents in a school, the VAL-ED can provide useful results for the purposes of evaluating the performance of a principal and also identifying leadership behaviors for improvement. When used two or more times across years, the VAL-ED has the potential to address questions about behavior change and about the effects of programs designed to improve learning-centered leadership behaviors. The results from the VAL-ED address fundamental questions such as:

- Who participated in the assessment of the principal's leadership behavior?
- What evidence did these respondents report using to make their effectiveness ratings of the principal?
- How effective is the principal's leadership behavior judged in comparison to a national sample of principals?

- How effective is the principal's leadership behavior in comparison to the VAL-ED proficiency standards?
- To what degree did the three respondent groups—teachers, supervisor, and principal—agree with regard to effectiveness ratings?
- Which areas of leadership behavior represent relative strengths and which represent areas for possible improvement?

The chapter is organized as follows: We begin with the theoretical framework for the VAL-ED by introducing our model of school leadership. The VAL-ED model is presented along with a conception of leadership behaviors that fits within a larger context of leadership assessment, school performance, and student success. We provide a detailed review of how the construction of the VAL-ED focuses on topics related to instructional leadership by clearly defining and measuring the leader behaviors that can improve learning. We then discuss the empirical evidence for the validity and reliability of the VAL-ED collected through a series of research studies. Lastly we provide practitioner-oriented guidance on implementation and interpretation of results.[1]

Theoretical Framework

The conceptual model of the VAL-ED shows that leadership knowledge and skills, personal characteristics, and values and beliefs inform the actual leadership behaviors exhibited by individuals or teams in performing their leadership responsibilities (see Figure 1). These leadership behaviors (the constructs measured in our assessment instrument and reviewed in detail later) then lead to school performance on core components such as providing a rigorous curriculum and high-quality instruction. These school performances, in turn, lead to student success. Student success is defined as value-added, for example, improvements in student achievement, student attendance, student graduation rates, and college enrollment.

Consistent with the empirical research (Hallinger & Heck, 1996; Heck & Hallinger, 1999; Leithwood et al., 2004), the VAL-ED assessment model does not envision direct effects of leadership behaviors on student success. Rather, the leadership behaviors lead to changes in school performance, which in turn lead to student success. This leadership model also posits that there are aspects of the context within which leadership and schooling takes place that bear on leadership evaluation (Murphy & Meyers, 2008). Levels of experience, student body composition, staff composition, level of schooling, and geographic setting of the school can all have bearing on high-quality education leadership.

16 | TOOLS FOR IMPROVING PRINCIPALS' WORK

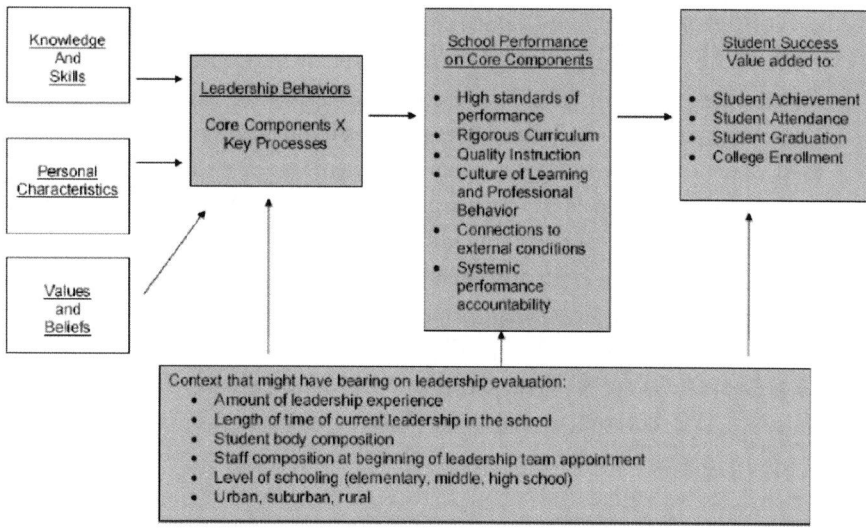

Figure 1. Conceptual Framework for the VAL-ED (Porter et al., 2006).

	Key Processes					
Core Components	Planning	Implementing	Supporting	Advocating	Communicating	Monitoring
High Standards for Student Learning						
Rigorous Curriculum (content)						
Quality Instruction (pedagogy)						
Culture of Learning & Professional Behavior						
Connections to External Communities						
Systems Performance Accountability						

Figure 2. The VAL-ED Constructs of Core Components and Key Processes (Porter et al., 2006).

The conceptual framework that drives our leadership assessment instrument focuses on two key dimensions of leadership behaviors. We refer to these two dimensions as *core components* and *key processes*. We propose to assess the intersection of *what* principals or leadership teams must accomplish to improve academic and social learning for all students (the core components), and *how* they create those core components (the key processes). The framework establishes that school leadership assessment should include measures of the intersection of these dimensions. Inside the conception model, principals' leadership behaviors is defined by the intersection of six core components of school performance and six key processes (see Figure 2). As we discuss below, a substantial research base supports the constructs of the core components and key processes (see Knapp et al., 2003; Leithwood et al., 2004; Murphy et al., 2007; Goldring et al, 2009 for recent reviews).

Core Components

In our framework, core components refer to characteristics of schools that support the learning of students and enhance the ability of teachers to teach. Following a systems view of organizations, we acknowledge the core components are interconnected, recursive, and reactive to one another, but for purposes of our assessment and descriptive analysis we review each individually.

High Standards for Student Learning. We defined high standards for student learning as the extent to which leadership ensures there are individual, team, and school goals for rigorous student academic and social learning. There is considerable evidence that a key function of effective school leadership concerns shaping the purpose of the school and articulating the school's mission (Hallinger & Heck, 2002; Knapp et al., 2003; Murphy et al., 2007). In our framework, we do not assess the mere presence of goals for student learning, but specifically emphasize the quality of the school goals, namely the extent to which there are *high* standards and *rigorous* learning goals. The research literature over the last quarter century has consistently supported the notion that high expectations for all, including clear and public standards, is one key to closing the achievement gap between advantaged and less advantaged students, and for raising the overall academic achievement of all students (Betts & Grogger, 2003; Brookover & Lezotte, 1977; Newmann, 1997; Purkey & Smith, 1983).

Rigorous Curriculum. We define a rigorous curriculum as the content of instruction, as opposed to the pedagogy of instruction, which is dealt with in the following section. Rigorous curriculum is defined as ambitious academic content provided to all students in core academic subjects. School leaders play a crucial role in setting high standards for student performance in their schools. These high standards, however, must be translated into ambitious academic content represented in the curriculum students experience. Murphy and colleagues (2007) argued that school leaders in productive schools are knowledgeable about and deeply involved in the school's curricular program (Marzano et al., 2005). These leaders work with colleagues to ensure that the school is defined by a rigorous curriculum program in general and that each student's program, in particular, is of high quality (Newmann, 1997; Ogden & Germinario, 1995). Learning-centered leaders ensure that each student has an adequate opportunity to learn rigorous content in all academic subjects (Boyer, 1983).

Quality Instruction. A rigorous curriculum (i.e., ambitious academic content) is insufficient to ensure substantial gains in student learning; quality instruction (i.e., effective pedagogy) is also required (Leithwood et al., 2004). Quality instruction is defined as effective instructional practices that maximize student academic and social learning. This component reflects research findings over the course of the past few decades about how people learn (National Research Council, 1999). That work makes clear that teachers' pedagogical practices must draw out and work with the pre-existing understanding that students bring to the classroom. Effective instructional leaders understand the properties of quality instruction and find ways to ensure that quality instruction is experienced by all students in their schools. They spend time on the instructional program, often through providing feedback to teachers and supporting teachers to improve their instruction (Marzano et al., 2005; Wellisch, MacQueen, Carriere, & Duck, 1978).

Culture of Learning and Professional Behavior. Another core component in our assessment framework is leadership that ensures there are integrated communities of professional practice in the service of student academic and social learning—that is, a healthy school environment in which student learning is the central focus. Research has demonstrated that schools organized as communities, rather than bureaucracies, are more likely to exhibit academic success (Bryk & Driscoll, 1988; Lee, Smith, & Croninger, 1995; Louis & Miles, 1990). Further research supports the notion that effective professional communities are deeply rooted in the academic and social learning goals of the schools (Little, 1982; Rosenholtz, 1989). Often termed teacher professional communities, these collaborative cultures are defined by elements such as shared goals and values, focus on student learning, shared work, deprivatized practice, and reflective dialogue (Louis & Kruse, 1996). School leadership plays a central role in the extent to which a school exhibits a culture of learning and professional behavior and includes integrated professional communities (Bryk, Camburn, & Louis, 1999; Louis, Marks, & Kruse, 1996).

Connections to External Communities. Leading a school with high expectations and academic achievement for all students requires robust connections to the external community. There is a substantial research base that has reported positive relationships between family involvement and social and academic benefits for students (Henderson & Mapp, 2002). A study of standards-based reform practices, for instance, found that teacher outreach to parents of low-performing students was related to improved student achievement (Westat and Policy Studies Associates, 2001). Similarly, schools with well-defined parent partnership programs show achievement gains over schools with less robust partnerships (Shaver & Walls, 1998). Learning-centered leaders play a key role in both establishing and supporting parental involvement and community partnerships.

Systemic Performance Accountability. There is individual and collective responsibility among the leadership, faculty, students, and community for achieving the rigorous student academic and social learning goals. Accountability stems from both external and internal accountability systems (Adams & Kirst, 1999). External accountability refers to performance expectations that emerge from outside the school and the local community. Simultaneously, schools and districts have internal accountability systems with local expectations and individual responsibilities. Internal goals comprise the practical steps that schools must take to reach those targets. Schools with higher levels of internal accountability are more successful within external accountability systems, and they are more skillful in areas such as making curricular decisions, addressing instructional issues, and responding to various performance measures (Bryk & Schneider, 2002; Elmore, 2005). Learning-centered leaders integrate internal and external accountability systems by holding their staffs accountable for implementing strategies that align teaching and learning with achievement goals and targets set by policy.

Key Processes

Our conceptual framework features six key process constructs. Key processes are leadership behaviors, most notably aspects of transformational leadership traditionally associated with processes of leadership that raise organizational members' levels of commitment and shape organizational culture (Burns, 1978; Conley & Goldman, 1994; Leithwood, 1994). Equally following the systems view of organizations, we review each key process individually.

Planning. An essential process of leadership is planning. We define planning as articulating shared direction and coherent policies, practices, and procedures for realizing high standards of student performance. Planning helps leadership focus resources, tasks, and people. Learning-centered leaders do not see planning as a ritual or as overly bureaucratic. They engage in planning as a mechanism to realize the core components of the school. Effective principals are highly skilled planners and, in fact, they are proactive in their planning work (Leithwood & Montgomery,

1982). Planning is needed in each of the core components; it is an engine of school improvement that builds common purpose and shared culture (Goldring & Hausman, 2001; Teddlie, Stringfield, Wimpelberg, & Kirby, 1989).

Implementing. After planning, leaders implement; they put into practice the activities necessary to realize high standards for student performance. In a comprehensive review of the research on implementation of curriculum and instruction, Fullan and Pomfret (1977) concluded that "implementation is not simply an extension of planning…it is a phenomenon in its own right" (p. 336). Effective leaders take the initiative to implement and are proactive in pursuing their school goals (Manasse, 1985). Learning-centered leaders are directly involved in implementing policies and practices that further the core components in their schools (Knapp et al., 2003). For example, effective leaders implement joint planning time for teachers and other structures as mechanisms to develop a culture of learning and professional behavior (Murphy, 2005). Similarly, they implement programs that build productive parent and community relations as a way to achieve connections to external communities (Leithwood & Jantzi, 2005).

Supporting. Leaders create enabling conditions; they secure and use the financial, political, technological, and human resources necessary to promote academic and social learning. Supporting is a key process that ensures the resources necessary to achieve the core components are available and used well. This notion is closely related to the transformational leadership behaviors associated with helping people be successful (Leithwood & Jantzi, 2005). The literature is clear that learning-centered leaders devote considerable time to supporting teachers in their efforts to strengthen the quality of instruction (Conley, 1991; Leithwood & Jantzi, 2005). This support takes varied forms. Leaders demonstrate personal interest in staff and make themselves available to them (Marzano et al., 2005). Leaders also provide support for high-quality instruction by ensuring that teachers have guidance as they work to integrate skills learned during professional development into their instructional behaviors (Murphy et al., 2007).

Advocating. Leaders promote the diverse needs of students within and beyond the school. Advocating for the best interests and needs of all children is a key process of learning-centered leadership (Murphy et al., 2007). Learning-centered leaders advocate for a rigorous instructional program for all students. They ensure that policies in the school do not prevent or create barriers for certain students to participate in classes that are deemed gateways to further learning, such as algebra. They ensure that special needs students receive content-rich instruction. Similarly, effective leadership ensures that all students are exposed to high-quality instruction; they manage the parental pressures that often create favoritism in placing students in particular classes. Both the instruction and content of the school's educational programs honor diversity (Ogden & Germinario, 1995; Roueche, Baker, Mullin, & Boy, 1986). Through advocacy, learning-centered leadership works with teachers and other professional staff to ensure that the school's culture both models and supports respect for diversity. (Butty, LaPoint, Thomas, & Thompson, 2001; Goldring & Hausman, 2001).

Communicating. Leaders develop, utilize, and maintain systems of exchange among members of the school and with its external communities. In studying school change, Loucks, Bauchner, Crandal, Schmidt, and Eisman (1982) found that "principals played major communication roles, both with and among school staff, and with others in the district and in the community" (p. 42). Learning-centered leaders communicate unambiguously to all the stakeholders and constituencies both in and outside the school about the high standards of student performance (Leithwood & Montgomery, 1982; Knapp et al., 2003). Leaders communicate regularly and through multiple channels with families and community members, including businesses, social service agencies, and faith-based organizations (Edmonds & Frederiksen, 1978; Garibaldi, 1993; Marzano et al., 2005). Through ongoing communication, schools and the community serve as resources for one another that inform, promote, and link key institutions in support of student academic and social learning.

Monitoring. Leaders systematically collect and analyze data to make judgments that guide decisions and actions for continuous improvement. This is monitoring. Early on, the effective schools literature identified monitoring school progress in terms of setting goals, assessing the curriculum, and evaluating instruction as a key role of instructional leadership (Hallinger & Murphy, 1985; Purkey & Smith, 1983). Learning-centered leaders monitor the school's curriculum, ensuring alignment between rigorous academic standards and curriculum coverage (Eubanks & Levine, 1983). They monitor students' programs of study to ensure that all students have adequate opportunity to learn rigorous content in all academic subjects (Boyer, 1983; Hallinger & Murphy, 1985). Learning-centered leadership also undertakes an array of activities to monitor the quality of instruction, such as ongoing classroom observations (Heck, 1992). Monitoring student achievement is central to maintaining systemic performance accountability.

The VAL-ED and ISLLC Alignment

The learning-centered leadership conceptual framework and the corresponding VAL-ED are anchored by and aligned with the ISLLC 2008 Educational Leadership Policy Standards (CCSSO, 2008).

The ISLLC standards were developed between 1994 and 1996 under the direction of the National Policy Board for Educational Administration (NPBEA), a consortium of the 10 national organizations associated with school leadership in the United States. They were adopted by the NPBEA in December 1996 and were reauthorized by the board in December 2007. Currently, they are used as the foundation for school leadership in over 40 states. Consequently, they have had a major influence on the shape and texture of school leadership in the United States. They have shaped the type of education that prospective and practicing school leaders receive, the ways in which educators are licensed and relicensed into the profession of school administration, how preparation programs in school leadership are accredited, the hiring criteria employed by school districts, and so forth. At their core, the ISLLC standards are an empirically anchored and value-based statement about what the profession of school leadership should look like at the dawn of the twenty-first century. They were crafted in an effort to move school leadership from the orbit of management toward the gravitational pull of learning and school improvement. They are broad statements designed to apply to all school leaders (Murphy, 2005).

We elected to align the VAL-ED to the ISLLC standards for two reasons, one practical and one conceptual. First, the standards provide the leadership scaffolding for 40 states, all the members of the NPBEA, and thousands of individual school districts. Therefore, an assessment system of leadership that was not coordinated with them would be largely ignored. Second, and more importantly, the intellectual foundation of the standards is nearly isomorphic with the foundation used to craft the conceptual framework of the assessment.

In both cases, the base is the research on schools where all students are effective in meeting ambitious learning targets. Figure 3 shows the intersection between the conceptual framework and the ISLLC standards. One key difference between the ISLLC standards and our conceptual framework is that the standards typically refer to a person in a leadership position (a school administrator), whereas our framework pertains to both individuals and leadership teams. Another difference is that our conceptual framework makes finer-grained distinctions than do the ISLLC standards.

Here we present some examples (e.g., ISLLC Standards 1 and 2) of how our conceptual framework is aligned with the ISLCC standards. ISLCC Standard 1 refers to setting a widely shared vision of learning. Specifically, "an education leader promotes the success of every student by facilitating the development, articulation, implementation, and stewardship of a vision of learning that is shared and supported by all stakeholders" (CCSSO, 2008, p. 14). The components of professional practice that are embedded in this standard include developing, communicating, implementing, and monitoring the vision. In our conceptual framework, the core components—high standards for student performance and systemic performance accountability—and the their intersection with the key processes of planning,

ISLLC Standards	VAL-ED Core Components	Examples of VAL-ED Items (not included in Form A or Form C)
1. Setting a widely shared vision for learning	• High standards for student learning • Systemic performance accountability	• Develops a plan for collecting data to review student learning against high standards. • Promotes recognition and rewards for students who achieve high standards of academic learning.
2. Developing a school culture and instructional program conducive to student learning and staff professional growth	• Rigorous curriculum (content) • Quality instruction (pedagogy) • Culture of learning & professional behavior	• Develops procedures for reviewing student work to assess the rigor of the curriculum. • Implements the use of research-based instructional strategies.
3. Ensuring effective management of the organization, operation, and resources for a safe, efficient, and effective learning environment	• Culture of learning & professional behavior	• Uses faculty expertise and knowledge in making decisions. • Implements school-wide rules and consequences to manage student behavior.
4. Collaborating with faculty and community members, responding to diverse community interests and needs, and mobilizing community resources	• Connections to external communities	• Plans with social service agencies for safety nets in support of student learning. • Creates opportunities for parents to work with teachers on their child's instruction.
5. Acting with integrity, fairness, and in an ethical manner	• Culture of learning & professional behavior • Systemic performance accountability	• Plans data collection to hold school leaders accountable for student academic and social learning. • Listens to faculty feedback about its accountability programs.
6. Understanding, responding to, and influencing the political, social, legal, and cultural context	• High standards for student learning • Connections to external communities	• Challenges parents to offer quality instructional experiences at home. • Advocates on behalf of families to express their opinions and needs.

Figure 3: The VAL-ED Components and Processes by ISLLC Standards Alignment.

implementing, supporting, advocating, communicating, and monitoring are consistent with Standard 1. VAL-ED items that measure the intersection of high standards for student performance and planning and supporting, such as *developing a plan for collecting data to review student learning against high standards* and *promoting recognition and rewards for students who achieve high standards of academic learning*, are rooted in Standard 1. These items provide evidence of leadership behavior that develops and implements a vision (for student performance).

ISLLC Standard 2 refers to the school culture and teaching and learning. Specifically, Standard 2 states, "An education leader promotes the success of every student by advocating, nurturing, and sustaining a school culture and instructional program conducive to student learning and staff professional growth" (CCSSO, 2008, p. 14). Included in this standard are such leadership behaviors as valuing students and staff, developing and sustaining a culture of learning, ensuring an inclusive culture, and monitoring and evaluating the culture. In our conceptual framework, Standard 2 is covered in a number of areas, but primarily in the intersection of the core components of Rigorous Curriculum, Quality Instruction, and Culture of Learning and Professional Behavior with the key processes of planning, implementing, supporting, advocating, communicating, and monitoring. Examples of the types of behaviors in our framework that are aligned with Standard 2 include *developing procedures for reviewing student work to assess the rigor of the curriculum* and *implementing the use of research-based instructional strategies.*

There are important differences between our framework and the ISLLC standards as well. Our conceptual framework makes systematic distinctions not captured in the standards; specifically, it distinguishes among rigorous curriculum, quality instruction, and culture of learning and professional behavior. The ISLLC Standards do not. Further, our framework systematically considers each of the six key processes for each core component; the ISLLC standards do not. Generally, there is quite good correspondence between an ISLLC standard and one of our core components.

Validity and Reliability

The VAL-Ed is designed, developed and tested to yield scores that are reliable (i.e., provide accurate measurement) and valid (i.e., measure leadership behaviors that lead to improved student achievement). To accomplish these goals, we followed a multi-stage development process that involved cognitive labs, pilot tests, and field tests. The design of the validity and reliabilit y studies is directly influenced by technical standards for high-quality assessments (American Educational Research Association, American Psychological Association, & National Council on Measurement in Education [AERA, APA, & NCME], 1999), principles of universal design (National Center on Education Outcome [NCEO], September 2006), and time-tested practices of item and test development (Downing & Haladyna, 2006; Haladyna, Downing, & Rodriguez, 2002). At each stage of the design and development process, the properties of the instrument were examined through empirical studies and expert reviews. Overall study results indicated strong content validity and guided further item revisions.

Specifically, the development of the VAL-ED involved (a) specifying the purposes of the assessment; (b) defining content assessed; (c) writing items; (d) developing test specifications for validity evidence plans; (e) designing instructions and response format; (f) piloting test forms; (g) designing scoring and interpretation frameworks for scores; (h) conducting studies that yield evidence for the reliability and validity of the scores; (i) refining items, format, and score interpretation procedures; (j) field-testing forms with a representative sample; (k) developing norms and standards to guide interpretation of results; and (l) writing a technical manual that summarizes technical characteristics and sound uses of the assessment.

Using classic test theory methodology, as well as item analyses tactics from Item Response Theory, we conducted a set of studies that provided substantial evidence for the reliability and validity of VAL-ED score inferences. These studies are described in detail in several research articles (Porter et al., 2010a, 2010b; Polikoff et al., 2009) and in the VAL-ED technical manual (Porter, Murphy, Goldring, & Elliott, 2008). Collectively, the studies create the technical foundation for the VAL-ED scores and thus make it possible to use the instrument with confidence to evaluate principals' leadership behaviors. Furthermore, the professional documents and the published research on test development and high-quality assessment of human performance provide strong guidelines for designing a high-quality and successful assessment program for school leaders.

Instrument Development and Pilot Testing

The development of the VAL-ED was embedded in a research paradigm. First, items were written to fit each of the 36 cells in the core components by key processes conceptual framework. As many items were written as leadership behaviors could be identified. For some cells more than 10 behaviors were identified and items written. Principals were asked to sort items into cells as a second check on the content validity of the items; sorting accuracy was good but some items were dropped and some rewritten for clarity of the target cell. Two rounds of cognitive interviews were conducted in three districts each. In each case, principals, teachers, and principals' supervisors from elementary, middle, and high schools participated in the cognitive interviews. Based on the results, the instrument was revised. When the instrument was judged to be ready, a nine-school pilot test was conducted in one district involving elementary, middle, and high schools. Based on that pilot, the instrument was seen to have good internal consistency reliability, good construct validity, good face validity, but the 108-item instrument was too long and the effectiveness scale was not being used across its full range. The instrument was revised to be shorter and have different benchmarks for the effectiveness scale. Cognitive interviews were conducted using the online instrument (the paper-and-pencil and online instruments are virtually identical). The positive results led to piloting the instrument once again, this time in 11 schools, again across elementary, middle, and high school. The results for this second pilot were encouraging. The reliability remained high. More of the range of the response scale was used. Completion time was seen as less of a problem, and confirmatory factor analysis on the teacher data supported the conceptual framework against which the items were written.

A fairness review of the VAL-ED instructions and items was conducted to identify and remove aspects of test items or directions that might hinder respondents from completing the instrument. The fairness review was based on the fairness guidelines published and used by Educational Testing Service. A panel of nine individuals completed the fairness review. The results indicated no fairness concerns in the instructions or introductory content. Three items on Form A and one item on Form C were identified as requiring some edits to improve their fairness characteristics and these edits were made.[2]

National Trial

With Form A and Form C of the VAL-ED assessment of school leadership in final form, a national field trial was undertaken to establish the psychometric properties of the assessment, to establish percentile ranks for reporting; to build an item-ordered booklet for the Bookmark performance standard setting; to investigate further the perceived feasibility of the instrument, and to investigate design factors, including level of schooling, locale, and the parallelness of Forms A and C. The target was set at 300 schools: 100 elementary, 100 middle, and 100 high schools. The obtained sample had principal data on 235 schools, supervisor data on 253, and teacher data on 245. For 218 schools, there were data from all three respondent groups.

Based on the national field trial, supervisors were seen as slightly more positive on principal effectiveness than were principals with teachers in between. Controlling for other factors, high school principals were seen as slightly less effective than elementary or middle school principals, but the difference was small. Suburban school principals were seen as more effective than rural school principals, and no significant differences were found between Forms A and C.

Confirmatory factor analysis, exploratory factor analysis with oblique factor rotations, and investigations of mean differences among core components, key processes, and their interactions were conducted to investigate the construct validity of the instrument. Confirmatory factor analysis supported both core components and key processes. Exploratory factor analysis identified factors for Performance Accountability, Connections to External Communities, and Culture of Learning and Professional Behavior, as well as the key processes of supporting and advocating. There were significant differences between the means of the core components, with the exception that Rigorous Curriculum and Performance Accountability were not significantly different from one another, nor were Quality Instruction and Culture of Learning and

Professional Behavior. For key processes, supporting was significantly different from all other key processes, but the other key processes were not significantly different from one another. Of the 630 pairs of contrasts among the 36 cells, for Form A 44% were significant, and for Form C 47% were significant. Finally, two analyses of the reliability of the difference between subscales were conducted. In the traditional analysis, the reliability of the difference of core components from the total score was generally good, and the reliability of the difference of key processes from the total score was generally poor. When comparing across core components and key processes, it was found that the reliability of the difference between core component subscales was quite strong, with mixed evidence as to the reliability of the difference between key process subscales. A second analysis used generalizability theory to investigate the reliability of contrasts between core components and between key processes. The reliabilities of the differences were surprisingly good given the notoriously low reliability of different scores. The results were similar to the results from the exploratory factor analysis. The reliabilities contrasting Culture of Learning and Professional Behavior, Connections to External Communities, Performance Accountability, and Rigorous Curriculum were all strong. For key processes, the reliabilities contrasting supporting and advocating were both strong. For total score, the internal consistency reliability ranged from .98 to .99. Internal consistencies were slightly lower for principals (.87 to .93) than for supervisors or teachers (.93 to .97), and the reliabilities for key processes (.87 to .90) based on principal data were slightly lower than the reliabilities for core components (.89 to .93). The conclusion is that there is strong internal consistency reliability for both total score and each of the 12 subscales, as based on national field trial data.

The national trial studies found empirical support for the conceptual framework. There were four sources of evidence: (a) the extent to which effectiveness ratings differed in their mean value among the core components (or key processes); (b) the reliability of contrasting a core component (or key process) from the overall total score with the criterion being reliabilities of .50 or greater; (c) using generalizability theory of finding that the core component (or key process) has significant unique variance; and (d) exploratory factor analysis using oblique notation indicating a clear factor on both forms (indicated with a double plus) or a clear factor on one form but not the other (indicated with a single plus).

The relationship between responses from principals, supervisors, and teachers was also investigated. All three respondent groups were positively intercorrelated with the highest intercorrelation between principals and teachers (approximately .25). The correlation between supervisors and teachers was lower, and the lowest correlation was between principals and supervisors. Clearly, the information from one respondent group was not redundant with the information from the other respondent groups, a finding that supports the 360-degree approach to assessment.

Moreover, investigations of the use of sources of evidence, the "Don't know" option on the effectiveness scale, and a variety of possible errors that could be made in filling out the instrument revealed no problems.

Nine questions were asked of respondents after they completed the assessment. All three respondent groups indicated that they found the instrument to be easy to use and the items to be (a) focusing on important leadership behaviors, (b) understandable, (c) not biased, and (d) appropriate for elementary, middle, and high school levels. Similarly, all respondent groups agreed that teachers should have input into the assessment of principal leadership, but they neither agreed nor disagreed that the VAL-ED should be used to hold principals accountable in their district. Perhaps had the item asked about formative as well as summative evaluations, the responses would have been more enthusiastic about use of the instrument.

A Bookmark method was used to set performance standards for distinguished, proficient, basic, and below basic. A national panel of 22 experts participated. Ultimately, the standards were set yielding 17% of the national field trial principals below basic, 50% below proficient, and 86% below distinguished.

With the completion of the national field trial, the VAL-ED has been documented to have excellent reliability, strong validity, initial national norms for reporting percentile ranks, and performance standards to identify *distinguished, proficient, basic,* and *below basic* principals. The norms and the proficiency levels apply to both Form A and C, which can be used interchangeably, and for a paper-and-pencil as well as an online version of the assessment.[3]

Short Form of the VAL-ED

With multiple teachers in the school, we investigated the possibility of having a random half of the teachers complete a random half of the 72 items on a form of the VAL-ED and the other random half of the teachers complete the other random half of the 72 items.

A 2x2 framework of six core components and six key processes forms 36 cells to guide the construction of the VAL-ED with two items for each of the cells. Parallel half forms for teachers were created by randomly assigning one item (from the original Form A or C) in a cell to one half form and the other item to another half form. Using data from the national field trial, we investigated the reliability of this approach. For total score when aggregating across teachers, one half form correlates 0.8 with the other half form. For subscales, half-form correlations range from 0.81 to 0.70. Because in reporting for the school the two half forms are averaged, these correlations were seen as of sufficient size to merit modifying the instrument. As a result teacher response time has been cut by 40% with no loss of information.

Discovery Education Assessment has implemented the random half-form approach for teachers, resulting in greater efficiency of assessment.

Ongoing Validation Studies

Work to enhance the psychometric properties of the VAL-ED is ongoing with support from the U.S. Department of Education's Institute for Education Sciences. During the period 2008 to 2012, the following studies were being conducted:

> *Known Groups:* This validity study identifies school principals who are considered most or least successful by their supervisors and examines whether VAL-ED accurately distinguishes the groups.
>
> *Test/Retest:* This study estimates the reliability of VAL-ED scores over time.
>
> *Convergence/Divergence:* This validity study investigates the degree to which VAL-ED survey measures are *similar* to an established measure of instructional leadership, i.e., the Principal Instructional Management Rating Scale (Hallinger and Murphy, 1985), and the extent to which VAL-ED measures instructional leadership *differently* from those identified as trait emotional intelligence as measured by the Trait Emotional Intelligence Questionnaire (Petrides, Pérez-González, & Furnham, 2007).
>
> *Consequences:* This validity study involves districts that have used VAL-ED for at least one year and examines what uses are made of VAL-ED results and to what effect.
>
> *Longitudinal Effect:* Schools that have used the VAL-ED in two consecutive springs are included in this study that examines whether VAL-ED results can be used to predict value-added to student achievement.

Assessment Procedures

The VAL-ED as an evaluation tool is available in both a paper and an online version. The instrument is a 360-degree assessment: for each school, the principal completes a self-evaluation, the teachers in the school evaluate the principal, and the supervisor of the principal evaluates the principal, all using the same 72-item instrument, which requires 20–30 minutes to complete.[4]

Results from the VAL-ED are reported in terms of mean item effectiveness on a 5-point effectiveness rating scale. Percentile ranks are based on available national data and performance standards. There is a total aggregate score, which is a function of the responses to all 72 items across the supervisor, the principal, and the teachers, where supervisor, principal, and teachers are weighted equally. Results are also reported separately for each respondent group and for each core component and each key process.

Respondents

The VAL-ED is designed to be completed by three types of respondents: *teachers, supervisors of principals,* and *principals themselves.* All individuals completing the instrument should know the principal and have worked with the principal in the same school for at least 2 months prior to the completion of the instrument. With regard to the teacher group, we encourage a broad definition so as to include faculty or staff who are actively engaged in an effort to improve the social and academic learning of students. This may include some individuals who typically are not considered teachers, but support teachers such as librarians, subject specialists, and counselors. In some school districts, principals may have more than one supervisor. If so, all official supervisors are encouraged to participate in the evaluation of the principal. Finally, the principal being evaluated conducts a self-evaluation. When teachers, supervisors, and the principal, are included in rating the principal, what is commonly called a 360 assessment is achieved.

Desired Teacher Participation. The VAL-ED is designed to have all teachers in a school rate the effectiveness of a principal's behavior. The representativeness and size of the group of teachers participating in the assessment of a principal's leadership behaviors matter. The goal should be to have all teachers participate. We consider response rates of 75% or higher as high. When the response rate is below 50% of teachers, one must be concerned about the validity of the resulting scores. Missing respondents from those eligible provokes a number of possible questions about the administration procedures and the relationships among respondents and a principal. Thus, it is important to take steps to ensure a high rate of participation.

Issues Influencing Response Rates. Three issues highly related to achieving a representative and large response rate to the VAL-ED are (1) time and timing of the assessment, (2) guarantee of anonymity of teachers' responses to the VAL-ED, and (3) appointment of an evaluation coordinator who does not participate in the assessment and is seen as objective. The 72-item VAL-ED typically requires 20 to 25 minutes to complete once the directions have been read and the example items examined. Thus, a period of up to 45 minutes is recommended to ensure complete and thoughtful responses to all items from all participants. When using the paper version of the instrument, a good practice is large-group administration, such as during a faculty meeting. If the respondents are completing the VAL-ED online or the paper administration is being conducted within an "assessment period" (e.g., 1 week), then the specified amount of time needed to complete the instrument may be less of a challenge.

Regardless of the amount of time to complete the VAL-ED or the timing in the school year when it is completed, the response rate from teachers is strongly affected by the guaranteed confidentiality of responses. Such a guarantee begins with the appointment of an evaluation coordinator who provides an accurate statement about the purpose and use of the assessment, ensures there is no connection of respondents' names to response forms or individual score summaries, ensures the VAL-ED response forms or data files are secure from beginning to end of the assessment process, and limits the role of the principal in the administration and management process by allowing him or her to provide only positive encouragement to participate and possible evidence for consideration when completing effectiveness ratings. The principal should not be present when teachers are completing the VAL-ED. A principal's actions to encourage positive ratings or to suggest negative consequences for not completing a VAL-ED response form is unprofessional and likely will result in an invalid assessment.

Directions for Completing the VAL-ED

Respondents are asked how effective the principal is at specific actions that affect core components of learning-centered leadership. The effectiveness ratings range from 1 = Ineffective to 5 = Outstandingly Effective for each of 72 behaviors. These behaviors sample all 36 cells of our conceptual model of leadership equally and thus serve as indicators of the construct of leadership we desire to measure. Respondents rate the extent to which the principal ensures behaviors and actions are taken in the school, thus acknowledging that principals do not necessarily perform the behavior themselves, but often designate and distribute these leadership practices and behaviors throughout the school. If a respondent does not have any evidence upon which to make an effectiveness rating, he or she must rate the principal as *Ineffective*.

The specific directions given to principal respondents are:

1. Read each item describing a leadership behavior. In some cases, you may not have actually performed the behavior, but you have ensured that it was done by others in the school. Either way the behavior should be rated.

2. Check the key **Sources of Evidence** you use for the basis of your assessment.

Note, at least one source of evidence must be checked for an item before you make an Effectiveness rating. If you check **No Evidence**, then **Ineffective** must be marked in the Effectiveness column.

3. If you check any sources of evidence other than No Evidence, always make an Effectiveness rating. The number of **Sources of Evidence** checked is **not** necessarily indicative of the Effectiveness rating.

4. Circle the **1 to 5 Effectiveness Rating** to indicate how effectively the behavior was performed. **Outstandingly effective** means you (or your designee) has carried out a particular behavior (e.g., providing necessary support) with a very strong, positive effect on the targeted area of school activity (e.g., rigorous curriculum). **Ineffective** means you (or your designee) has either not done the particular behavior (e.g., not provided necessary support) or has carried out the behavior with very low quality that does not have a positive effect on the targeted area of school activity (e.g., rigorous curriculum).

A set of four items and the response format for the VAL-ED is illustrated in Figure 4. The higher the score, the more effective a principal is in exhibiting the desired leadership behaviors. The end goal of the interpretation is to be able to make a reliable and valid attribution about a principal based on the input from multiple respondents who have observed and interacted with him or her.

Rigorous Curriculum (content)	Sources of Evidence Check Key Sources of Evidence						Effectiveness Rating Mark One Circle to Indicate How Effective				
	Reports from Others	Personal Observations	School Documents	School Projects or Activities	Other Sources	No Evidence	Ineffective	Minimally Effective	Satisfactorily Effective	Highly Effective	Outstandingly Effective
- There is ambitious academic content provided to all students in core academic subjects.											
How effective am I at ensuring the school...											
Planning — 13. develops a rigorous curriculum for all students.	☐	☐	☐	☐	☐	☐	○ 1	○ 2	○ 3	○ 4	○ 5
14. plans access to rigorous curricula for students with special needs.	☐	☐	☐	☐	☐	☐	○ 1	○ 2	○ 3	○ 4	○ 5
Implementing — 15. creates rigorous sequences of learning experiences/courses.	☐	☐	☐	☐	☐	☐	○ 1	○ 2	○ 3	○ 4	○ 5
16. implements a rigorous curriculum in all classes	☐	☐	☐	☐	☐	☐	○ 1	○ 2	○ 3	○ 4	○ 5

Figure 4: Sample VAL-ED Items on Principal Form.

Behavior Ratings and Evidence for Ratings of Effectiveness of Leadership Behavior

As with any assessment tool, rating scales have limitations and should be used as part of a more comprehensive database to increase the likelihood that their resulting scores are reliable and valid. Perhaps an important limitation is that without tangible evidence about a principal's behavior, we do not know if self-reports and ratings by others are associated with what the principal actually does. Normative press and social desirability are also potentially problematic influences on the validity of self-report assessments. Most of the potential shortcomings of rating scales can be overcome with the use of evidence-based, multirater systems that utilize objective scoring rubrics and repeated measures of performance. In addition, when items are phrased in behavioral terms and results reported in ways that lead to opportunities for improvement, research has found that rating scale methods can be highly efficient and valid measures of human behavior (Desimone, 2009).

Thus, the VAL-ED uses rating scale methodology *and* encourages respondents to recall, document, and evaluate evidence of leadership behaviors from their interactions with the principal. There is not a requirement to actually collect the evidence, although a respondent could do so or a principal could provide a portfolio of evidence he or she has developed as part of the evidential bases for effectiveness judgments. The actual evidence available to most respondents is substantial and takes the form of work products, observations, interviews, and school events. In summary, samples of tangible and reliable evidence documented by respondents play an important role in the assessment of a principal's leadership behavior. The VAL-ED assessment process is designed to be evidence- based and honors the reports of respondents who have substantial interactions with the principal whom they are assessing.

To achieve the VAL-ED's potential to inform principals and others interested in their leadership behaviors, it must be implemented with integrity. This means that the VAL-ED needs to be used for its intended purposes and be administered as designed. The following summarizes the key implementation guidance:

1. The VAL-ED measures leadership behaviors, not attitude or personal characteristics.

2. Scores based on respondents who represent fewer than 50% of those invited to assess the principal may be unrepresentative and should be used with caution.

3. Scores based on respondents who report high rates of No Evidence or Don't Know responses may be unrepresentative and should be used with caution.

4. The results of the VAL-ED provide technically sound scores, but they should be used along with other information when making important personnel decisions or they should be repeated to confirm original conclusions.

Principal's VAL-ED Report and Interpretation

The VAL-ED provides an evidence-based, multirater method for assessing learning-centered leadership behaviors of a school's principal. The instrument privileges behaviors that influence the practices of teachers and staff, and in turn are related to increases in student achievement. The use of multiple respondents—teachers, supervisors, and principals themselves—who work in the same environment, effectively surrounding the principal, and the requirement for effectiveness ratings to be based on tangible observations or reports of behavior, both help to enhance the salience and the comprehensiveness of the resulting scores.

The VAL-ED behavior inventory provides information on a total score, six subscales for core components, and six subscales for key processes separately for each respondent group and overall averaged across respondent groups. The core components and key processes are based on the same information, so while their information is redundant, the two separate profiles offer diagnostic information as to how a principal's behaviors might be improved, leading to a more effective school and, in turn, improved student achievement.

The most fundamental score resulting from the VAL-ED is the Principal's Overall Total Effectiveness score. This score is based on the average ratings of all respondents where each respondent group is equally weighted and is reported in the 5-point effectiveness metric used to rate each of the 72 items on the instrument. Thus, the Principal's Overall Total Effectiveness score and the Core Component and Key Process subscale scores are all reported on a continuous scale from a low of 1.0 (Ineffective) to a high of 5.0 (Outstandingly Effective).

The VAL-ED results are reported on the Principal's Report Form and interpreted against both norm-referenced and standards-referenced criteria that highlight areas of strength and possible areas for improvement. A leadership development plan can be developed based on these results. The VAL-ED provides technically sound scores when used as designed. However, it is recommended that it be used along with other information when making important evaluative decisions. The report addresses questions such as: Who responded? What evidence was used to evaluate the principal? What do the results say about the principal's current leadership behaviors? We illustrate and explain the evaluation results in the report samples in Figures 5–9.[5]

Who Responded and What Evidence Did They Use?

A response rate of greater than or equal to 75% is high, 50% to 74% is moderate, and below 50% is low. When response rates are low, resulting scores should be interpreted with caution.

Ratings of a principal's behaviors should be based on evidence that is recent, relevant, and representative. Evidence comes in many forms (e.g., observations of behavior, review of documents that record leadership actions, and communications with people who have directly observed the principal's behavior). After reflecting on a sample of evidence, respondents' effectiveness ratings of leadership behaviors are behaviorally anchored and more accurate. Figure 5 summarizes each type of evidence used as a basis for effectiveness ratings of the leadership behaviors by teachers. The bars display the sources of evidence for each item used by all responding teachers in the school. Percentages are based on number of items for which a source of evidence was checked; these percentages need not sum to 100 across sources. How the principal and the supervisor use the evidences is also presented in the report.

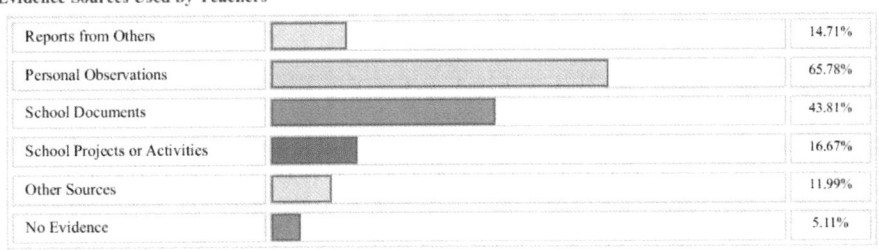

Figure 5: Sample Report (Part 1)—Evidence Used by Teachers.

What Are the Results of the Assessment?

The VAL-ED provides a total score across all respondents as well as separately by respondent group. In the sample report provided in Figure 6, the Principal's Overall Total Effectiveness score based on the averaged ratings of all respondents is 3.47. Remember, this score is based on a 5-point effectiveness scale where 1 = Ineffective; 2 = Minimally Effective; 3 = Satisfactorily Effective; 4 = Highly Effective; 5 = Outstandingly Effective. The scores from the teachers are based on the average across all teacher respondents. It is important to recognize that all scores on all tests have some *error* associated with them. As required by the *Testing Standards for Educational and Psychological Testing* (AERA, APA, & NCME, 1999), the standard error of measurement (SEM) for the VAL-ED's mean total score is +.05. This SEM can be used to create a confidence band for each score on the VAL-ED. For important decisions a 95% confidence band is recommended. Using this criteria, we suggest users consider a range of scores (observed score + .05) rather than just a raw effectiveness single-point score.

Figure 6 presents the effectiveness scores, the performance level, and the percentile rank. The total score and the component and key process effectiveness ratings are interpreted against a national representative sample that included principals, supervisors, and teachers, providing a percentile rank. The results are also interpreted against a set of performance standards ranging from *Below Basic* to *Distinguished*. The scores associated with performance levels were determined by a national panel of principals, supervisors and teachers.

Overall Effectiveness Score		
Mean Score	Performance Level	Percentile Rank
3.47	Basic	31.9

The standard error of measurement is .05

Summary of Core Components Scores					Summary of Key Processes Scores			
	Mean	Performance Level	Percentile Rank			Mean	Performance Level	Percentile Rank
High Standards for Student Learning	3.53	Basic	34.6		Planning	3.47	Basic	37.8
Rigorous Curriculum	3.53	Basic	44.2		Implementing	3.35	Basic	20.9
Quality Instruction	3.69	Proficient	50.6		Supporting	3.64	Proficient	38.7
Culture of Learning & Professional Behavior	3.48	Basic	22.8		Advocating	3.42	Basic	36.0
Connections to External Communities	3.04	Below Basic	15.9		Communicating	3.49	Basic	33.3
Performance Accountability	3.40	Basic	41.0		Monitoring	3.45	Basic	37.8

Figure 6: Sample Report (Part 2)—Scores, Performance Level, and Percentile Rank.

Norm-Referenced Scores. To facilitate interpretation of the total and subscale scores we translate total mean scores for each respondent's form of the VAL-ED to a percentile rank score based on our 2008 national field trial in 218 schools. These original norms are created separately for teacher responses, principal responses, supervisor responses, and a combination of all three of these respondent groups on both Forms A and C of the VAL-ED. The resulting normative information allows for the comparison of a principal's behaviors on total score and subscale profiles to a national sample of principals who lead elementary, middle, and high schools representative of urban, suburban, and rural locales in all regions of the country. The norms for the VAL-ED will be updated periodically to ensure sensitivity to changes in leadership behavior and schools nationally.

Percentile ranks indicate the percentage of individuals in the norm group who scored at or below a given raw score. Percentiles range from 1 to 99. A percentile rank of 50 indicates that the individual's score is average in his or her group. Percentiles are widely used because they can be described in a simple manner and are understood by most educators. It is important, however, to recognize the limitations of percentiles. Unlike standard scores, which are equal interval measures, percentiles represent a rank-order type of measure. Score units are unequal; thus, percentiles cannot be arithmetically manipulated like standard scores.

Criterion-Referenced Scores. For our criterion-referenced interpretive framework, we defined proficiency levels and used a national panel of educational leaders to establish the scores (i.e., cut scores) that were needed to marginally meet each level. These proficiency cut scores were set on total score mean item response, using an equal-weight average across the three respondent groups. We used a modified Bookmark approach to setting proficiency standards (Cizek, 2001) for the following four proficiency levels:

- *Below Basic*—A leader at the *below basic* level of proficiency exhibits leadership behaviors of core components and key processes at levels of effectiveness that over time are unlikely to influence teachers to bring the school to a point that results in acceptable value added to student achievement and social learning for students.

- *Basic*—A leader at the *basic* level of proficiency exhibits leadership behaviors of core components and key processes at levels of effectiveness that over time are likely to influence teachers to bring the school to a point that results in acceptable value added to student achievement and social learning for some subgroups of students, but not all.

- *Proficient*—A *proficient* leader exhibits leadership behaviors of core components and key processes at levels of effectiveness that over time are likely to influence teachers to bring the school to a point that results in acceptable value added to student achievement and social learning for all students.

- *Distinguished*—A *distinguished* leader exhibits leadership behaviors of core components and key processes at levels of effectiveness that over time are virtually certain to influence teachers to bring the school to a point that results in strong value added to student achievement and social learning for all students.

The current three cut scores were set based on the 2008 national trial data. They are used to differentiate these four levels of leadership proficiency: 3.29 between asic and Below Basic 3.60 between Basic and Proficient; and 4.00 between Proficient and Distinguished. The result of these cut scores is that principals who earn a mean item response score averaged across all respondent groups in the range of 1.0 to 3.28 will be described as behaving at the Below Basic level. Principals who earn a mean item response score averaged across all respondent groups in the range of 3.29 to 3.59 will be described as behaving at the Basic level. Principals who earn a mean item response score averaged across all respondent groups in the range of 3.60 to 3.99 will be described as behaving at the Proficient level. And, finally, principals who earn a mean item response score averaged across all respondent groups in the range of 4.00 to 5.00 will be described as behaving at the Distinguished level. Based on our national field trial with 300 principals, these cut scores resulted in 17% of principals at the Below Basic level, 33% at the Basic level, 36% at the Proficient level, and 14% at the Distinguished level of proficiency.

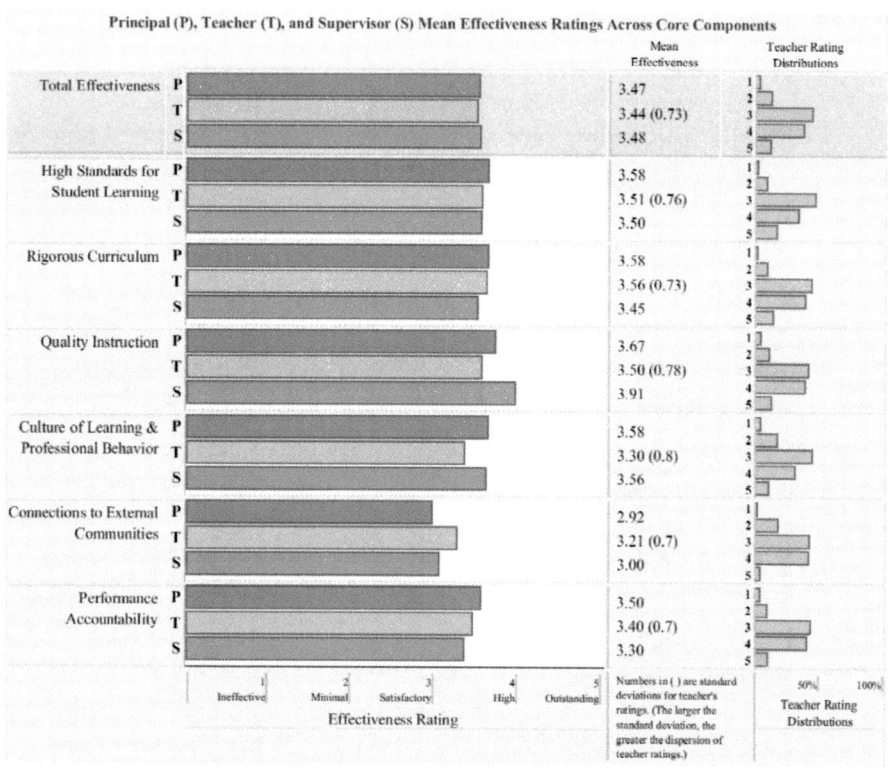

Figure 7: Sample Report (Part 3)—Core Component Scores and Respondent Comparisons.

Assessment Profile and Respondent Comparisons

The principal's relative strengths and areas for development can be determined by comparing scores for each of the six core components and six key processes across different respondent groups. Figure 7 presents an integrated visual summary of the results, specifically the mean effectiveness score associated with each core component. These scores can be interpreted by (a) comparisons among the six core components; (b) examination of scores among respondent groups; (c) comparisons to the mean effectiveness scale; and (d) distribution of ratings among teachers.

For each of the six core components in Figure 7, examine the effectiveness ratings. The ratings for a core component are based on twelve items. The higher the ratings, the more effective the leadership behaviors of the principal. When there are large differences between respondent groups, the focus should be on the results for each respondent group rather than the overall effectiveness score. Contrary to anecdotal fears that teachers may give subjective ratings to their principals, the 2008 national trial data indicates that among the VAL-ED users included in the sample, principals tended to give themselves the most stringent effectiveness ratings as compared with the teachers and the supervisors (Porter et al., 2010b).

Using Results to Plan for Professional Growth

The matrix in Figure 8 provides an integrated summary of the principal's relative strengths and areas for growth based on the mean item scores for the intersection of core components by key processes across the three respondent groups. Cells that are dark gray represent areas of behavior that are "proficient" or "distinguished" (P). Cells that are light gray represent areas of behavior that are "basic" (B). Cells that are black represent areas of behavior that are "below basic" (BB).

The Principal's Report Form also points out areas listed in each cluster that are 'below basic' (marked with "BB") by listing leadership behaviors in the assessment item pool for possible improvement. For example, in this sample profile, weak performance areas include the core component of *Connections to External Communities* and its intersection with the six key processes. Figure 9 shows one set of suggested leadership behaviors that address the core component of *Connections to External Communities* and the key process of *Advocating*. The behaviors that are in boldface type are those that were actually assessed in the evaluation. The other behaviors represent the entire pool of VAL-ED behaviors for each core component by key process. All of these behaviors are relevant targets for improvement.

Core Components	Key Processes					
	Planning	Implementing	Supporting	Advocating	Communicating	Monitoring
High Standards for Student Learning	B	B	P	BB	P	B
Rigorous Curriculum	B	BB	P	P	BB	B
Quality Instruction	B	P	P	B	P	P
Culture of Learning & Professional Behavior	P	B	B	P	B	BB
Connections to External Communities	BB	BB	BB	BB	BB	BB
Performance Accountability	B	BB	P	BB	B	B

Figure 8: Sample Report (Part 4)—Performance Profile for Professional Growth.

Connections to External Communities X Advocating

- Advocates for social services needed by students and families.
- Advocates for students in need of special services with the external community.
- **Challenges teachers to work with community agencies to support students with low achievement.**
- Challenges barriers from outside the school that can inhibit learning.
- Advocates to district decision makers to promote the needs of all students.
- **Promotes mechanisms for reaching families who are least comfortable at school.**

Figure 9: Sample Report (Part 5)—Suggestions for Possible Improvement.

Summary

The purpose of this chapter is to introduce the VAL-ED as a new evaluation tool for principal performance. This new assessment focuses exclusively upon leadership behaviors linked to student learning.

Reviews of research on leadership, professional standards for school leaders, and instruments currently being used across the country provide the rationale and content design imperatives for a new assessment instrument. We present the conceptual framework that drives our leadership assessment development work. We are assessing school leadership behaviors at the intersection of core components (i.e., what principals or leadership teams must accomplish to improve academic and social learning for all students) and key processes (i.e., how principals or leadership teams create those core components). Using this conceptual framework, we develop a leadership behavior inventory that will provide profiles of performance across each of the core components and across each of the key processes. Our overall conception of a leadership assessment system is broader than our core components by key processes assessment of leadership behaviors.

Our assessment model gives weight to how successful a school is in terms of achieving core components. For example, does the school have a rigorous curriculum or a culture of learning and professional behavior? In assessing the quality of school leadership, we also give weight to evidence of student accomplishment. For example, does the school have a relatively large value added to student achievement? Finally, our assessment model recognizes that context matters when it comes to assessing the quality of education leadership. For example, how long has the principal been at the school? What is the composition of the student body? Are we assessing leadership at a high school or an elementary school?

Our model for assessment of leadership in education hypothesizes that school leadership behaviors defined by our core components and key processes lead over time to a school improving in terms of high standards for student learning, rigorous curriculum, quality instruction, the culture of learning and professional behavior, connections to external communities, and systemic performance accountability. A school having these core components in turn leads to the school having improved student achievement, attendance, graduation and the like.

This chapter also documents that each of our core components and each of our key processes is based in research on how leadership behaviors add value to student achievement. Further, we have shown that our conceptual framework, defined by the intersection of our six core components and six key processes, is consistent with the ISLLC standards, though not redundant. For example, our conceptual framework makes systematic distinctions not captured in the ISLLC standards. Our framework distinguishes among rigorous curriculum, quality instruction, and culture of learning and professional behavior. The ISLLC standards do not. Further, for each core component we distinguish among leadership behaviors for each of the six key processes, whereas the ISLLC standards do not.

We discuss the research studies (in brief) to establish the VAL-ED as an instrument that (a) works well in a variety of settings and circumstances, (b) is unbiased, (c) is construct valid, (d) is reliable, (e) is feasible for widespread use (both online and paper-and-pencil versions), (f) provides accurate and useful reporting of results, (g) yields a diagnostic profile for formative purposes, and (h) can be used to measure progress over time in the development of leadership.[6]

With the practitioners that may be interested in implementing the VAL-ED in mind, we also emphasize the necessary considerations for administering the survey to multiple respondents as intended by the design team. Moreover, we illustrate the usage of the VAL-ED Principal Report Form and provide a set of suggestions for making the best use of the results.[7]

In January 2008, *Education Week* reported that researchers with Learning Point Associates, a nonprofit educational consulting firm based in suburban Chicago, reviewed eight principal-performance instruments being used by school districts and concluded that VAL-ED comes closest to measuring the leadership attributes and behaviors that research finds to be associated with how well students perform (Maxwell, 2009). VAL-ED also was rated the best among the instruments for validity and reliability, meaning that the assessment measures what it is supposed to measure and yields consistent results by the same report. We hope that the ongoing validation studies will further enhance the psychometric properties of the VAL-ED as an evaluation instrument and serve as an effective tool for leadership assessment and development.

Notes

[*]The authors gratefully acknowledge the generous support of the Wallace Foundation. The research reported here was supported by the Institute of Education Sciences, U.S. Department of Education, through grant R305C050041–05 to the University of Pennsylvania. The opinions expressed are those of the authors and do not represent views of the Institute or the U.S. Department of Education. The VAL-ED instrument is authored by Drs. Porter, Murphy, Goldring, and Elliott and copyrighted by Vanderbilt University, all of whom receive a royalty from its sales by Discovery Education Assessment. The VAL-ED authors and their research partners have made every effort to be objective and data based in statements about the instrument, and value the independent peer review process of their research. With any publication, readers in the end must judge the facts and related materials for themselves.

1. This chapter is based on previously published research on the VAL-ED. Sources are cited accordingly throughout. More can be found at http://valed.com/research.html.
2. A full report on the development and pilot studies for the VAL-ED can be found at www.valed.com or reference Porter et al., (2010a).
3. A full report on the national trial studies for the VAL-ED can be found at www.valed.com or reference Porter et al., (2010b).
4. Teachers as a group provide ratings on all 72 items, but to save time each individual teacher rates only a subset of 36 items.
5. Information on score reports is from a comprehensive, integrated Principal Report available online at www.valed.edu and in the VAL-ED Technical Manual and Users' Guide.

6. Because the validation of all tests and assessments is an ongoing process designed to refine technical features and understand long-term consequential aspects of the use of assessment, we encourage researchers and practitioners alike to consult our website (www.valed.com) for periodic updates about the VAL-ED.
7. For implementation and usage tips consult the VAL-ED Technical Manual and Users' Guide at www.valed.com.

References

Adams, J. E., & Kirst, M. W. (1999). New demands and concepts for educational accountability: Striving for results in an era of accountability. In J. Murphy & K. Louis (Eds.), *Handbook of research on educational administration, 2nd edition* (pp. 463–489). San Francisco: Jossey-Bass.

American Educational Research Association, American Psychological Association, & National Council on Measurement in Education (AERA, APA, & NCME). (1999). *Standards for educational and psychological testing*. Washington, DC.

Betts, J. R., & Grogger, J. (2003). The impact of grading standards on student achievement, educational attainment, and entry-level earnings. *Economics of Education Review, 22*, 343–352.

Boyer, E. L. (1983). *High school: A report on secondary education in America*. New York: Harper & Row.

Brookover, W. B., & Lezotte, L. W. (1977). *Changes in school characteristics coincident with changes in student achievement*. East Lansing: College of Urban Development, Michigan State University.

Bryk, A., Camburn, E., & Louis, K. S. (1999). Professional community in Chicago elementary schools. Facilitating factors and organizational consequences. *Educational Administration Quarterly, 35*, 751–781.

Bryk, A. S., & Driscoll, M. E. (1988). *The high school as community: Contextual influences and consequences for students and teachers*. Madison: National Center on Effective Secondary Schools, University of Wisconsin-Madison.

Bryk, A. S., & Schneider, B. (2002). *Trust in schools: A core resource for improvement*. New York: Russell Sage.

Burns, J. M. (1978). *Leadership*. New York: Harper & Row.

Butty, J., LaPoint, V., Thomas, V., & Thompson, D. (2001). The changing face of after school programs: Advocating talent development for urban middle and high school students. *NASSP Bulletin, 58*(262), 22–34.

Cizek, G. J. (2001). *Setting performance standards: Concepts, methods, and perspectives*. Mahwah, NJ: Erlbaum.

Conley, D. T. (1991). Lessons from laboratories in school restructuring and site-based decision making. *Oregon School Study Council Bulletin, 34*(7), 1–61.

Conley, D. T., & Goldman, P. (1994). Ten propositions for facilitative leadership. In J. Murphy & K. S. Louis (Eds.), *Reshaping the principalship: Insights from transformational reform efforts*. Thousand Oaks, CA: Corwin Press, 237–262.

Council of Chief State School Officers (CCSSO). (1996). *Interstate school leaders licensure consortium standards for school leaders*. Washington, DC: Author.

Council of Chief State School Officers. (2008). *Educational leadership policy standards: 2008*. Washington DC: Author.

Desimone, L. M. (2009). Improving impact studies of teachers' professional development: Toward better conceptualizations and measures. *Educational Researcher, 38*(3), 181–199.

Downing, S., & Haladyna, T. M. (2006). *Handbook of test development.* Mahwah, NJ Lawrence Erlbaum Assoc Inc.

Edmonds, R., & Frederiksen, J. R. (1978). *Search for effective schools: The identification and analysis of city schools that are instructionally effective for poor children.* Cambridge, MA: Center for Urban Studies, Harvard University.

Elmore, R. F. (2005). Accountable leadership. *The Educational Forum, 69,* 134–142.

Eubanks, E. E., & Levine, D. U. (1983, June). A first look at effective schools projects in New York City and Milwaukee. *Phi Delta Kappan, 64*(10), 697–702.

Fullan, M., & Pomfret, A. (1977). Research on curriculum and instructional implementation. *Review of Educational Research, 47,* 335–397.

Garibaldi, A. M. (1993). *Improving urban schools in inner-city communities* (Occasional Paper No. 3). Cleveland, OH: Levine College of Urban Affairs, Urban Child Research Center, Cleveland State University.

Goldring, E., Cravens, X., Murphy, J., Porter, A., Elliott, S., & Carson, B. (2009). The evaluation of principals: What and how do states and urban districts assess leadership? *Elementary School Journal, 110*(1), 19–39.

Goldring, E., & Hausman, C. (2001). Civic capacity and school principals: The missing link in community development. In R. Crowson & B. Boyd (Eds.), *Community development and school reform.* Greenwich, CT: JAI Press.

Goldring, E., Porter, A., Murphy, J., Elliott, S. N., & Cravens, X. (2009). Assessing learning-centered leadership: Connections to research, professional standards, and current practices. *Leadership and Policy in Schools, 8,* 1–36.

Haladyna, T. M., Downing, S. M., & Rodriguez, M. C. (2002). A review of multiple choice item-writing guidelines for classroom assessment. *Applied Measurement in Education, 15*(3), 309–334.

Hallinger, P., & Heck, R. (1996). Reassessing the principal's role in school effectiveness: A review of empirical research, 1980–1985. *Educational Administration Quarterly, 32*(1), 5–44.

Hallinger, P., & Heck, R. H. (2002). What do you call people with visions? The role of vision, missions, and goals in school improvement. In K. Leithwood, P. Hallinger, G. Furman, J. MacBeath, B. Mulford, & K. Riley (Eds.), *The second international handbook of educational leadership and administration.* Dordrecht, The Netherlands: Kluwer.

Hallinger, P., & Murphy, J. (1985). Assessing the instructional management behavior of principals. *Elementary School Journal, 86,* 217–247.

Heck, R. (1992). Principals' instructional leadership and school performance: Implications for policy development. *Educational Evaluation and Policy Analysis, 14*(1), 21–34.

Heck, R. H., & Hallinger, P. (1999). Next generation methods in the study of leadership and school improvement. In J. Murphy, & K. S. Louis (Eds.). *Handbook of research on educational administration* (2nd ed., pp. 141–162). San Francisco: Jossey-Bass.

Henderson, A. T., & Mapp, K. L. (2002). *A new wave of evidence: The impact of school, family, and community connections on student achievement.* Austin, TX: Southwest Educational Development Laboratory.

Knapp, M. S., Copland, M. A., & Talbert, J. (2003). *Leading for learning: Reflective tools for school and district leaders.* Seattle: Center for the Study of Teaching and Policy, University of

Washington.
Leithwood, K. (1994). Leadership for school restructuring. *Educational Administration Quarterly, 30*, 498–518.
Leithwood, K., & Jantzi, D. (2005). A review of transformational school leadership research, 1996–2005. *Leadership and Policy in Schools, 4*, 177–199.
Leithwood, K., Louis, K. S., Anderson, S., & Wahlstrom, K. (2004). *How leadership influences student learning*. Minneapolis: University of Minnesota.
Leithwood, K., & Montgomery, D. J. (1982). The role of the elementary school principal in program improvement. *Review of Educational Research, 52*(3), 309–339.
Lee, V. E., Smith, J. B., & Croninger, R. G. (1995). *Another look at high school restructuring: More evidence that it improves student achievement and more insights into why*. Madison, WI: Center on Organization and Restructuring of Schools.
Little, J. W. (1982, Fall). Norm of collegiality and experimentation: Work-place conditions of school success. *American Educational Research Journal, 19*(3), 325–340.
Loucks, S. F., Bauchner, J. E., Crandal, D., Schmidt, W., and Eisman, J. (1982). *Portraits of the changes, the players, and the contexts. A study of dissemination efforts supporting school improvement. People, policies, and practices: Examining the chain of school improvement*. Andover, MA: The Network, Inc.
Louis, K. S., Marks, H., & Kruse, S. (1996). Teachers' professional community in restructuring schools. *American Educational Research Journal, 33*(4), 757–798.
Louis, K. S., & Miles, M. B. (1990). *Improving the urban high school: What works and why*. New York: Teachers College Press.
Manasse, A. L. (1985). Improving conditions for principal effectiveness: Policy implications for research. *The Elementary School Journal, 85*, 439–463.
Marzano, R. J., Waters, T., & McNulty, B. A. (2005). *School leadership that works: From leadership to results*. Alexandria, VA: Association for Supervision and Curriculum Development.
Maxwell, L. A. (2009). Review backs new tool for principal evaluation: Vanderbilt's new assessment receives high marks, but many are not linked to students' learning. *Education Week, 29*(16), 8.
Murphy, J. (2005). Unpacking the foundations of ISLLC Standards and addressing concerns in the academic community. *Educational Administration Quarterly, 41*, 154–191.
Murphy, J., Elliott, S. N., Goldring, E., & Porter, A. C. (2007). Leadership for learning: A research-based model and taxonomy of behaviors. *School Leadership & Management, 27*(2), 179–201.
Murphy, J., & Hallinger, P. (1985). Effective high schools: What are common characteristics? *NASSP Bulletin, 69*(477), 18–22.
Murphy, J., & Meyers, C. V. (2008). *Turning around failing schools: Leadership lessons from the organizational sciences*. Thousand Oaks, CA: Corwin.
National Research Council. (1999). *How people learn: Bridging research and practice*. Washington, DC: National Academy Press.
Newmann, F. M. (1997). How secondary schools contribute to academic success. In K. Borman & B. Schneider (Eds.), *Youth experiences and development: Social influences and educational challenges*. Berkeley, CA: McCutchan.
Ogden, E. H., & Germinario, V. (1995). *The nation's best schools: Blueprints for excellence*. Lancaster, PA: Technomic.

Petrides, K. V., Pérez-González, J. C., & Furnham, A. (2007). On the criterion and incremental validity of trait emotional intelligence. *Cognition and Emotion, 21*, 26–55.

Polikoff, M. S., May, H., Porter, A. C., Elliott, S. N., Goldring, E., & Murphy, J. (2009). An examination of differential item functioning in the Vanderbilt Assessment of Leadership in Education. *Journal of School Leadership, 19*(6), 661–679.

Porter, A. C., Goldring, E. B., Murphy, J., Elliott, S. N., & Cravens, X. (2006). A framework for the assessment of learning-centered leadership. New York, NY: Wallace Foundation.

Porter, A. C., Murphy, J., Goldring, E. B., Elliott, S. N., Polikoff, M. S., & May, H. (2008). *VAL-ED: Technical Manual (Version 1.0)*. Nashville: Discovery Education Assessments.

Porter, A. C., Polikoff, M., Goldring, E. B., Murphy, J., Elliott, S. N., & May, H. (2010a). Developing a psychometrically sound assessment of school leadership: The VAL-ED as a case study. *Educational Administration Quarterly, 46*(2), 135–173.

Porter, A. C., Polikoff, M. S., Goldring, E., Murphy, J.; Elliott, S. N.; & May, H. (2010b) Investigating the validity and reliability of the Vanderbilt Assessment of Leadership in Education. *Elementary School Journal, 111*(2), 282–313.

Purkey, S. C., & Smith, M. S. (1983). Effective schools: A review. *The Elementary School Journal, 83*(4), 426–452.

Rosenholtz, S. J. (1989). *Teachers' workplace: The social organization of schools.* New York: Longman.

Roueche, J. E., Baker, G. A., Mullin, P. L., & Boy, N. H. O. (1986). *Profiling excellence in America's schools.* Arlington, VA: American Association of School Administrators.

Shaver, A. V., & Walls, R. T. (1998). Effect of Title I parent involvement on student reading and mathematics achievement. *Journal of Research and Development in Education, 31*(2), 90–97.

Teddlie, C., Stringfield, S., Wimpelberg, R., & Kirby, P. (1989). Contextual differences in models for effective schooling in the United States. In B. Creemers, T. Peters, & D. Reynolds (Eds.), *School effectiveness and school improvement: Selected proceedings from the Second Inferential Congress* (pp. 117–130). Amsterdam: Swets and Zeitlinger.

Wellisch, J. B., MacQueen, A. H., Carriere, R. A., & Duck, G. A. (1978, July). School management and organization in successful schools. *Sociology of Education, 51*, 211–226.

Westat and Policy Studies Associates. (2001). *The longitudinal evaluation of change and performance in Title I schools.* Washington, DC: U.S. Department of Education, Office of the Deputy Secretary, Planning and Evaluation Service.

• 3 •

A Data-Driven Approach TO Assess AND Develop Instructional Leadership WITH THE PIMRS

PHILIP HALLINGER

Among the global trends in educational leadership and management that have emerged over the past 50 years, few have been more significant, widespread or persistent than the focus on understanding linkages between school leadership and learning (Bell, Bolam, & Cubillo, 2003; Bridges, 1967; Gross & Herriot, 1965; Hallinger & Heck, 1996a, 1996b; Leithwood, Anderson, Mascall & Strauss, 2011; Robinson, Lloyd & Rowe, 2008; Witziers, Bosker, & Kruger, 2003). The "elusive search" (Witziers et al., 2003) for understanding the nature of leadership that makes a difference for student learning has engaged scholars in studying a wide variety of leadership models. These include instructional leadership (e.g., Bossert, Dwyer, Rowan & Lee, 1982; Hallinger & Murphy, 1985a), transformational and transactional leadership (e.g., Leithwood & Jantzi, 2000), strategic leadership (e.g., Davies, Ellison & Bowring-Carr, 2005), teacher leadership (e.g., Barth, 2001; Lambert, 2002; York-Barr & Duke, 2004), collaborative leadership (Hallinger & Heck, 2010) and distributed leadership (Spillane, 2006). Recent research syntheses support the conclusion that, among these competing models, instructional leadership has demonstrated the greatest impact on student learning (e.g., Hallinger, 2011b; Leithwood, Day, Sammons, Harris, & Hopkins, 2006; Robinson et al., 2008). This conclusion has further enhanced the prominence of instructional leadership as a focus for policy and practice, and provides a rationale for why school personnel *should* focus on strengthening instructional leadership as a lever for school improvement (Hallinger, 2003; Leithwood et al., 2011; Printy, n.d.).

The broad purpose of this chapter is to offer a data-driven, research-informed approach to understanding, assessing and strengthening principal instructional leadership. The chapter begins with a brief review of the historical evolution of the instructional leadership construct. This leads into the introduction of a specific conceptual model of instructional leadership and presentation of an instrument for assessing the practice of instructional leadership, the *Principal Instructional Management Rating Scale* (*PIMRS*; Hallinger, 1982). Given the goal of strengthening system-wide capacity for instructional leadership at the school level, we also consider some of the barriers that impede or lead principals away from enacting this role in practice. Finally, the chapter discusses how the instrument has been used by school systems to assess and develop instructional leadership.

Instructional Leadership as a Key Domain of Educational Management

During the early and middle years of the 20th century, practical wisdom shared by principals, school superintendents, teachers and parents in the United States conveyed the belief that "good schools have good principals" (e.g., Grobman & Hynes, 1956; Gross & Herriot, 1965; Lipham, 1961; Miller, 1960; Stuart, 1950; Tyack & Hansot, 1982; Uhls, 1962). The definitive example was a book published by James Lipham in the early 1960s, aptly titled *Effective Principal, Effective School* (Lipham, 1961). As stated by Lipham:

> In summarizing findings on the principal's role in the school, this monograph assumes that the principal is a pivotal figure in the school and is the one who most affects the quality of teacher performance and student achievement. The author concludes that the studies reviewed demonstrate that the principal is a key factor in the success of the school. (Lipham,,1961, p. 3)

Yet, despite formulating this conclusion, Lipham (1961) also acknowledged that the "studies" on which his conclusions were based consisted largely of opinion surveys and case studies rather than "scientific" inquiry. Several years later, Edwin Bridges (1967) offered a more pointed critique of the practical wisdom of the times.

> Of the seven major task areas for which principals have responsibility, curriculum and instruction has generated the most sound and fury. On the one hand, the principal has been exhorted to exert instructional leadership, while on the other hand, he has been

told flatly that such a role is beyond his or any other human being's capacity. The problem with these disputations is that the exponents of a given position have neither defined sharply what is signified by the concept of instructional leadership nor made their assumptions explicit. (1967, p. 136)

Consequently, this practical wisdom, though widely accepted, lacked anything approaching a sound empirical knowledge base. It was, therefore, unable to offer reliable guidance for policymakers, educators of leaders, or school leaders themselves (Bridges, 1967, 1982; Erickson, 1967). Nonetheless, a perusal of the professional and scholarly literatures of the ensuing era suggests that support for this practical wisdom continued unabated (Bridges, 1982).

The next significant point in the historical evolution of this construct came at the dawn of the effective schools era in the USA in the early 1980s (Edmonds, 1979). Researchers studying instructionally effective schools identified "strong instructional leadership by the principal" as a hallmark of effective urban elementary schools in the United States (Bossert et al., 1982; Edmonds, 1979; Purkey & Smith, 1983). Although this conclusion found a ready reception among American policymakers, there were significant limitations in the research designs employed in these studies. Consequently, the research finding of "strong instructional leadership by the principal" continued to yield considerable ambiguity concerning both the nature of the role and its contribution to school improvement (Barth, 1986; Barth & Deal, 1982; Bossert et al., 1982; Cuban, 1984; Leithwood & Montgomery, 1982; Murphy, Hallinger & Mitman, 1983; Rowan, Bossert & Dwyer, 1983). Limitations noted by reviewers of this literature included:

- Lack of clearly explicated conceptual frameworks;
- Lack of valid and reliable instrumentation for studying the role;
- Lack of theoretical models that articulated how this role influenced student learning;
- Reliance on weak research designs, ill-equipped to test for causal effects.

These limitations were cause for concern in light of burgeoning attempts to embed emerging this research finding into government policies and principal training curricula in the USA (Barth, 1986; Cuban, 1984). Moreover, in a reprise of Bridges' earlier critique, highly respected scholar-practitioners continued to evince skepticism concerning the extent to which instructional leadership represented a leadership model that could be broadly applied to the principalship in all schools (e.g., Barth, 1986; Barth & Deal, 1982; Cuban, 1984, 1988).

During this same period, Stephen Bossert and colleagues (1982) at the Far West Lab in San Francisco published a seminal literature review that synthesized findings from empirical studies that had focused more specifically on investigating school leadership and learning. While the authors acknowledged these methodological limitations, they also claimed to see the foundation within this literature for a productive program of research targeting instructional leadership and its effects on learning. Bossert's "instructional management framework" subsequently became a valuable lens used by other scholars for conceptualizing how leadership for learning is enacted in schools. We note that the findings from the Bossert review were largely supported by other contemporary reviews of this literature (e.g., Leithwood & Montgomery, 1982; Hallinger & Murphy, 1985a; Murphy, Hallinger & Mitmal, 1983; Purkey & Smith, 1983).

Subsequently, during the 1980s and 1990s a growing number of largely North American scholars began to undertake more intentionally designed empirical investigations of the principal's instructional leadership role (e.g., Blasé, 1987; Dwyer, Lee, Rowan, & Bossert 1983; Eberts & Stone, 1988; Hallinger, Bickman & Davis, 1996; Hallinger & Murphy, 1985a, 1985b; Hallinger, Taraseina & Miller, 1994; Heck, Larson & Marcoulides, 1990; Howe, 1995; Jones, 1987; Krug, 1986; Leitner, 1994; Leithwood & Montgomery, 1982; Leithwood & Stager, 1989; O'Day, 1986). This was facilitated, in no small part, by development of new conceptual frameworks (e.g., Bossert et al., 1982; Hallinger, Murphy, Weil, Mesa, & Mitman, 1983) and the first research instruments (e.g., Hallinger & Murphy, 1985a; Villanova, Gauthier, Proctor, & Shoemaker, 1981) developed to assess instructional leadership. These developments signaled the emergence of instructional leadership as a research-based construct, and highlighted its potential for contributing to the profession's understanding of how principal leadership impacts student learning (Hallinger & Heck, 1996a; Leithwood, Begley, & Cousins 1990). As a result, by the mid-1990s, Hallinger and Heck (1996a, 1996b, 1998) observed that instructional leadership had become the most prevalent perspective adopted by researchers engaged in the study of school leadership effects in North America.

At the same time, however, it is interesting to note that prior to the turn of the millennium interest in instructional leadership was a largely North American phenomenon.[1] Indeed, it has been only in the last decade that the term *instructional leadership* and its cousin, *leadership for learning*, have gained broad international currency. This is reflected in research and policy publications from the UK (Bell et al., 2003; Day et al., 2009; Hunter Foundation, 2005; MacBeath & Cheng, 2008; Southworth, 2002), continental Europe (Krüger, Witziers, & Sleegers, 2007; Witziers et al., 2003), East Asia (Chan & Cheng, 1993; Kim, 1988; Hallinger et al., 1994; Ratchaneeladdajit, 1997; Poovatanikul, 1993; Wongtrakool, 1995) and Australia/New

Zealand (Mulford & Silins, 2009; Robinson et al., 2008). This reflects the growing global interest in understanding the ways in which school leaders contribute to school improvement and student learning (Hallinger & Heck, 2011a).

This growing global interest in instructional leadership has subsequently generated an expanding body of empirical research and continuing advances in clarifying its contribution to improvements in teaching and learning (e.g., see Bryk, Sebring, Allensworth, Luppescu, & Easton, 2009; Datnow & Castellano, 2001; Hallinger & Heck, 2010; Krüger et al., 2007; Knapp, Copland, Honig, Plecki, & Portin, 2009; Marks & Printy, 2003; May & Supovitz, 2011; Mulford & Silins, 2009; Nettles & Herrington, 2007; Opdenakker, & Van Damme, 2007; Printy, Marks, & Bowers, 2009; Silva, White, & Yoshida, 2011; Spillane, 2006; Wahlstrom & Louis, 2008; Wiley, 2001). Thus, we conclude that 50 years after publication of *Effective Principal, Effective School* (Lipham, 1961), instructional leadership has become increasingly accepted globally as a normative expectation in the principalship.

Instructional Leadership: A Conceptual Framework

The quotation from Bridges (1967) noted earlier highlighted the importance of starting with a sound definition of what is meant by instructional leadership. In their review article, Bossert and colleagues (1982) began to define this construct, which they termed *instructional management*. They selected the term *instructional management* because they inferred that this role of the principal revolved around core managerial functions concerned with the "coordination and control" of curriculum and instruction (e.g., Cohen & Miller, 1980).

Nonetheless, over time, *instructional leadership* became the term more commonly used by scholars and practitioners. The formal distinction between these terms lies in the sources of power by which the leader achieves results. *Instructional leadership* became the preferred term due to the recognition that principals who operate from this frame of reference rely more upon expertise and influence than on formal authority and position power to achieve a sustainable impact on staff motivation and behavior, and student learning (e.g., Blasé, 1987; Hallinger, 2003; Hallinger & Heck, 1996a; Leithwood et al., 1990).

Another early attempt to provide a clear definition of instructional leadership came from Hallinger and Murphy in the early 1980s (Murphy, Hallinger, Weil, & Mitman, 1983; Hallinger et al., 1983; Hallinger & Murphy, 1985a). Our proposed conceptual framework incorporated three dimensions in this role: *Defining the School's Mission, Managing the Instructional Program*, and *Promoting a Positive School Learning Climate* (Hallinger et al., 1983; Hallinger & Murphy, 1985a; see Figure 1). These dimensions were further delineated into 10 instructional leadership functions.

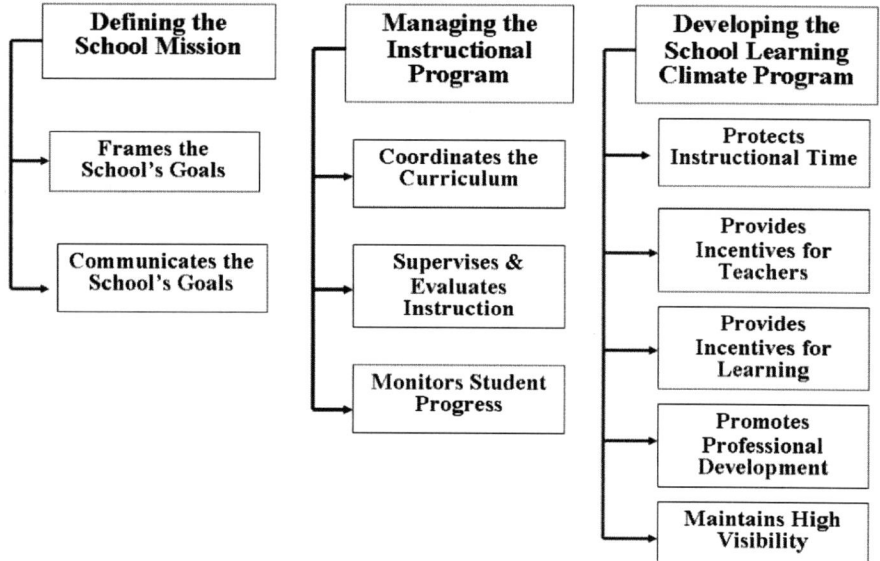

Figure 1. PIMRS Conceptual Framework.

Two functions, Framing the School's Goals and Communicating the School's Goals, comprise the dimension *Defining the School's Mission*. These concern the principal's role in working with staff to ensure that the school has a clear mission and that the mission is focused on the academic progress of its students. Note that this dimension does not assume that the principal defines the school's mission alone. Instead it proposes that the principal is responsible for ensuring that such a mission exists, for communicating it widely to staff, and ensuring that there is a shared purpose underlying staff efforts to improve teaching and learning in the school. This dimension is the starting point for creating a learner-centered school.

The second dimension is *Managing the Instructional Program*. This incorporates three leadership functions: Supervising and Evaluating Instruction, Coordinating the Curriculum, and Monitoring Student Progress. This dimension focuses on the role of the principal in "managing the technical core" of the school (Hallinger et al., 1983; Murphy, Hallinger, Weil & Mitman, 1983). Although in larger schools it is clear that the principal is not the only person involved in monitoring and developing the school's instructional program, the principal is expected to ensure that these tasks are carried out.

The third dimension, *Promoting a Positive School Learning Climate*, includes several functions: Protecting Instructional Time, Promoting Teacher Professional Development, Maintaining High Visibility, Providing Incentives for Teachers, and Providing Incentives for Learning. This dimension is broader in scope and intent than the second dimension and overlaps with dimensions incorporated into transformational leadership frameworks (Hallinger, 2003; Leithwood et al., 2006). It conforms to the notion that successful schools create an "academic press" through the development of high standards and expectations, and a culture that fosters and rewards continuous learning and improvement (Bossert et al., 1982; Hallinger & Murphy, 1985a; Murphy, Hallinger, Weil & Mitman, 1983; Purkey & Smith, 1983).

These three dimensions and their composite functions represent a research-informed framework for conceptualizing the principal's role as an instructional leader. Although this framework proposes that coordination and control of the academic program of the school remains a key leadership responsibility of the principal, in practice many specific activities and tasks may be shared, delegated, or distributed (e.g., Hallinger, 2003; Marks & Printy, 2003; Spillane, 2006). Indeed, over the past three decades the field has increasingly recognized that the scope of tasks involved in enacting instructional leadership often goes beyond the principal's responsibility (Barth, 2001; Hallinger & Heck, 2010; Lambert, 2002; Marks & Printy, 2003; Printy, n.d.; Spillane, 2006).

The rationale for this conclusion is grounded in the importance of this role to the school's improvement, the scope of work involved, the extent of expertise required, the time available to the principal, and the need to develop capacity for future leadership in the school (e.g., Barth, 2001; Donaldson, 2001; Grubb & Flessa, 2009; Lambert, 2002; Marks & Printy, 2003; Spillane, 2006). Thus, although this chapter focuses on the instructional leadership of the principal, we assert that the same framework can be applied beyond the principal to encompass the broader set of actors who collaborate to provide instructional leadership for their schools (Hallinger & Heck, 2010). The next section of the chapter will examine barriers to enacting these instructional leadership functions in practice.

Barriers to Instructional Leadership

Despite the fact that practical wisdom and research support the belief that instructional leadership is important to school improvement, it was earlier noted that some scholars and practitioners questioned both its relevance and viability as a guiding metaphor for school leadership (e.g., Barth, 1986; Cuban, 1984). These scholars observed that despite decades of rhetorical support for this role in the professional literature, its implementation in practice was more aptly characterized by its scarcity than by its prevalence. Four obstacles have been identified that constrain principals from exercising strong instructional leadership: lack of expertise in curriculum and instruction, professional norms, system expectations, and role diversity.

Lack of Expertise in Curriculum and Instruction

Educators have long assumed that principals have the tools to provide instructional leadership because they were once teachers themselves. Unfortunately, preparation as a teacher neither ensures that a prospective principal is capable of leading others nor that he or she has specific expertise in curriculum and instruction. Moreover, school principals were not traditionally selected on the basis of their instructional leadership potential. Finally, university-based preparation programs have not generally developed these capacities in the depth required for principals to engage teachers productively in changing their teaching practice. Consequently, upon assuming their administrative role, many principals lack the expertise and confidence to focus on this part of the job.

Professional Norms

Long-standing professional norms that state that educational decision making is the teacher's domain may also militate against the exercise of instructional leadership (Barth & Deal, 1982; Marshall, 1996). Principals often informally trade their authority over curriculum and instruction for compliance by teachers on other issues (Cuban, 1988). This trade-off is formalized in some districts through collective bargaining agreements. Whether formal or informal, these "negotiated treaties" result in territorial boundaries that create a "force field" around the classroom that limits the frequency and depth of principals' classroom visitations as well as their initiative in consulting with teachers about instructional matters (Marshall, 1996, 2004).

System Expectations

It has also been the case that most school systems have traditionally placed a higher priority on managerial efficiency and political stability than on instructional leadership (Cuban, 1988; March, 1978). This is reflected in norms implicitly understood by both principals and system administrators. Principals typically receive few formal rewards for actively engaging in curriculum and instructional change, and in the past suffered few sanctions if they ignored this domain. Conversely, central office supervisors are likely to address community or management-related problems through quick, firm communications to the principal involved.

Consistent with these observations is the finding that promotions into administrative positions are just as often associated with gender, political clout, and visibility as with instructional leadership potential (Cuban, 1988). Thus, the administrative norms in most school systems still reinforce the informal negotiation of treaties with teachers concerning domains of practice, further inhibiting instructional leadership (Barth & Deal, 1982; Cuban, 1988; Marshall, 1996, 2004). While there is evidence of recent changes with respect to this obstacle in the USA (see Silva et al., 2011), it is too soon to tell how deep and long-lasting they will be.

Role Diversity

It is well documented that the principal's workday comprises many brief, fragmented interactions with different actors (Dwyer, 1986; Horng, Klasik, & Loeb, 2010; Lee & Hallinger, in press; Marshall, 1996; Martin & Willower, 1981; Peterson, 1977–78). It is often difficult for principals to schedule the uninterrupted blocks of time necessary for planning and assessing curriculum, observing lessons, and conferencing with teachers. In addition, teachers, parents, students, and central office staff hold widely varying expectations of the principal (Marshall, 1996, 2004). This multiplicity of roles and expectations tends to act as a counterforce, fragmenting both the principal's vision and allocation of time.

These barriers are worthy of note since they reflect both structural (e.g., role definitions) and sociocultural norms (e.g., norms of classroom privacy) that principals must strive to overcome if they are intent upon enacting instructional leadership in their schools. As implied above, we observe that in many parts of the world today the press to "be an instructional leader" has taken on greater urgency. For example, recently adopted policies in the United States levy sanctions on principals whose schools do not meet annual learning targets. While on the surface it would seem that these policies should impact principal allocation of time and attention towards instructional leadership, there remains wide variance both in the USA and internationally in principals' allocation of time to instructional leadership (Horng et al., 2010; Lee & Hallinger, in press). Thus, we note that school cultures change slowly and the barriers noted above will continue to hold sway in many school systems for years to come.

Assessing the Practice of Instructional Leadership

This chapter proposes a data-driven approach to the development of instructional leadership capacity in schools and school systems. In order to design such an approach, however, one needs a reliable means of gathering data on the principal's instructional leadership practice. Let us briefly examine some of these approaches.

Approaches to Assessing Principal Instructional Leadership

We begin by noting that it is possible to gather data on the principal's instructional leadership practice through a variety of means including direct observation, interviews, and questionnaires (Goldring, Porter, Murphy, Elliot, & Cravens, 2009; Hallinger & Murphy, 1985a, 1987). Each method has advantages and disadvantages in terms of efficiency (i.e., time and effort) and effectiveness (i.e., quality of information).

Systematic use of direct observation was pioneered in principal professional development in the United States as long ago as the 1980s. Researchers at the Far West Lab in San Francisco developed the Peer-Assisted Leadership program, or PAL (Barnett & Long, 1986). This professional leader learning program grew out of the research process employed in early observational studies of instructional leadership carried out at the Far West Lab by Bossert and his colleagues (Dwyer, 1986; Dwyer et al., 1983). In this program principals use a combination of semistructured observation and reflective interviewing to gather information and provide nonjudgmental feedback to peers. This process was geared toward stimulating the principal to reflect on personal patterns of instructional leadership practice and link these to important goals, as well as to create a more intentional awareness among principals of their approach to instructional leadership.

The trend towards using peer coaching and mentoring in leader learning programs has gathered force in recent years. Thus, in many parts of the world today, peer coaching and mentoring have been introduced into training and development programs for school leaders (e.g., Browne-Ferrigno & Muth, 2004; Ehrich, Hansford, & Tennent, 2004; Goldring, 2010; Walker et al., 2002). These programs train principals in formal coaching skills that they can then use with peers as means of stimulating on-the-job learning and development.

While observation offers possibly the most direct means of obtaining data on leadership practice, it is time-consuming. Multiple observations are needed to generate valid results. Observational data are not easily synthesized to provide a picture of performance across individuals. For these reasons, we view direct observation as a useful, but supplementary method of generating data on principal practice. In addition, we suggest observation of the principal may be more suitably employed for the purpose of professional development than for personnel evaluation.

Interviews with stakeholders can be employed to generate a picture of the principal's instructional leadership. Again, however, interviews are time consuming and of limited validity when used as the sole method of assessment. Respondents may be reluctant to make direct statements during interviews concerning the practices of their superordinate. Concerns over confidentiality may also inhibit the validity of responses.

Questionnaires represent a commonly used means of generating perceptual data. They are efficient, since it generally takes less time to complete and score a questionnaire than to conduct a single observation. Although questionnaires rely on the staff's perceptions rather than observed behavior, numerous studies have found that they can provide reliable, valid data on managerial behavior (Latham & Wexley, 1981).

Issues arise concerning who should complete questionnaires that provide data on principal practice (e.g., the principal, teachers, supervisors, parents). This is important in that the assumption behind a behavioral questionnaire is that it provides a "perceptual sampling" of the principal's behavior. Therefore, respondents must have had sufficient opportunities to "observe" the principal in practice if they are to provide valid data in response to questionnaire items (Hallinger & Murphy, 1985a, 1987; Latham & Wexley, 1981).

The PIMRS Instrument

As noted earlier, interest in instructional leadership preceded the availability of tools that could reliably capture the construct in practice. The (*PIMRS*, Hallinger, 1982) was developed 30 years ago as a tool that could be used by both researchers and school practitioners in the measurement of this construct. It is based upon the conceptual framework presented earlier in this chapter. The instrument has subsequently been employed by numerous school systems as well as by more than 200 researchers in published studies and doctoral dissertations focusing on principal instructional leadership (Hallinger, 2011a).

Sample *PIMRS* Rating Subscale: Teacher Form
To what extent does your principal. . . ?
I. FRAME THE SCHOOL GOALS

	Almost Never				Almost Always
1. Develop a focused set of annual school-wide goals	1	2	3	4	5
2. Frame the school's goals in terms of staff responsibilities for meeting them	1	2	3	4	5
3. Use needs assessment or other systematic methods to secure staff input on goal development	1	2	3	4	5
4. Use data on student academic performance when developing the school's academic goals	1	2	3	4	5
5. Develop goals that are easily translated into classroom objectives by teachers	1	2	3	4	5

Figure 2. Sample Items from the PIMRS.[2]

The original form of the PIMRS[3] (Hallinger, 1982) contained 11 subscales and 72 "behaviorally anchored" items. Subsequent revision of the instrument reduced the instrument to 10 subscales and 50 items. For each item, the rater assesses the frequency with which the principal enacts a behavior or practice associated with that particular instructional leadership function. Each item is rated on a Likert-type scale ranging from (1) almost never to (5) almost always (see Figure 2). The instrument is scored by calculating the mean for the items that comprise each subscale. This results in a profile that portrays perceptions of principal performance on each of the 10 instructional leadership functions (see Figure 3).

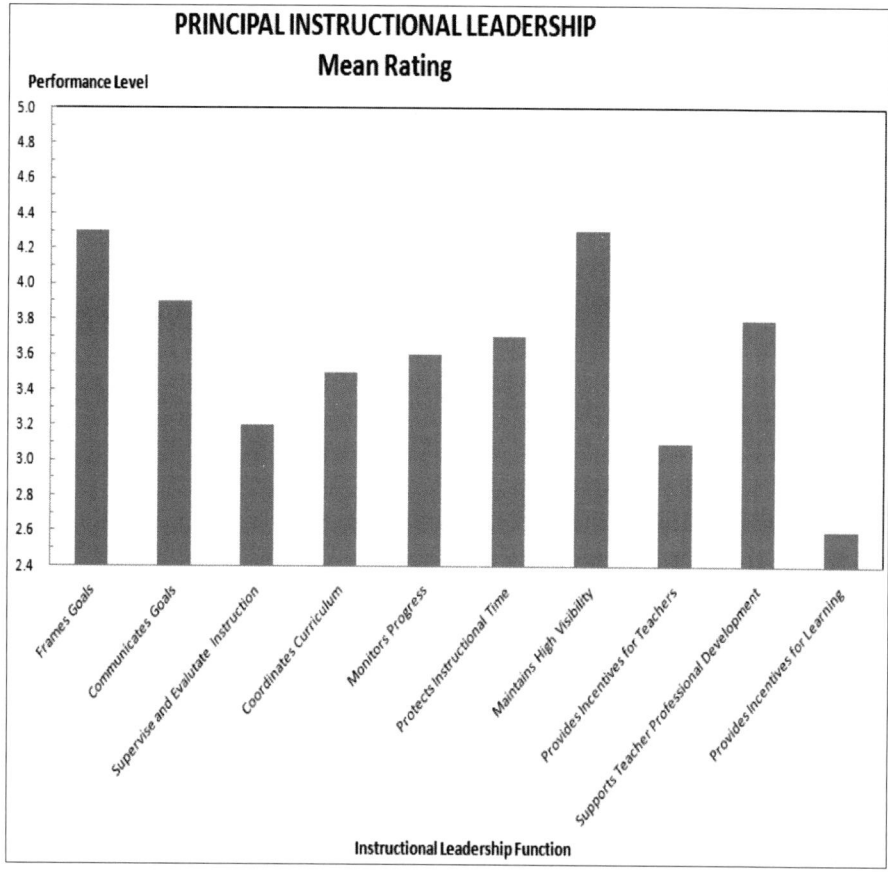

Figure 3. Rating of an Individual Principal with the PIMRS.

Three parallel forms of the instrument have been developed and tested: a self-assessment form to be completed by the principal, a teacher form and a supervisor form. The items that comprise each form are identical; only the stems change to reflect the differing perspectives of the role groups. Early studies found significant differences in perceptions across role groups (Hallinger & Murphy, 1985a; Krug, 1986; O'Day, 1983). Validation studies in the United States indicate that the *PIMRS* form that solicits teachers' perceptions provides the most valid data of the three forms.

The original validation study found that the *PIMRS* met high standards of reliability (Hallinger, 1983). All ten subscales exceeded .80 using Cronbach's test of internal consistency. Subsequent studies have generally substituted Ebel's (1951) test for calculating inter-rater reliability for Cronbach's formula. This test provides a more accurate test of reliability for ratings aggregated from a set of schools where respondents within schools (e.g., teachers) are rating a feature of the school (i.e., the principal).

These studies have supported the original validation study in its conclusion that the scale provides reliable data on instructional management (e.g., Dunn, 2010; Fulton, 2009; Hallinger et al., 1994; Harris, 2002; Howe, 1995; Jones, 1987; Leitner, 1994; Mercer, 2004; Moore, 2003; O'Day, 1984). Studies have further tested the *PIMRS* for face validity, content validity and discriminant validity. Initially, the instrument was judged to be a valid measurement tool for use at the elementary school level. Subsequent studies referred to in this chapter expanded on the instrument's validation (e.g., Hallinger et al., 1994; Howe, 1995; Jones, 1987; Leitner, 1994; O'Day, 1984). It suffices to conclude that the instrument appears to have provided a reliable and valid means of assessing the instructional leadership of school principals.

Using Data to Strengthen Instructional Leadership

According to Duke and Stiggins (1985), the type of data needed in assessing leadership practice varies with the purpose of the assessment. Where assessments are used for personnel evaluation and other accountability-oriented purposes, the data must meet specific legal and professional standards of reliability and validity (Latham & Wexley 1981). Few principal evaluation systems even approach such standards, and the procedures used seldom meet the criteria administrators must apply to the evaluation of teachers (Goldring, Cravens, Murphy, & Elliot, 2009). Where assessments are used only for professional improvement, there can be greater leeway in the nature of the data used (Duke & Stiggins, 1985). Within the scope of this chapter, we focus primarily on employing the *PIMRS* for the latter purpose.

The *PIMRS* can be administered to a principal as a self-assessment instrument as well as to supervisors and teachers to provide a broader picture of the principal's leadership. The choice of appraisers depends on the purposes of the assessment. When professional improvement is the sole concern, self-report data from the principal are acceptable, at least as a starting point. However, greater care must be exercised when collecting data as part of the evaluation process. A sample self-report profile of an individual principal on the 10 instructional leadership functions was shown in Figure 3.

There are several features to keep in mind when interpreting this particular profile. First, the analysis focuses on functional responsibilities rather than the broader dimensions (e.g., Defining the Scholl's Mission) or specific items. From the perspectives of both measurement and practical experience, this often offers a useful level of detail for users, whether they are principals or system-level personnel. Second, we note that the scale is based on a level of frequency of demonstrating the specified behaviors. While moderately high ratings are preferred, a rating of 5 may not reflect the optimal quality of performance. Therefore, the fact that a principal has not achieved a profile of 'full marks' should not be interpreted as a 'personal deficit.'[4] Thus, a principal would typically approach the interpretation of this profile in terms of an identification of 'relative strengths' in the 10 functional areas of instructional leadership.

In order to maximize the validity of the *PIMRS* assessment results, we do suggest that both teachers and the principal complete the scale. This not only yields more valid information, but also additional interpretive perspectives for principals to consider. A sample profile comparing the perceptions of teachers and a principal is shown in Figure 4.

This comparative profile of the principal's instructional leadership offers an opportunity for the principal to compare his or her self-perceptions with those of the teaching staff and/or a supervisor(s). Thus, in Figure 4, the principal would not only identify areas of relative strength with respect to the 10 instructional leadership functions, but also differences between self-perceptions and those of one's colleagues. If we accept coaching as a process of data gathering, feedback and self-reflection (Barnett & Long, 1986; Goldring, 2010), then these differences in perception can be employed as a stimulus for reflection, goal-setting, action steps, and further data gathering. Notably, the use of the profile also offers a data-driven approach to assessing change over time in the principal's practice in specific areas within this key domain of the role.

System administrators can also aggregate data obtained across a number of schools in order to identify system-wide strengths and weaknesses. This information can be used for the purposes of planning staff development for principals, recruitment and selection of new principals and middle-level leaders, succession planning, and revision of system policies. For example, Figure 5 offers a different data display for 10 principals from the same school system, this time focusing analysis on the three instructional leadership dimensions.

A DATA-DRIVEN APPROACH TO ASSESS AND DEVELOP INSTRUCTIONAL LEADERSHIP | 61

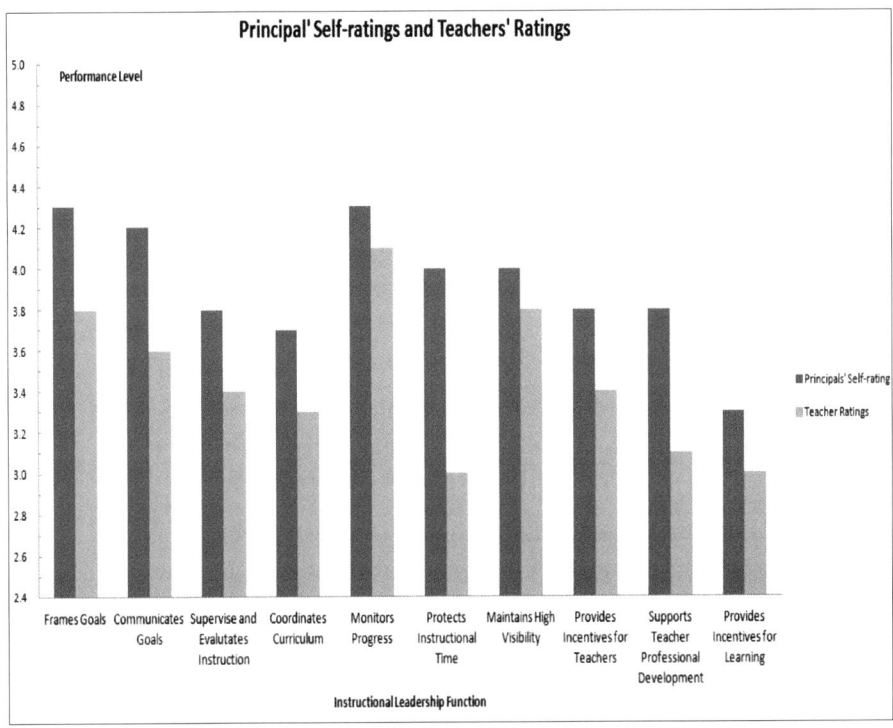

Figure 4. Comparing Teacher and Principal
Perceptions on Instructional Leadership Functions.

Interpretation of Figure 5 would focus on mean performance as well as variability of performance across the principals on the three dimensions. For example, we can see that the principals as a whole appear considerably stronger in terms of establishing a clear mission than in managing the instructional program or developing the school learning climate. This is reflected in a stronger overall mean performance (not tabled) as well as the fact that this dimension was strongest for every principal, regardless of their personal mean rating.

The profile also highlights differences among principals. Thus, we can see that #5 appears to stand out as an instructional leader, while principals #9 and #10 appear to be relatively weaker. Based on this profile, one could subsequently drill down to examine these performance trends in terms of the 10 leadership functions, as well as individual performance profiles. These illustrative profiles are offered in order to indicate the direction that school systems have taken in employing these data, both to stimulate individual principal learning and development and for planning system-wide training and policy revisions.

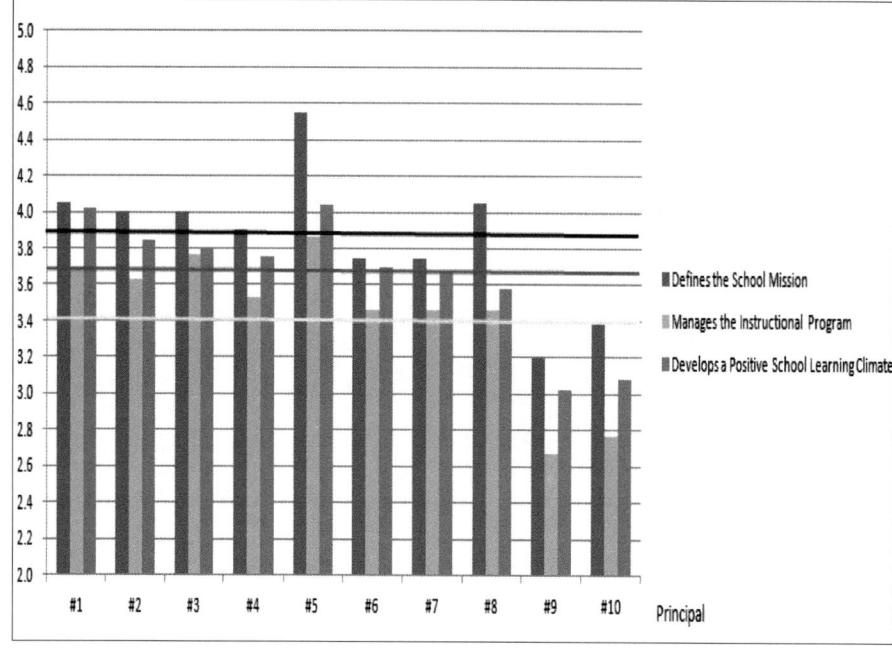

Figure 5. Comparison of Instructional Leadership Profiles among 10 Principals.

Conclusion

Traditionally principals have been offered few incentives and encountered many hazards for venturing into the instructional leadership domain (Cuban, 1988). A weak knowledge base in curriculum and instruction, fragmented system expectations, territorial treaties negotiated with teachers, and diverse roles have tended to keep many site administrators from actively engaging in this role (Bridges, 1967; Cuban, 1988; Hallinger, 2011b; March, 1978; Marshall, 1996, 2004). The implication of this observation is that school systems should not view lack of capacity in instructional leadership as an individual deficit but as an organizational challenge.

At the same time, in today's accountability-driven context, a continuing lack of engagement in this role seems untenable. Pressures to meet annual targets for student learning have created a new context or paradigm within which principals are working, at least in the United States. This makes the principal's active engagement in the instructional leadership role both a moral and a survival imperative (Bryk et al., 2009; Nettles & Herrington, 2007; Silva et al., 2011).

In this chapter, I have sought to present a rationale, conceptual framework, and tool for developing a data-driven approach to improving instructional leadership capacity in schools and school systems. This yields several recommendations for school systems interested in supporting and developing instructional leadership capacity:

1. Define the instructional leadership role so that principals and other leaders at the school level clearly understand what is expected.
2. Remove barriers through revision of relevant policies and provision of tangible support.
3. Establish staff development programs for principals that are research-based and engage principals in learning how to coach each other (e.g., Barnett & Long, 1986; Goldring, 2010; Walker et al., 2002).
4. Provide support by ensuring that instructional leadership is provided not only by the principal but by other colleagues as well (e.g., Hallinger, 2003; Lambert, 2002; Printy, n.d.; Spillane, 2006).
5. Develop leadership succession plans that seek to identify future leaders and build instructional leadership skills among middle leaders before they ascend to the principalship.
6. Use an assessment system that provides data on principal instructional leadership that are valid for accountability purposes and contribute to professional improvement.

This chapter suggests that the *PIMRS* could have a place in this data-driven approach. When used in conjunction with training and development, this systematic, research-based tool provides information principals can use to identify areas for their own professional development and to make decisions regarding the school program. School principals and school systems can use the instrument for planning and evaluating staff development programs, and as a part of a comprehensive approach to principal evaluation.

Notes

*The author wishes to acknowledge the funding support of the Research Grant Council (RGC) of Hong Kong for its support through the General Research Fund (GRF 841711).
1. Van de Grift's (1990) research in the Netherlands was a notable exception to this trend.
2. The full scale can be obtained from the author by e-mail at Hallinger@gmail.com.
3. A variety of resources related to the use of the *PIMRS* can be accessed at the author's personal website: http://philiphallinger.com/pimrs.html. The *PIMRS* instrument can be obtained by contacting the author directly at Hallinger@gmail.com.
4. The author is in the process of revalidating the scale, a process that will yield standards of desirable performance within each of the functions.

References

Barnett, B., & Long, C. (1986). Peer-assisted leadership: Principals learning from each other. *Phi Delta Kappan, 67*(9), 672–675.

Barth, R. (1986). On sheep and goats and school reform. *Phi Delta Kappan, 68*(4), 293–296.

Barth, R. (2001). Teacher leader. *Phi Delta Kappan, 82*(6), 443–449.

Barth, R., & Deal, T.E. (1982). *The principalship: Views from without and within*. Prepared for the national conference on the principalship convened by the National Institute of Education. ERIC Document 224176.

Bell, L., Bolam, R., & Cubillo, L. (2003). *A systematic review of the impact of school headteachers and principals on student outcomes*. London: EPPI-Centre, Social Science Research Unit, Institute of Education.

Blasé, J. (1987). Dimensions of effective school leadership: The teacher's perspective. *American Educational Research Journal, 24*(4), 589–610.

Bossert, S., Dwyer, D., Rowan, B., & Lee, G. (1982). The instructional management role of the principal. *Educational Administration Quarterly, 18*(3), 34–64.

Bridges, E. (1967). Instructional leadership: A concept re-examined. *Journal of Educational Administration, 5*(2), 136–147.

Bridges, E. (1982). Research on the school administrator: The state-of-the-art, 1967–1980. *Educational Administration Quarterly, 18*(3), 12–33.

Browne-Ferrigno, T., & Muth, R. (2004). Leadership mentoring in clinical practice: Role socialization, professional development, and capacity building. *Educational Administration Quarterly, 40*, 468–494.

Bryk., A., Sebring, P., Allensworth, E., Luppescu, S., & Easton, J. (2009). *Organizing schools for improvement: Lessons from Chicago*. Chicago, IL: University of Chicago Press.

Chan, Y.C., & Cheng, Y.C. (1993). A study of principals' instructional leadership in Hong Kong secondary schools. *Educational Research Journal, 8*, 56–67.

Cohen, E., & Miller, R. (1980). Coordination and control of instruction in schools. *Pacific Sociological Review, 4*, 446–473.

Cuban, L. (1984). Transforming the frog into a prince: Effective schools research, policy, and practice at the district level. *Harvard Educational Review, 54*(2), 128–151.

Cuban. L. (1988). *The managerial imperative and the practice of leadership in schools*. Albany, NY: SUNY Press.

Datnow, A., & Castellano, M. (2001). Managing and guiding school reform: Leadership in success for all schools. *Educational Administration Quarterly, 37*(2), 219–249.

Davies, B., Ellison, L., & Bowring-Carr, C. (2005). *School leadership in the 21st century: developing a strategic approach*. London: Routledge-Falmer.

Day, C., Sammons, P., Hopkins, D., Harris, A., Leithwood, K., Gu, Q., Brown, E., Ahtaridou, E., & Kingston, A. (2009). The *impact of school leadership on pupil outcomes, Final Research Report*, DCSF-RR108. London: Department for Children, Schools and Families.

Donaldson, G.A. (2001). *Cultivating leadership in schools: Connecting people, purpose, and practice*. New York: Teachers College Press.

Duke, D., & Stiggins, R. (1985). Evaluating the performance of principals: A descriptive study. *Educational Administration Quarterly, 21*(4), 71–98.

Dunn, A. (2010). *A quantitative study of the perceptions of school leadership preparation in the State of Georgia*. Unpublished doctoral dissertation, Walden University, Minneapolis., MN

Dwyer, D. (1986). Understanding the principal's contribution to instruction. *Peabody Journal of Education, 63*(1), 3–18.

Dwyer, D., Lee, G., Rowan, B., & Bossert, S. (1983). *Five principals in action: Perspectives on instructional management*. San Francisco, CA: Far West Laboratory for Educational Research. ERIC Document No. 231085.

Ebel, R. (1951). Estimation of the reliability of ratings. *Psychometrika, 16*, 407–424.

Eberts, R.W., & Stone, J.A. (1988). Student achievement in public schools: Do principals make a difference? *Economics of Education Review, 7*, 291–299.

Edmonds, R. (1979). Effective schools for the urban poor. *Educational Leadership, 37*(1), 15–24.

Ehrich, L., Hansford, B., & Tennent, L. (2004). Formal mentoring programs in education and other professions: A review of the literature. *Educational Administration Quarterly, 40*, 518–540.

Erickson, D. (1967). The school administrator. *Review of Educational Research, 37*(4), 417–432.

Fulton, T. (2009). *High school principal instructional leadership behavior in high and low need and high and low achievement schools*. Unpublished doctoral dissertation, Dowling College, Oakdale, NY.

Goldring, E., Cravens, X., Murphy, J., & Elliot, S. (2009). The evaluation of principals: What and how do states and urban districts assess leadership? *Elementary School Journal, 110*(1), 19–39.

Goldring, E. (2010). *The next generation of principal professional development: Feedback and coaching as a tool for leadership development*. Keynote paper presented at the conference The Challenges and Prospects of School Improvement in the New Era, Taipei, Taiwan.

Goldring, E., Porter, A., Murphy, J., Elliot, S. N., & Cravens, X. (2009). Assessing learning-centered leadership: Connections to research, professional standards, and current practices. *Leadership and Policy in Schools, 8*, 1–36.

Grobman, H., & Hynes, V. (1956). What makes a good principal? *NASSP Bulletin, 40*(223), 5–16.

Gross, N., & Herriot, R. (1965). *Staff leadership in schools*. New York: Wiley.

Grubb, W.N., & Flessa, J. (2009). "A job too big for one": Multiple principals and other non-traditional approaches to school leadership. In K. Leithwood, B. Mascall, and T. Strauss (Eds.), *Distributed leadership according to the evidence* (pp. 137–164). London: Routledge.

Hallinger, P. (1982, 1990). *Principal Instructional Management Rating Scale*. Sarasota, FL: Leading Development Associates.

Hallinger, P. (1983). *Assessing the instructional management behavior of principals*. Unpublished doctoral dissertation, Stanford University, Stanford, CA. ERIC Document No. 8320806.

Hallinger, P. (2003). Leading educational change: Reflections on the practice of instructional and transformational leadership. *Cambridge Journal of Education, 33*(3), 329–351.

Hallinger, P. (2011a). A review of three decades of doctoral studies using the *Principal Instructional Management Rating Scale*: A lens on methodological progress in educational leadership. *Educational Administration Quarterly, 47*(2) 271–306.

Hallinger, P. (2011b). Leadership for learning: Lessons from 40 years of empirical research. *Journal of Educational Administration, 49*(2), 125–142.

Hallinger, P., Bickman, L., & Davis, K. (1996). School context, principal leadership and student achievement. *Elementary School Journal, 96*(5), 498–518.

Hallinger, P., & Heck, R.H. (1996a). Reassessing the principal's role in school effectiveness: A review of empirical research, 1980–1995. *Educational Administration Quarterly, 32*(1), 5–44.

Hallinger, P., & Heck, R.H. (1996b). The principal's role in school effectiveness: An assessment of methodological progress, 1980–1995. In K. Leithwood et al. (Eds.), *International handbook of research in educational leadership and administration* (pp. 723–784). New York: Kluwer Press.

Hallinger, P., & Heck, R.H. (1998). Exploring the principal's contribution to school effectiveness: 1980–1995. *School Effectiveness and School Improvement, 9*(2), 157–191.

Hallinger, P., & Heck, R.H. (2010). Collaborative leadership and school improvement: Understanding the impact on school capacity and student learning. *School Leadership and Management, 30*(2), 95–110.

Hallinger, P., & Heck, R. (2011). Conceptual and methodological issues in studying school leadership effects as a reciprocal process. School Effectiveness and School Improvement, 22(2), 149-173.

Hallinger, P., & Murphy, J. (1985a). Assessing the instructional leadership behavior of principals. *Elementary School Journal, 86*(2), 217–248.

Hallinger, P., & Murphy, J. (1985b). What's effective for whom? School context and student achievement. *Planning and Changing, 16*(3), 152–160.

Hallinger, P., & Murphy, J. (1987). Assessing and developing principal instructional leadership. *Educational Leadership, 45*(1), 54–62.

Hallinger, P., Murphy, J., Weil, M., Mesa, R.P., & Mitman, A. (1983). Effective schools: Identifying the specific practices and behaviors of the principal. *NASSP Bulletin, 67*(463), 83–91.

Hallinger, P., Taraseina, P., & Miller, J. (1994). Assessing the instructional leadership of secondary school principals in Thailand. *School Effectiveness and School Improvement, 5*(4), 321–348.

Harris, E. (2002). *The relationship between principals' instructional leadership skills and the academic achievement of high-poverty students.* Unpublished doctoral dissertation, University of South Carolina, Columbia.

Heck, R.H., Larson, T., & Marcoulides, G. (1990). Instructional leadership and student achievement: Validation of a causal model. *Educational Administration Quarterly, 26*(2), 94–125.

Horng, E.L., Klasik, D., & Loeb, S. (2010). Principal time-use and school effectiveness. National Center for the Analysis of Longitudinal Data in Education Research. Retrieved June 1, 2010, from www.stanford.edu/.../Principal%20Time-Use%20Research%20Paper%20(revised).pdf

Howe, W. (1995). *Instructional leadership in Catholic elementary schools: An analysis of personal, organizational, and environmental correlates.* Unpublished doctoral dissertation, Stanford University, Stanford, CA. ERIC Document No. 9611976.

Hunter Foundation. (2005). New drive to improve school leadership in Scotland. http://www.thehunterfoundation.co.uk/projects/?project_id=5.

Jones, P. (1987). *The relationship between principal behavior and student achievement in Canadian secondary schools.* Unpublished doctoral dissertation, Stanford University, Stanford, CA.

Kim, Y.M. (1988). *The relationship of principals' instructional leadership to student achievement in academic private high schools in Seoul, Korea.* Ed.D. dissertation, University of Southern California, Los Angeles, California. Retrieved March 4, 2011, from Dissertations & Theses: A & I (Publication No. AAT 0563753).

Knapp, M., Copland, M., Honig, M., Plecki, M., & Portin, B. (2009). *Learning-focused leadership* and leadership support: Meaning and practice in urban systems. Seattle Center for the Study of Teaching and Policy, University of Washington.

Krug, F. (1986). *The relationship between the instructional management behavior of elementary school principals and student achievement.* Unpublished doctoral dissertation, University of San Francisco, San Francisco, CA. ERIC Document No. 8722942.

Krüger, M., Witziers, B., & Sleegers, P. (2007). The impact of school leadership on school level factors: Validation of a causal model. *School Effectiveness and School Improvement, 18*(1), 1–20.

Lambert, L. (2002). A framework for shared leadership. *Educational Leadership, 59*(8), 37–40.

Latham, G., & Wexley, K. (1981). *Increasing productivity through performance appraisal.* Menlo Park, CA: Addison Wesley.

Lee, M.S., & Hallinger, P. (in press). Exploring the impact of national context on principals' time use: Economic development, societal culture, and educational system. *School Effectiveness and School Improvement.*

Leithwood, K., Anderson, S., Mascall, B., & Strauss, T. (2011). School leaders' influences on student learning: The four paths. In T. Bush, L. Bell & D. Middlewood (Eds.), *The principles of educational leadership and management,* 13–30. London: Sage.

Leithwood, K., Begley, P. & Cousins, B. (1990). The nature, causes and consequences of principals' practices: An agenda for future research. *Journal of Educational Administration, 28*(4), 5–31.

Leithwood, K., Day, C., Sammons, P., Harris, A., & Hopkins, D. (2006). *Seven strong claims about successful school leadership.* Nottingham, UK: National College for School Leadership.

Leithwood, K., & Jantzi, D. (2000). The effects of transformational leadership on organizational conditions and student engagement with the school. *Journal of Educational Administration, 38*(2), 112–129.

Leithwood, K. & Montgomery, D. (1982). The role of the elementary principal in program improvement. *Review of Educational Research, 52*(3), 309–339.

Leithwood, K., & Stager, M. (1989). Expertise in principal's problem-solving. Educational Administration Quarterly, 25(2) 126-161.

Leitner, D. (1994). Do principals affect student outcomes: An organizational perspective. *School Effectiveness and School Improvement, 5*(3), 219–238.

Lipham, J. (1961). *Effective principal, effective school.* Reston, VA: National Association of Secondary School Principals.

MacBeath, J., & Cheng, Y.C. (2008). *Leadership for learning: International perspectives.* Rotterdam: Sense Publishers.

March, J.G. (1978). The American public school administrator: A short analysis. *School Review, 86*(2), 217–250.

Marks, H., & Printy, S.M. (2003). Principal leadership and school performance: An integration of transformation and instructional leadership. *Educational Administration Quarterly, 39*(3), 370–397.

Marshall, K. (1996). How I confronted HSPS (Hyperactive Superficial Principal Syndrome) and began to deal with the heart of the matter. *Phi Delta Kappan, 76*(5), 336–345.

Marshall, K. (2004). How I recovered from HSPS (Hyperactive Superficial Principal Syndrome: A progress report. *Phi Delta Kappan, 84*(9), 701–709.

Martin, W., & Willower, D. (1981). The managerial behavior of high school principals. *Educational Administration Quarterly, 17*(1), 69–90.

May, H., & Supovitz, J. (2011). The scope of principal efforts to improve instruction. *Educational Administration Quarterly, 47*(2) 332–352.

Mercer, S. (2004). *The relationship of teachers' perceptions of principals' instructional leadership skills and school performance in four high-poverty South Carolina middle schools.* Unpublished doctoral dissertation, University of South Carolina, Columbia SC.

Miller, G. (1960, April). *What is the role of the principal in promoting good relationships with staff?* Proceedings of the annual meeting of the National Association of Secondary School Principals, 19–22.

Moore, Q. (2003). *Teachers' perceptions of principals' leadership skills in selected South Carolina secondary schools.* Unpublished doctoral dissertation, University of South Carolina, Columbia, SC.

Mulford, B., & Silins, H. (2009). Revised models and conceptualization of successful school principalship in Tasmania. In B. Mulford & B. Edmunds (Eds.), *Successful school principalship in Tasmania* (pp. 1–19). Launceston: Faculty of Education, University of Tasmania.

Murphy, J. (1988). Methodological, measurement and conceptual problems in the study of instructional leadership. *Educational Evaluation and Policy Analysis, 10*(2), 117–139.

Murphy, J., Hallinger, P., & Mitman, A. (1983). Problems with research on educational leadership: Issues to be addressed. *Educational Evaluation and Policy Analysis, 5*(3), 297–306.

Murphy, J., Hallinger, P., Weil, M., & Mitman, A. (1983). Instructional leadership: A conceptual framework. *Planning and Changing, 14*(3), 137–149.

Nettles, S., & Herrington, C. (2007). Revisiting the importance of the direct effects of school leadership on student achievement: The implications for school improvement policy. *Peabody Journal of Education, 82*(4), 724–736.

O'Day, K. (1983). *The relationship between principal and teacher perceptions of principal instructional management behavior and student achievement.* Unpublished doctoral dissertation, Northern Illinois University, Normal, IL. ERIC Document No. 8426701.

Opdenakker, M., & Van Damme, J. (2007). Do school context, student composition and school leadership affect school practice and outcomes in secondary education? *British Educational Research Journal, 33*(2), 179–206.

Peterson, K.D. (1977–78). The principal's tasks. *Administrator's Notebook, 26*(8), 1–4.

Pitner, N. (1988). The study of administrator effects and effectiveness. In N. Boyan (Ed.), *Handbook of research in educational administration* (pp. 106–132). New York: Longman.

Poovatanikul, V. (1993). *Analyses of the perceptions of Thai principals and teachers as to the principal's role as instructional leader.* Unpublished doctoral dissertation, Southern Illinois University, Carbondale.

Printy, S.M. (n.d.). *How principals influence instructional practice: Leadership levers.* Unpublished paper. East Lansing, MI: Michigan State University.

Printy, S. M., Marks, H.M., & Bowers, A. (2009). *Integrated leadership: How principals and teachers share instructional influence.* Unpublished manuscript, Michigan State University, East Lansing.

Purkey, S. & Smith, M. (1983). Effective schools: A review. *Elementary School Journal, 83*(4), 427-52.

Ratchaneeladdajit, R. (1997). *Perceptions of Thai principals and teachers toward the principals' role* as *instructional leaders in private schools in Bangkok, Thailand*. Unpublished doctoral dissertation, Southern Illinois University, Carbondale, IL.

Robinson, V., Lloyd, C., & Rowe, K. (2008). The impact of leadership on student outcomes: An analysis of the differential effects of leadership types. *Educational Administration Quarterly, 44*(5), 635–674.

Rowan, B., Bossert, S., & Dwyer, D. (1983). Research on effective schools: A cautionary note. *Educational Researcher, 12*, 24–31.

Silva, J., White, G., & Yoshida, R. (2011). The direct effects of principal–student discussions on eighth grade students' gains in reading achievement: An experimental study. *Educational Administration Quarterly*, published online April 5, 2011.

Southworth, G. (2002). Instructional leadership in schools: Reflections and empirical evidence. *School Leadership and Management, 22*(1), 73–92.

Spillane, J.P. (2006). *Distributed leadership*. San Francisco: Jossey-Bass.

Stuart, J. (1950). *The thread that runs so true*. New York: Scribner's Sons.

Tyack, D., & Hansot, E. (1982). *Managers of virtue*. New York: Basic Books.

Uhls, H. (1962). What's important Mr. Principal? *NASSP Bulletin, 46*(273), 108–111.

Van de Grift, W. (1990). Educational leadership and academic achievement in elementary education. *School Effectiveness and School Improvement, 1*(3), 26–40.

Villanova, R., Gauthier, W., Proctor, P., & Shoemaker, J. (1981). *The Connecticut school effectiveness questionnaire*. Hartford, CT: Bureau of School Improvement, Connecticut State Department of Education.

Wahlstrom, K., & Louis, K.S. (2008). How teachers experience principal leadership: The roles of professional community, trust, efficacy, and shared responsibility. *Educational Administration Quarterly, 44*(4), 458–495.

Walker, A., Chan, A., Cheung, R., Chan, D., Wong, C., & Dimmock, C. (2002). *Principals developing principals: Principal professional development in Hong Kong*. Invited paper presented at the National College of School Leadership 1st Invitational International Conference, Nottingham, UK.

Wiley, S. (2001). Contextual effects on student achievement: School leadership and professional community. *Journal of Educational Change, 2*(1), 1–33.

Witziers, B., Bosker, R., & Kruger, M. (2003). Educational leadership and student achievement: The elusive search for an association. *Educational Administration Quarterly, 34*(3), 398–425.

Wongtrakool, P. (1995). *Instructional leadership of principals and student achievement in private lower secondary schools of Thailand*. Ph.D. dissertation, Illinois State University, Normal, Retrieved March 4, 2011, from Dissertations & Theses: A&I. (Publication No. AAT 9604384).

York-Barr, J., & Duke, K. (2004). What do we know about teacher leadership? Findings from two decades of scholarship. *Review of Educational Research, 74*(3), 255–316.

· 4 ·

Identifying Leadership AND Organizational Processes Related TO School Outcomes AND Improvement

Validating an Instrument

RONALD H. HECK & GEORGE A. MARCOULIDES

A large body of research accumulated over the past 30 years supports the view that school leadership facilitates growth in student learning (Bossert et al., 1982; Leithwood et al., 2006; Robinson, Lloyd, & Rowe, 2008; Witziers, Bosker, & Kruger, 2003). One primary pathway is by shaping conditions in the school that foster the school's capacity to provide effective teaching and learning. Examples include facilitating the development of school values that support learning, establishing educational partnerships, increasing teacher collaboration regarding curriculum development and organization, enhancing professional development opportunities, and fostering more effective assessment practices (e.g., Hallinger, Bickman, & Davis, 1996; Leithwood et al., 2004; Robinson et al., 2008; Supovitz, Sirinides, & May, 2010). Leadership, therefore, serves as a key *mediating* construct between the school's context (e.g., community values, support, involvement) and structure and its organizational values, behaviors, and instructional practices, which directly influence student outcomes (Bossert et al., 1982; Hallinger et al., 1996; Heck, Larsen, & Marcoulides, 1990; Heck & Marcoulides, 1996b; Heck & Moriyama, 2010; Leithwood et al., 2004; Ogawa & Bossert, 1995). School leaders targeting organizational improvement must facilitate school changes that are embraced and owned by the teachers, who are essentially the ones responsible for implementation in classrooms (Barth, 2001; Hall & Hord, 2001).

Research within the educational effectiveness area has directed attention toward the identification of school factors that support teaching and learning, classroom and school learning environments, support networks, and the ongoing evaluation of strategic efforts to implement changes in the school's instructional practices (Creemers & Kyriakides, 2008). One criticism of this previous research, however, is that the interrelationships among school factors have generally been neglected; that is, in past studies all school factors (i.e., context, composition climate, leadership, organizational values, and instructional processes) have generally been assumed to influence outcomes *directly* (Opdenakker & Van Damme, 2007). Despite the large number of studies conducted over the past 30 years, there has been no consensus about how various types of environmental, structural, school-level processes and classroom-level variables fit together to determine levels of student outcomes, although a few attempts have been made to unify the conceptual components of these factors into a theory that explains outcomes (e.g., Bossert et al., 1982; Creemers, 1994; Creemers & Kyriakides, 2008; Hallinger et al., 1996; Heck et al., 1990; Heck & Marcoulides, 1996a; Mortimore, 1993b; Leithwood, Patten, & Jantzi, 2010; Reynolds & Packer, 1992; Teddlie & Reynolds, 2000).

The usefulness of past theory and research in identifying and organizing promising school characteristics that impact student learning has therefore been somewhat limited in establishing a solid knowledge base (Creemers & Kyriakides, 2008; Heck & Marcoulides, 1996b; Heck & Moriyama, 2010; Scheerens & Bosker, 1997; Teddlie & Reynolds, 2000). As Opdenakker and Van Damme (2007) summarize these limitations:

> While in the past researchers often concentrated on one specifically effectiveness-enhancing factor (e.g., school leadership), or investigated the influence of several factors on outcomes without taking into account the possibility that factors relate to each other, nowadays there are calls to pay attention to the interrelatedness of factors, the direct and indirect effects of factors, the mediated effects of factors and to use time-ordered modeling procedures like path analysis or structural equation modeling. So a plea for more complex models is made. (pp. 179–180)

More typically, only school-level relations are examined; that is, a number of leadership studies have identified various mediators measured at the school level that influence school-level achievement. Leithwood and his colleagues (2010) provide one such summary of pathways of school leadership influence on mediating processes that may affect outcomes. Although school-level improvement is *assumed* to influence what teachers do in classrooms, there have been few empirical tests of this hypothesis that capture the hierarchical complexity of classrooms nested within schools and students nested within classrooms. Examining relationships among school processes, classroom practices, and outcomes clearly requires more complex research designs, instruments, and modeling procedures that can incorporate not only direct and indirect effects, but mediated effects, measurement error, and also accommodate longitudinal data collection (Heck & Marcoulides, 1996b; Heck & Moriyama, 2010; Opdenakker & Van Damme, 2007). Unfortunately, however, previous research on the effectiveness of educational processes has several shortcomings in producing knowledge that can be directly implemented to produce improved school outcomes.

Building on this line of conceptual and empirical work concerning the delineation of relationships between school and classroom factors and student outcomes, in this chapter we present results from several studies we have conducted to identify ways in which school leadership and organizational processes (e.g., values, governance structures, curricular organization, teacher attitudinal and behavioral processes) may intersect in ways that explain student outcomes. These variables all appear to be elements in a conceptual framework that suggests the importance of a school's culture (i.e., its values, rituals and history, academic and social organization, policies, and problem-solving processes) in determining student learning. How school staff, parents, and students are able to organize and coordinate the work life of the school (e.g., its goals, curriculum, instructional techniques, student groupings, decision making) shapes not only the learning experiences and achievement of the students, but also the environment in which this work is carried out (Heck et al., 1990). We present a discussion of the rationale behind the development of our proposed model of organizational relationships and feature an instrument for measuring school processes. We also provide a summary of some of our findings focused on identifying these relationships in different organizational settings. In a broad way, these types of processes and practices we attempt to measure have been referred to as organizational culture (e.g., Hofstede et al., 1990; Schein, 1990), and we have shown that they influence outcomes in a variety of different organizational settings (Gomez, Marcoulides, & Heck, 2012; Heck et al., 1990; Heck & Marcoulides, 1996b; Marcoulides & Heck, 1993; Marcoulides, Heck, & Papanastasiou, 2005).

Defining the Conceptual Model

We note that our proposed model is part of a multilevel conceptual framework of schooling suggests that cultural processes may permeate the school on several levels. For example, at the school level Opdenakker and Van Damme (2007) identified three sets of school factors as context (e.g., school structure, size, and facilities), composition (e.g., student in-take variables, teaching and administrative staff), and school practices (e.g., mission, goals, and values; management and decision-making practices; academic and social organization; climate, and school-community partnerships). Heck and Moriyama (2010) found leadership serves as a mediating construct between the school's context and its instructional practices. Leadership influenced subsequent instructional practices, and instructional practices directly influenced subse-

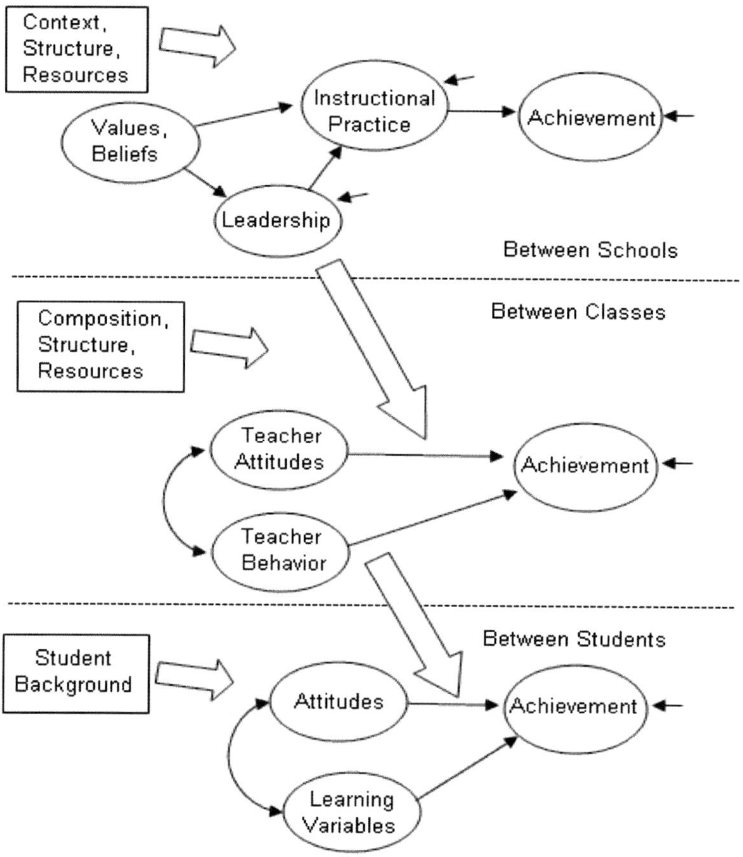

Figure 1. Specifying a multilevel model of context, process, and outcomes.

quent academic outcomes. Similarly, the school's instructional practices mediated leadership, contextual, and compositional effects on outcomes. In another examination of school leadership and capacity-building effects on learning improvement, the effectiveness of school leadership strategies aimed at improving instructional practices and teacher classroom effectiveness (e.g., attitudes, beliefs, and values about student learning, classroom processes, and professional development) moderated individual teachers' effects on student learning (Heck & Hallinger, 2010). Importantly, this finding suggests that collective effort to facilitate school-wide improvement can coordinate the *individual* behavior of teachers within their classrooms. This suggests school improvement strategies should likely consider the importance of identifying ways to create linkages between behavior at one level of the organization to changing attitudes and behavior of individuals at other levels. We summarize some of the beliefs, values, and intervening processes that comprise this type of multilevel school organizational system in Figure 1.

Organizational Culture

Organizational culture provides one means for thinking about how beliefs, values, and behavior may influence the particular strategies that organizations use to produce outcomes. For over 50 years, researchers have attempted to conceptualize the nature of the workplace culture in order to determine its relationship to the productivity and satisfaction of employees (Hoy, Hannum, & Tschannen-Moran, 1998; Moran & Volkwein, 1992). In the 1950s, Argyris (1954) studied variations in work environments within the financial banks. He noted that an atmosphere built on trust and openness would help unearth conflict and make it easier to implement changes that would improve the organization. Since this study, an extensive literature has developed on organizational culture. It is defined as patterns of shared values and beliefs that produce behavioral norms (e.g., policies, processes) adopted in solving problems (Hofstede et al., 1990; Schein, 1990). Schein (1990) notes that culture is a body of solutions to problems that have worked consistently and are taught to new members as the correct way to perceive, think about, and feel in relation to those problems. The sum of these shared philosophies, assumptions, values, and norms binds the organization together.

Organizational culture, therefore, can be thought of as the manner in which an organization solves problems to achieve its specific goals and maintain itself over time. Moreover, culture is holistic, historically determined, socially constructed, and, hence, difficult to change (Hofstede et al., 1990). Empirically validating the specific parameters of this multidimensional construct, however, has been problematic. As Trice and Beyer (1984) noted, early research examining culture focused primarily on single discrete elements of culture, while generally ignoring its multidimensional nature. Another problem has been that research has not always been clear on whether the association between various aspects of organizational culture and performance reflects any type of causal relationship (Saffold, 1988), or are merely associations between levels of outcomes and particular views of processes associated with those outcomes. Hence, while there has been some general agreement on what the concept means, there has been less agreement on how it should be measured, especially across multiple layers of organizational structure and process, and how it may be related to organizational performance. In one preliminary study on product and service organizations, we proposed and tested a model of some important aspects of organizational culture that explained differences in organizational performance (Marcoulides & Heck, 1993).

We noted that organizational culture consisted of three interrelated dimensions—a *sociocultural* system of the perceived functioning of the organization's leadership processes, strategic actions, and practices; an underlying *value and belief* system; and an individual belief, attitude, and *behavioral* system of those who work within the organization (Allaire & Firsirotu, 1984; Schein, 1990). We specified five latent factors that together comprised measurable aspects of school culture and that, in concert, were related to organizational performance (Marcoulides & Heck, 1993). In a subsequent test within school settings, we confirmed that our proposed model was also positively related to student achievement (Heck & Marcoulides, 1996a). In this latter test, consistent with Figure 1, we also defined a number of contextual (e.g., school size, school type) and compositional (e.g., collective staff factors, student composition) factors that exerted some independent effects on the component variables in our model. We found that although leadership is certainly an important construct in developing and maintaining effective organizational practices, it is certainly not the only factor that contributes to school outcomes. Of course, most of this influence was found to be *indirect*; that is, other organizational process variables mediate its effects on outcome. As a number of school leadership studies have similarly indicated (Hallinger et al., 1996; Heck et al., 1990; Leithwood et al., 1993, 2010; Supovitz et al., 2010), there are additional school processes, loosely constituting an organization's culture, that contribute to outcomes including classroom structure, teaching practices, teaching attitudes, and resource allocation (Bossert, 1988).

Other studies have also found that school culture affects the morale, productivity, and satisfaction of teachers, consequently having a positive or negative effect on the long term learning environment of a school (Brown, Lemus, & Pickett, 1999; Taylor & Tashakkori, 1995). The culture that exists within a school can facilitate positive teacher social relationships and attitudes that may translate into increased academic achievement (Holt & Smith, 2002; Sweetland & Hoy, 2000; Heck, 2000; Hoy et al., 1998; Lumsden, 1998; Hoy, Tarter, & Bliss, 1990). Furthermore, Lumsden (1998) established that it is the principal who is most influential in creating a school culture that impacts the morale of the teachers. Firestone and Louis (1999) and others (e.g., Bossert et al., 1982; Hallinger & Heck, 1996; Ogawa & Bossert, 1995; Heck et al., 1990; Leithwood et al., 2010) concur with these findings and further suggest that school administrators can influence the school's surrounding culture, the school's orderliness, and ensure that teachers focus on student achievement.

Hence, it is relatively clear, despite a number of different names used for describing such school process factors, that researchers have isolated a number of school processes that are consistently related to school outcomes and growth in student learning. Less is known, however, about how such strategies to change various cultural and instructional processes unfold over time in order to bring about school improvement. We believe that monitoring the implementation of chosen school improvement strategies and examining their impact over time on measured school processes can also provide useful information for school leaders about the implementation of such improvement strategies and their impact on changing the normative structure (i.e., culture) as well as the work structure (e.g., classroom activities, teacher knowledge and instructional pedagogy) of the school.

Our Instrumentation

Because we have tested our model across different types of organizations (e.g., product and service organizations, high schools, middle and elementary schools) and with various groups of respondents (e.g., employees of businesses, teachers, students) we have used a number of different instruments to define our proposed model. As a result, we believe we have achieved some initial success in our original goal "to begin to develop a 'roadmap' that suggests possible relationships among variables comprising organizational culture and to estimate their relative effects on performance" (Heck & Marcoulides, 1993, p. 213). Also, it is important to understand that both culture and climate are affected by different spheres of influence and that researchers cannot simply investigate single spheres when attempting to explain outcomes.

For purposes of defining relationships among school leadership, culture, instructional practices, and outcomes, we developed an instrument we refer to as the "Organization of the School and Teacher Satisfaction with Their Work Environment" (OSTSWE). We provide a copy of the current version of it in the appendix. We provided preliminary results from this model in 1996 (Heck & Marcoulides, 1996a). This instrument was created based on our earlier research about how organizational culture can make a difference in for-profit organizational productivity (Marcoulides & Heck, 1993). The instrument was designed to measure a variety of strategic interactions between school leaders (e.g., principals, teacher leaders) and teachers, focusing on how the school is structured and governed, how it is organized instructionally, and how teachers perceive elements of its culture, climate, and their classroom instructional practices. The OSTSWE has already been shown to possess good psychometric properties and a number of its dimensions have been shown to be directly or indirectly associated with school achievement (e.g., Heck & Marcoulides, 1996a; Gomez et al., 2012). We note that any attempt to model the richness of organizational life must begin with some admissions of its limitations. There is really no universal paradigm or theory for examining organizational behavior that is valid in all contexts (Marcoulides & Heck, 1993). Proposed theories often become problematic when they attempt to model the actual detail of real organizations, because organizations are socially constructed realities with complex sets of interrelationships among their internal and environmental processes. Researchers may also lack the ability to isolate and measure some important organizational variables or to ensure that the survey items used adequately reflect member participation in important organizational processes. Although this reduction of reality can be considered a limitation, we believe there is a definite usefulness to such an approach, since it helps make the social construction of underlying organizational processes somewhat more accessible (Hofstede et al., 1990; Schein, 1990). We discuss this instrument in more detail in the next section.

Latent Dimensions

In developing our constructs comprising culture, we incorporated three interrelated subsystems of culture from the work of Allaire and Firsirotu (1984). The first is a sociocultural subsystem composed of perceptions about formal organizational structures (e.g., its authority system and decision-making structure), strategies (e.g., particular choices it may make in pursuing improvement), policies, and management/leadership practices relative to its work that have been consistently successful, and, therefore, permanently established. In managing the core technology (e.g., improving teaching and the instructional environment surrounding classroom practices), leaders facilitate the pursuit of goals, develop strategies to achieve goals through effective decision making, and organize the workforce to achieve organizational goals (Thompson, 1967). In school settings, central to this pursuit is the extent to which the leadership team (e.g., administrators, teachers, community's and parents) organize the school's core pursuits (e.g., hiring, organizing the curriculum and assigning teachers to groups of students, allocating learning resources, setting discipline policies). Ingersoll (1994) suggests that in secondary schools, principals are far more often in control of key activities within their schools than their faculties. However, more democratic (and distributed) leadership (focusing on collaboration, teamwork, and participation in decision making) seems to characterize higher-achieving schools (Heck et al., 1990; Heck & Hallinger, 2010; Lee & Croninger, 1994; Leithwood et al., 2010).

A second subsystem is an organizational belief system that embodies the myths, rituals, and ideologies of the organization (Allaire & Firsirotu, 1984). Leaders attempt to influence the development of values and define the organization's purposes, policies, and strategies to organize the work structure. Bolman and Deal (1984) identified the mythological roles that leaders as ceremonial heads of organizations often play in the effort to clarify roles and responsibilities, clarify (or teach) organizational values, and promote the organization's mission to the organization and wider community. Such ceremonial behaviors often represent attempts to transmit organizational values at deeper levels of acculturation. One co-effect of the socialization of organizational values is climate, which can be defined as the perceptions held by members as to the nature of the organization's work environment including, for example, its social relations, communication processes, evaluation processes, and reward structures. These elements, as we might suspect, are more subject to changing conditions within the organization than are its deeper cultural norms, values, and socialization processes.

A final component of culture is an individual belief system. This is a function of the collective individuals within the organization who contribute their unique experiences, beliefs, goals, and personalities. As Hofstede et al. (1990) suggest, there appears to be a similarity in values and daily practices among people working in an organization. Hofstede et al. argue that these shared values are at least partially the result of founders and significant leaders. This is because the procedures of selection and socialization processes include organizational norms of behavior. Although the goal is to socialize new members into the organization, the process may not always be uniform. Thus, in our study teachers may be viewed as another potential source of variation affecting the school's academic performance through their individual attitudes and behavior (e.g., beliefs about student learning, standards for student performance, implementation of the required curriculum, assessment of students) in organizing their classrooms and conducting their instructional activities. We have identified differences in these more collective versus individual views within and across schools (e.g., Heck et al., 1990; Heck & Marcoulides, 1996a).

Figure 2 presents our representation of our structural model of organizational culture. The model proposes five factors that together comprise measurable elements of organizational culture adapted to school settings. The elements in concert are hypothesized to influence organizational performance and change in organizational performance over time. In most of our studies, the outcome has been school performance, as measured on standardized tests of reading and math (e.g., Heck & Marcoulides, 1996a; Marcoulides et al., 2005; Gomez et al., 2012). Organizational structure and organizational values are considered exogenous constructs, in that other factors outside the model (e.g., composition, context) determine their variability. We recognize that organizational structures and values are themselves dynamic processes; that is, subject to influence from other external and internal processes over time. With data collected at one, or a few points, in time, we have found that the school's structure (i.e., relative bureaucracy in terms of established rules and control mechanisms) and its values (i.e., core norms and beliefs) are relatively stable.

Organizational climate, managerial processes, and teacher attitudes/behavior are endogenous, in that other constructs in the model determine their variability. We note in Figure 2 that the effects of leadership processes on outcomes are most likely fully mediated (or partially mediated) by organizational climate and by teacher attitudes and behavior at the school and classroom levels (noted with a dotted line). We have noted in previous work (e.g., Marcoulides et al., 2005; Heck, 2007; Heck &

Hallinger, 2010) that these variables change over time, and such changes are often related to changes in student outcomes. The exogenous variables, therefore, indirectly affect organizational outcomes through the endogenous variables in our model. For example, we expect that organizational values at least *partially explain* teachers' attitudes (i.e., toward students, toward instruction) and classroom behavior because individual teachers are socialized into the organization as new members.

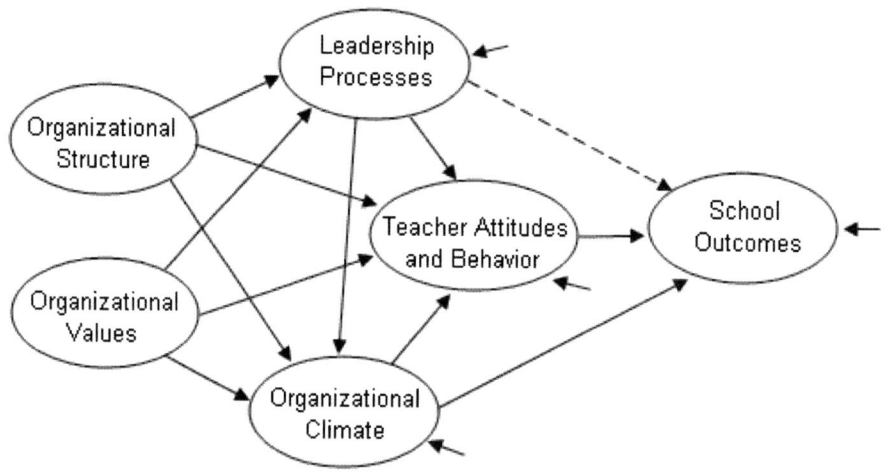

Figure 2. Proposed model of variables affecting school outcomes.

As a group, the set of factors in Fig. 1 are viewed as loosely comprising the three subsystems of culture (i.e., sociocultural, belief, individual attitudes and beliefs) suggested by Allaire and Firsirotu (1984). We believe these subsystems represent manifestations of what an organization is as it attempts to resolve the challenges it faces over time, for example, attempting to meet external demands for improved student achievement.

Sociocultural Subsystem

Organizational structure. At their most basic level, organizations are structured to achieve specific goals. Considerable work in organizational theory has been devoted to specifying the effects of the organization's structure, its technical capacity and goal orientations on the processes of administration (Marcoulides & Heck, 1993; Owens, 1998; Thompson, 1967). Owens further asserts that organizational structures may indirectly influence the achievement of outcomes. Extant studies suggest that some variables such as size, complexity of the administrative hierarchy, or presence of control mechanisms may impact administrative practices, teacher attitudes and behavior, and levels of performance (e.g., Heck et al., 1990; Ingersoll, 1994; Leithwood et al., 2004). We defined structure as attitudes and beliefs related to the organization's formal mechanisms to achieve goals, or desired results. Formalization refers to how rules are used in the school and the amount of deviation that is permitted from the stated procedures. To the extent that rules clarify expectations for teachers (e.g., regarding performance evaluation), dissatisfaction is unlikely, since a direction for their work activities is provided. If this results in excess control, however, so that rules are perceived as an infringement on teacher autonomy, dissatisfaction may ensue (Hoy et al., 1990; Ingersoll, 1994). Thus, structure refers to the basic organizational anatomy (e.g., relative bureaucracy of its structure) used to achieve school goals (e.g., improved student achievement). In the current version of our instrument (i.e., Gomez et al., 2012), the construct is defined by five items (items 2–5, 28), with an alpha of 0.70.

Leadership/managerial processes. This construct is measured by a variety of strategies, policies, and practices leaders use to organize and monitor the work structure of the organization in a manner that will maximize its performance. Such strategies include how new teachers are recruited and selected, how they are supported, supervised, and evaluated, the extent to which administrators identify and address school problems and are supportive of teachers, whether the school utilizes its available resources effectively, and whether teachers have opportunities to pursue challenging work in the school (e.g., professional development opportunities). Variables in this domain emphasize how the organization functions over time as a result of its particular structures, purposes, and value and belief systems. It is defined by three subscales including *resources available* (items 6, 7 and 46—alpha = .70), *principal responsiveness* (items 11–14, alpha = .86), and *leadership* (items 24–30, alpha = .79).

Organizational Value Subsystem

Organizational values. As Hofstede et al. (1990) indicate, organizational values (from previous leaders, upper management) often permeate the organization such that they are translated into the practices of people throughout the organization. It can therefore be asserted that an organization's collective culture influences both the attitudes and subsequent behaviors of its members, as well as the level of productivity it achieves. One would expect, therefore, a relatively high correlation between the stated (written and oral) practices, procedures, and leadership strategies, and values of an organization and the attitudes and behaviors of its individual members. It is difficult to operationalize all aspects of an organization's values system (e.g., Schein, 1990). We chose several values or activities representing values thought to be important in achieving school productivity. These include the extent to which innovation or risk taking is encouraged, whether support and time are provided for developing collaboration among faculty, and whether the school promotes greater (or lesser) teacher participation in decision making. This construct is measured by three subscales including *time for collaboration* (items 32–34, alpha = .70), *encouragement of innovation* (items 18, 19, 37, alpha = .70), and *participation in decision making* (items 15–17, alpha = .70).

Organizational climate. Hofstede et al. (1990) suggest that climate is a term that has often been misperceived as "culture," in the American management literature. Owens (1998), however, has drawn some useful distinctions between the two terms. Climate refers more to the perceptions of teachers and others about how the work environment is functioning including the quality of social interactions, the types of communication channels open to members, access to technology and resources, demands or stress placed on them to produce, and recognition of their efforts. As noted by Hoy and Hannum (1997), because of the broad number of definitions and terms for climate, there are also a number of instruments that "have been systemically developed to examine the organizational climate of schools" (Hoy & Hannum, 1997, p. 292). To make matters more complicated, each instrument seems to measure a different aspect of climate and each survey has its own terms used to describe the climate in organizations. Key aspects within the climate therefore include teacher and student morale, staff cohesiveness, and academic emphasis present within the school (Hoy & Feldman, 1999). This can be described in terms of the trust, friendliness, and enthusiasm that are exhibited by the staff and students. For example, a positive school work environment has been associated with fewer discipline referrals for misbehavior, fewer emotional problems, and lower antisocial behavior from students (Kuperminc et al., 1997). We expect that a more democratic type of leadership helps promote collegiality and collaborative relationships and builds more long-term commitment to the organization.

In our instrument, climate is more specifically defined as teachers' perceptions about a variety of these conditions in the school (e.g., their satisfaction with the social environment, communication channels, and collegiality). We therefore use the term *climate* more narrowly to describe perceptions about "how things are" in the organization on a day-to-day basis. Climate may change more readily—depending, for example, on the actions of administrators, teachers' colleagues, and parents—than the entire underlying system of constructs that comprise the school's culture. It is defined by three subscales including social relationships (items 40–45, alpha = .75), communication processes (items 8–10, alpha = .77), and teacher collegiality (items 20–23, alpha = .79).

Individual Belief Subsystem

Teacher attitudes and behavior. Organizational members bring their unique attitudes, values, and goals to the workplace (Marcoulides & Heck, 1993). While such attitudes and values are partially shaped by the organization as well as national culture (Hofstede et al., 1990), individuals may be thought of as possessing a wide range of perceptions about work-related and various social and political issues. These perceptions about such issues as teaching, implementing the curriculum, grouping students, and making strategic choices in working with students are central to teachers' behavior (and effectiveness) in the classroom. Importantly, we note that strategic leadership actions to coordinate teachers' classroom behavior, therefore, may be constrained by the sometimes divergent goals, attitudes, and behavior of individual teachers (Fuller et al., 1982). Teacher attitudes and classroom effectiveness have been found to be related to the achievement of students (Mortimore, 1993; Gomez et al., 2012; Heck, 2009; Heck & Hallinger, 2010; Heck & Marcoulides, 1996a). We focus specifically on teachers' attitudes about their classroom instruction, student ability, and student background. The construct is measured by two subscales including teachers' perceptions of students (items 35–36, 47, alpha = .73) and perceptions about parents (items 31, 38–39, alpha = .77). In our results presented, however, we only used a scale defining teachers' perceptions of their students to measure the construct.

Presenting Some Sample Results of Our Model Tests

Our purpose in developing the instrument was to identify variables in the schools' cultural environment that contribute to performance because administrators, teachers, and others promoting school improvement may be interested in monitoring and changing some of these variables. As Fullan (2006) notes, school improvement is an organizational process, with all that this entails both within the school and in relation to its external environment. Serious reform involves changing the culture and the structure of the school (Fullan, 2006; Sarason, 1982). As a means to this end, school leaders are asked to practice a distributive leadership style where teachers are empowered within their grade level or department to respond to common issues (e.g., curriculum organization, resource allocation, instructional strategies) without administrator interference (Harris, 2004; Lieberman, Saxl, & Miles., 2000). With the inception of a more consequential accountability system, teachers in successful schools have shifted from a dependency on managerial processes to one of vision and purpose. In Figure 3, we provide our initial model results from the 1996 study (for full details see Heck & Marcoulides, 1996a).

Several findings are of interest. First, as proposed, we found degree of bureaucratic organizational structure was negatively related to both perceptions about leadership processes and teacher attitudes about students. Second, organizational values were directly related to leadership processes and indirectly related to organizational climate. In turn, organizational climate was indirectly related to organizational performance (.11) through teacher attitudes. Third, leadership was positively related to organizational climate, and leadership was found to be significantly indirectly related to performance through climate and teacher attitudes. The size of the indirect effect, however, was small (.08) but consistent with leadership indirect effects ranging from .06 to .14 in similar research (e.g., Heck & Hallinger, 2010).

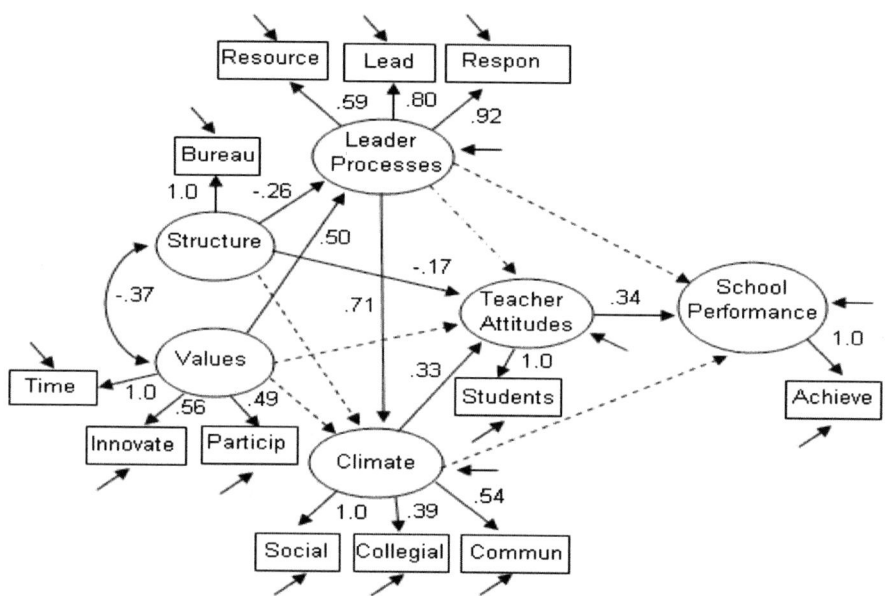

Figure 3. Standardized model estimates from secondary schools in Singapore (dotted lines indicate paths that were tested but were not significant).

In our latest use of the OSTSWE instrument to study possible differences in middle school versus K-8 school structures that might be related to differences in academic outcomes (Gomez et al., 2012), we found considerable support for the construct validity of our originally proposed model (Heck & Marcoulides, 1996a). More specifically, the results indicated that the component dimensions of a school's academic and social culture were positively related to each other and to student outcomes in schools serving young adolescents. This provides additional evidence of the proposed model's construct validity in describing educational processes and outcomes in these types of schools. This was particularly evident in terms of the positive indirect effects of organizational values (with separate indirect effects through specific mediated variables of .12, .31 and .50, $p < .05$) and school climate (.50, $p < .05$) associated with explaining school outcomes, and the direct effect of teacher attitudes associated with school outcomes—regardless of school type (see also Heck et al., 1990; Leithwood & Mascall, 2008; Leithwood et al., 2010). In Figure 4, we provide these results summarized across both types of school structures.

Overall, this model also provided support for the view that organizational culture consists of several related subsystems (i.e., sociocultural, organizational, individual) that can be positively related to outcomes. Our proposed model indicated all three subsystems were relevant to understanding differences in patterns of belief, behavior, and outcomes among the schools investigated. Our results therefore suggest initial clues about which component parts of schools' organizational cultures may be amenable to school-level action directed at improving outcomes. More specifically, teacher attitudes continue to be a consistent predictor of outcomes. We suggest that the attitudes teachers hold about students (e.g., expectations) may ultimately affect how classroom experiences are structured (grouping practices, access to curricu-

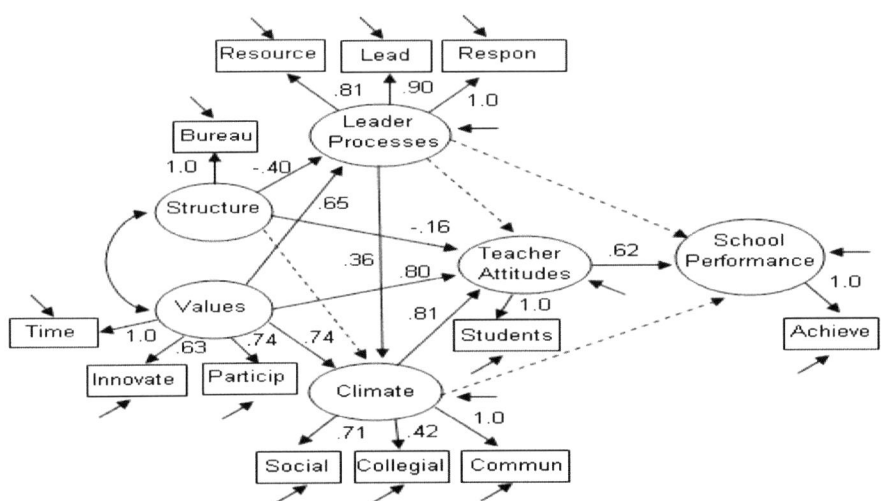

Figure 4. Standardized direct effects of model component variables in middle-level schools (dotted lines indicate paths that were tested but were not significant).

lum). This provides one potential place where school leaders can intervene to reshape teacher attitudes and implementation behavior regarding proposed changes in instruction within the school (e.g., using technology, adapting new curricular programs, adopting different grouping and assessment practices). Moreover, less rigidity at the school level in terms of policies and action that teachers can take was related to more positive attitudes about climate and leadership practices.

Since the proposed model was found to fit the teacher data from both types of school structures and because a statistically significant difference was determined in the eighth-grade performance, one can compare the specific aspects of the model across the two teacher groups, confirm which paths differ, and then infer that the higher performance may indeed be explained by the higher teacher perception on that particular path. Because some variables emerged as better predictors of performance according to teachers from each school type, strategic school improvement might result from becoming more aware of teachers' perceptions about key organizational processes (e.g., academic orientation underlying organizational values, organizational climate, and teacher attitudes) and also consider ways to change those aspects that appear to influence school performance. We provide these results for K-8 and middle schools in Figure 5.

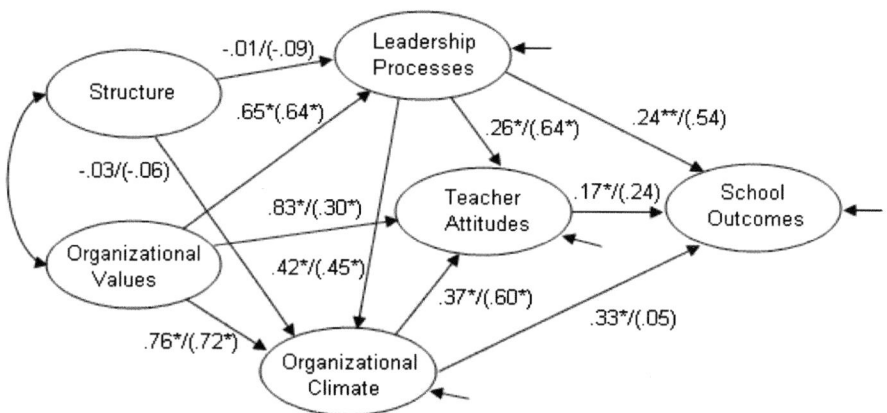

Figure 5. Examining standardized coefficients in the proposed model between K-8 and middle (coefficients in parentheses) schools. (Note: *p < .05, **p < .10).

First, organizational norms and values were indirectly related to higher outcomes in both settings. Schools that fostered innovation and risk taking, teacher participation in decision making, and provided time for collaboration were higher producing than schools where these variables were perceived in less positive terms. More specifically, in the K-8 group, for every 1-unit increase in *organizational values* and *organizational climate* we expect a 0.25 increase in school outcomes. These findings suggest that teachers in K-8 schools perceived to have higher levels of collaboration and involvement within their schools, which, in turn, resulted in higher staff communication and collaboration, which all indirectly was associated with higher school performance. Similarly, in the K-8 group, for every 1-unit increase in *organizational values* and *teacher attitudes* we expect a 0.14 increase in school outcomes. K-8 schools (more than middle schools) were perceived to have higher levels of collaboration and involvement at the school, which in turn results in higher teacher beliefs about their students, which indirectly was associated with higher school outcomes.

Second, teacher perceptions of social relations (climate) were positively related to higher outcomes in K-8 schools. Third, teacher attitudes appeared to be more consistent predictors of school outcomes in K-8 schools than in middle schools. This may have something to do with the different ways these two types of schools are organized for instruction. Especially in middle schools, students may pass through a greater number of teachers each day and a number of the courses may be more disconnected from standardized testing (which may only affect the English and math teachers). Teachers in K-8 schools may have a more direct role in this regard.

Of course, our data in this study only offer a glimpse of this different organizational phenomenon in K-8 and middle schools. It remains to be more thoroughly studied as to how the distribution of control within schools may affect the lives and behavior of teachers and students. Moreover, the linkages between schools and districts are also important to consider in sustaining programs to improve outcomes (Fullan, 1991). It is not clear from these data what might be possible reasons for systematic differences in organizational relationships across these two types of settings. We caution that simply changing leadership practices to mirror successful schools may not necessarily result in direct specific changes in outcomes; however, it is clear that discussions of best practices by leaders and staff, at least as perceived by teachers, must begin with an understanding of the important variables influencing school outcomes (Heck & Marcoulides, 1996a; Leithwood et al., 2010; Leithwood & Jantzi, 1997; Leithwood & Mascall, 2008). We should keep in mind also that there are several variables other than culture (e.g., student backgrounds, family socioeconomic status, student attitudes toward school) that were not specifically examined in this particular study but may also affect student performance. This is because the study was conducted at the teacher and school levels, as opposed to the individual student level.

Integrating Our Results

We found that the proposed model examined and tested in this latest study across teachers from two different types of middle-level school structures (i.e., Gomez et al., 2012) compared quite favorably with previous studies of organizational culture and performance in for-profit organizations (Marcoulides & Heck, 1993), at the high school level in Singapore (Heck & Marcoulides, 1996a), and across elementary and high school data obtained from the Trends in International Mathematics and Science Study (TIMSS) data (Marcoulides et al., 2005). Although the overall model tested in this study was determined to fit equally well with both types of middle grade structures examined, the actual magnitude of the parameter estimates within the model reflecting the effects across specific latent variables and on the outcome variable differed somewhat across the two school types. Based upon results obtained in past research studies spanning almost two decades, it appears that the observed variation of the parameter estimates across the two school types found can most likely be attributed to different school contexts considered.

Indeed, since the actual magnitude of effects within the model also changed once school configuration was taken into account, it is clear that the school configuration was the key factor bringing about these changes. For example, similar to the originally proposed model, in the total teacher sample the sole important direct factor in explaining school performance was teacher attitudes. In contrast for the K-8 group, the most important variables explaining school performance were organizational climate and teacher attitudes. In the middle school group, no significant direct effects to school performance were found.

Because structural types do not appear to account directly for differences in outcomes, but process variables do, as we have previously suggested, instead of comparing the pros and cons of different middle level structures, especially since organizational structure has been found not to affect school performance, school leaders are encouraged to focus on reshaping school values, school-wide student improvement goals, and school climate in order to raise teacher attitudes and collegiality (Heck & Marcoulides, 1993). Improving teacher attitudes and collegiality is important, as it is those variables that have been found to impact school performance in both school structures. As we noted, "Because time in the school day is limited, there are trade-offs associated with school management" (1993, p. 26). Hence, deciding on which variables are important in facilitating strong educational outcomes becomes a crucial aspect of school leadership aimed at facilitating school academic improvement (Leithwood et al., 2010).

Most importantly our model tests across a variety of elementary, middle, and high schools in different settings have achieved some similar results. Specifically, the model appears to differentiate schools based on their academic performance, although there is some difference in the size (and statistical significance) of particular paths. It is probably best not to put too much emphasis on this part of the findings, however, because of the potential effects of different sample sizes (and slight variations in the instruments) used to collect the data. The congruence of the model in terms of constructs, directions of paths, and overall goodness of fit indices provides more concrete evidence of its validity in monitoring internal school processes that are related to outcomes. These results add to its construct validity and suggest that at least some aspects of an organization's culture are predictive of its performance on a variety of outcome measures. The latent constructs all produced similar direct effects on each other and on individuals' outcomes.

Our results should be considered in relation to a few limitations. First, we were not able to obtain direct information about how teachers instruct in their classrooms. It is likely that differences in teachers' classroom effectiveness have a direct effect on student learning (as well differences in their attitudes). Second, although concerns can be raised about any attempt to reduce the complexity of complex day-to-day educational relationships in schools to a model of organizational culture and estimate its relationship to outcomes, there is a benefit in doing so if it helps to identify paths that might provide insight to strategic actions that can improve classroom instruction and the environment surrounding the school's instructional practices. These two areas have been identified in a recent meta-analysis of school factors that influence outcomes (Kyriakides et al., 2009).

Future Directions

Further research related to schools' leadership, organizational values, academic and social organization, and teacher attitudes and classroom behavior may help illuminate strategies for improving educational practices in schools that lead to increased outcomes for early students. This is because school climate, teacher attitudes, and organizational values appear to explain school performance more than the other latent variables (e.g., structure) in the considered model. An organization's culture is reflected in what is done, how it is done, and who is involved in these processes. Efforts directed toward the determination of the particular profile of organizational culture present in an organization may provide information about options that are available in managing, or changing, the determinant variables. By examining these processes, it may be possible to explain why some schools are not performing at desired levels. We are encouraged that our instrumentation appears to differentiate schools according to some important underlying values, leadership, and work-related processes in schools. Our view of leadership highlights school leadership's role in reducing bureaucratic control, building collaboration and teamwork, and as a result empowering others to share in the leadership of the school. We recognize that more collaborative and distributed types of school leadership appear to have particular advantages in helping others in the school organization commit to and implement changes in educational practices (Gronn, 2002; Leithwood et al., 2010).

Further research might pursue two different directions. First, we see our model as multilevel in nature (e.g., see Heck & Marcoulides, 1996a). It is clear that school processes (e.g., structures, values, leadership processes) have effects that may structure activity at other levels of the organization (e.g., individual teachers in classrooms). For example, in related analyses, we have examined how instructionally focused leadership appears to enhance teacher effectiveness in the classroom. It is clear also that classrooms may mediate school-level strategic efforts to change teacher attitudes and behavior, particularly if teachers are not part of the process of deciding and committing to implement such changes in instructional practices. Our proposed model opens up many new possibilities for examining mediation effects within and between organizational levels of the school.

Second, further research may also use our instrument to conduct a longitudinal study of the same schools using the instrument at different points in time to investigate if there are any differences in the parameter estimates of teacher perceptions about the component constructs with changes in school performance. We see organizational processes as dynamic, in that changes in the environment surrounding schools often lead to necessary adjustments in internal processes. Our initial efforts in this regard have indicated, for example, support for the temporal ordering of instructionally focused leadership, changes in school instructional practices, and resulting changes in math and reading outcomes (Heck & Moriyama, 2010). We could also foresee a study investigating "mixtures" (or subpopulations) of schools that might have similar cultural models and outcomes [see Marcoulides and Heck (2009) for further discussion of mixture models]. The concepts represented in our model represent one attempt to describe quantitatively various aspects of culture identified in previous theory and research on organizations. Expanding on these beginningsm, we believe, would be a profitable goal for further research.

Appendix: Survey Instrument as Implemented in Gomez, Marcoulides, and Heck's study (2012) of K-8 and Middle Schools

The concepts represented in our instrument represent one attempt to collect information from teachers and others about various aspects of schools' educational processes and leadership practices identified in previous theory and research on organizations. Organizational culture provides one type of organizing construct about how school personnel think about their school's governance structures, its educational practices, and its problem-solving processes. Interested readers could add a variety of different teacher or school demographics (e.g., teacher-level information, school context information) to adapt the instrument to their own specific research needs. It would also be possible to add a section that would focus on particular improvement strategies being pursued (e.g., reorganizing leadership practices to be more team-oriented and collaborative, focusing on changes in teacher classroom practices) or to provide more detailed information about a subset of the broad processes comprising the present instrument. An example might be obtaining more detailed information about the school's instructional practices. Readers with further questions about the instrument or its possible uses can contact the chapter's authors for further help.

The Organization of the School and Teacher Satisfaction with Their Work Environment

With this survey we will focus on teachers' perceptions of the current student learning environment at their school and how they relate to school performance. Thank you for your help in attempting to improve the education of your middle level students. With this survey we will focus on teachers' perceptions of the current student learning environment at their school and how they relate to school performance. Thank you for your help in attempting to improve the education of your middle level students.

1. In which type of school do you work?

☐ K-8 School
☐ Middle School/Junior High

2. Select the button on the scale below that reflects the accuracy of the following statement:

	Highly Inaccurate	Somewhat Inaccurate	Neither Inaccurate or Accurate	Somewhat Accurate	Highly Accurate
Teachers have to follow rules at this school that conflict with their best professional judgment.	☐ Highly Inaccurate	☐ Somewhat Inaccurate	☐ Neither Inaccurate or Accurate	☐ Somewhat Accurate	☐ Highly Accurate

3. Select the button on the scale below that reflects the accuracy of the following statement:

	Highly Inaccurate	Somewhat Inaccurate	Neither Inaccurate or Accurate	Somewhat Accurate	Highly Accurate
Teachers can take little action at this school until a superior approves it.	☐ Highly Inaccurate	☐ Somewhat Inaccurate	☐ Neither Inaccurate or Accurate	☐ Somewhat Accurate	☐ Highly Accurate

4. Select the button on the scale below that reflects the accuracy of the following statement:

	Highly Inaccurate	Somewhat Inaccurate	Neither Inaccurate or Accurate	Somewhat Accurate	Highly Accurate
Things are tightly controlled here and the best policy is to stick closely to the rules.	☐ Highly Inaccurate	☐ Somewhat Inaccurate	☐ Neither Inaccurate or Accurate	☐ Somewhat Accurate	☐ Highly Accurate

5. Select the button on the scale below that reflects the accuracy of the following statement:

Teachers have 'freedom within limits' at this school; that is, they know what is expected of them but they also have the freedom to be creative.

Highly Inaccurate	Somewhat Inaccurate	Neither Inaccurate or Accurate	Somewhat Accurate	Highly Accurate
☐ Highly Inaccurate	☐ Somewhat Inaccurate	☐ Neither Inaccurate or Accurate	☐ Somewhat Accurate	☐ Highly Accurate

6. Select the button on the scale below that reflects the accuracy of the following statement:

Teachers are able to get the instructional materials or assistance they need at the time they are needed.

Highly Inaccurate	Somewhat Inaccurate	Neither Inaccurate or Accurate	Somewhat Accurate	Highly Accurate
☐ Highly Inaccurate	☐ Somewhat Inaccurate	☐ Neither Inaccurate or Accurate	☐ Somewhat Accurate	☐ Highly Accurate

7. Select the button on the scale below that reflects the accuracy of the following statement:

Simple, time-saving procedures exist for the acquisition and use of resources (e.g., printing machine, paper, teaching materials, curriculum guides etc).

Highly Inaccurate	Somewhat Inaccurate	Neither Inaccurate or Accurate	Somewhat Accurate	Highly Accurate
☐ Highly Inaccurate	☐ Somewhat Inaccurate	☐ Neither Inaccurate or Accurate	☐ Somewhat Accurate	☐ Highly Accurate

IDENTIFYING LEADERSHIP AND ORGANIZATIONAL PROCESSES | 93

8. Select the button on the scale below that reflects the accuracy of the following statement:

	Highly Inaccurate	Somewhat Inaccurate	Neither Inaccurate or Accurate	Somewhat Accurate	Highly Accurate
Teachers always receive information concerning school-related matters first-hand and without ambiguity.	☐ Highly Inaccurate	☐ Somewhat Inaccurate	☐ Neither Inaccurate or Accurate	☐ Somewhat Accurate	☐ Highly Accurate

9. Select the button on the scale below that reflects the accuracy of the following statement:

	Highly Inaccurate	Somewhat Inaccurate	Neither Inaccurate or Accurate	Somewhat Accurate	Highly Accurate
There is effective, two-way communication between teachers and administrators.	☐ Highly Inaccurate	☐ Somewhat Inaccurate	☐ Neither Inaccurate or Accurate	☐ Somewhat Accurate	☐ Highly Accurate

10. Select the button on the scale below that reflects the accuracy of the following statement:

	Highly Inaccurate	Somewhat Inaccurate	Neither Inaccurate or Accurate	Somewhat Accurate	Highly Accurate
There are procedures open to me (that are easily followed) for going to a higher authority if a decision is made that seems unfair.	☐ Highly Inaccurate	☐ Somewhat Inaccurate	☐ Neither Inaccurate or Accurate	☐ Somewhat Accurate	☐ Highly Accurate

11. Select the button on the scale below that reflects the accuracy of the following statement:

	Highly Inaccurate	Somewhat Inaccurate	Neither Inaccurate or Accurate	Somewhat Accurate	Highly Accurate
This school's administration knows the problems faced by the staff.	☐ Highly Inaccurate	☐ Somewhat Inaccurate	☐ Neither Inaccurate or Accurate	☐ Somewhat Accurate	☐ Highly Accurate

12. Select the button on the scale below that reflects the accuracy of the following statement:

The school administration's behavior towards the staff is supportive and encouraging.

- ☐ Highly Inaccurate
- ☐ Somewhat Inaccurate
- ☐ Neither Inaccurate or Accurate
- ☐ Somewhat Accurate
- ☐ Highly Accurate

13. Select the button on the scale below that reflects the accuracy of the following statement:

Teachers do not hesitate to approach the administration with any school-related problems they may have.

- ☐ Highly Inaccurate
- ☐ Somewhat Inaccurate
- ☐ Neither Inaccurate or Accurate
- ☐ Somewhat Accurate
- ☐ Highly Accurate

14. Select the button on the scale below that reflects the accuracy of the following statement:

The administration is seldom sympathetic towards personal problems that the teachers face.

- ☐ Highly Inaccurate
- ☐ Somewhat Inaccurate
- ☐ Neither Inaccurate or Accurate
- ☐ Somewhat Accurate
- ☐ Highly Accurate

15. Select the button on the scale below that reflects the accuracy of the following statement:

Teachers participate in determining appropriate instructional methods and techniques in this school.

- ☐ Highly Inaccurate
- ☐ Somewhat Inaccurate
- ☐ Neither Inaccurate or Accurate
- ☐ Somewhat Accurate
- ☐ Highly Accurate

16. Select the button on the scale below that reflects the accuracy of the following statement:

	Highly Inaccurate	Somewhat Inaccurate	Neither Inaccurate or Accurate	Somewhat Accurate	Highly Accurate
In this school, teachers participate in determining the type and content of professional development (school-based workshops, seminars, talks) we have.	☐ Highly Inaccurate	☐ Somewhat Inaccurate	☐ Neither Inaccurate or Accurate	☐ Somewhat Accurate	☐ Highly Accurate

17. Select the button on the scale below that reflects the accuracy of the following statement:

	Highly Inaccurate	Somewhat Inaccurate	Neither Inaccurate or Accurate	Somewhat Accurate	Highly Accurate
While I obviously can't have a vote on every decision that is made in this school that affects me, I do feel that I can have important input into decisions.	☐ Highly Inaccurate	☐ Somewhat Inaccurate	☐ Neither Inaccurate or Accurate	☐ Somewhat Accurate	☐ Highly Accurate

18. Select the button on the scale below that reflects the accuracy of the following statement:

	Highly Inaccurate	Somewhat Inaccurate	Neither Inaccurate or Accurate	Somewhat Accurate	Highly Accurate
In this school, teachers are encouraged to experiment with their teaching rather than conform.	☐ Highly Inaccurate	☐ Somewhat Inaccurate	☐ Neither Inaccurate or Accurate	☐ Somewhat Accurate	☐ Highly Accurate

19. Select the button on the scale below that reflects the accuracy of the following statement:

Differences between individuals and groups are considered to contribute to the richness of this school.

Highly Inaccurate	Somewhat Inaccurate	Neither Inaccurate or Accurate	Somewhat Accurate	Highly Accurate
☐ Highly Inaccurate	☐ Somewhat Inaccurate	☐ Neither Inaccurate or Accurate	☐ Somewhat Accurate	☐ Highly Accurate

20. Select the button on the scale below that reflects the accuracy of the following statement:

Teachers are familiar with the content and specific goals of the courses taught by other teachers in their department and in other subject departments.

Highly Inaccurate	Somewhat Inaccurate	Neither Inaccurate or Accurate	Somewhat Accurate	Highly Accurate
☐ Highly Inaccurate	☐ Somewhat Inaccurate	☐ Neither Inaccurate or Accurate	☐ Somewhat Accurate	☐ Highly Accurate

21. Select the button on the scale below that reflects the accuracy of the following statement:

Every teacher in this school does his or her own work; there is little concern about coordinating what each teaches.

Highly Inaccurate	Somewhat Inaccurate	Neither Inaccurate or Accurate	Somewhat Accurate	Highly Accurate
☐ Highly Inaccurate	☐ Somewhat Inaccurate	☐ Neither Inaccurate or Accurate	☐ Somewhat Accurate	☐ Highly Accurate

IDENTIFYING LEADERSHIP AND ORGANIZATIONAL PROCESSES | 97

22. Select the button on the scale below that reflects the accuracy of the following statement:

	Highly Inaccurate	Somewhat Inaccurate	Neither Inaccurate or Accurate	Somewhat Accurate	Highly Accurate
Teachers from one subject area or level respect those from other subject areas or level.	☐ Highly Inaccurate	☐ Somewhat Inaccurate	☐ Neither Inaccurate or Accurate	☐ Somewhat Accurate	☐ Highly Accurate

23. Select the button on the scale below that reflects the accuracy of the following statement:

	Highly Inaccurate	Somewhat Inaccurate	Neither Inaccurate or Accurate	Somewhat Accurate	Highly Accurate
When I have a teaching problem, I can get help or advice from other teachers at my school very easily.	☐ Highly Inaccurate	☐ Somewhat Inaccurate	☐ Neither Inaccurate or Accurate	☐ Somewhat Accurate	☐ Highly Accurate

24. Select the button on the scale below that reflects the accuracy of the following statement:

	Highly Inaccurate	Somewhat Inaccurate	Neither Inaccurate or Accurate	Somewhat Accurate	Highly Accurate
The administrative team talks openly and frankly with all staff members about school-related matters.	☐ Highly Inaccurate	☐ Somewhat Inaccurate	☐ Neither Inaccurate or Accurate	☐ Somewhat Accurate	☐ Highly Accurate

25. Select the button on the scale below that reflects the accuracy of the following statement:

	Highly Inaccurate	Somewhat Inaccurate	Neither Inaccurate or Accurate	Somewhat Accurate	Highly Accurate
The administrative team deals effectively with pressures from outside the school that might interfere with my teaching.	☐ Highly Inaccurate	☐ Somewhat Inaccurate	☐ Neither Inaccurate or Accurate	☐ Somewhat Accurate	☐ Highly Accurate

26. **Select the button on the scale below that reflects the accuracy of the following statement:**

	Highly Inaccurate	Somewhat Inaccurate	Neither Inaccurate or Accurate	Somewhat Accurate	Highly Accurate
The administrative team knows what kind of school they want and communicate it effectively to the staff.	☐ Highly Inaccurate	☐ Somewhat Inaccurate	☐ Neither Inaccurate or Accurate	☐ Somewhat Accurate	☐ Highly Accurate

27. **Select the button on the scale below that reflects the accuracy of the following statement:**

	Highly Inaccurate	Somewhat Inaccurate	Neither Inaccurate or Accurate	Somewhat Accurate	Highly Accurate
The administrative team sets an example by working hard themselves.	☐ Highly Inaccurate	☐ Somewhat Inaccurate	☐ Neither Inaccurate or Accurate	☐ Somewhat Accurate	☐ Highly Accurate

28. **Select the button on the scale below that reflects the accuracy of the following statement:**

	Highly Inaccurate	Somewhat Inaccurate	Neither Inaccurate or Accurate	Somewhat Accurate	Highly Accurate
The administrative team rules the school with an iron fist.	☒ Highly Inaccurate	☐ Somewhat Inaccurate	☐ Neither Inaccurate or Accurate	☐ Somewhat Accurate	☐ Highly Accurate

29. **Select the button on the scale below that reflects the accuracy of the following statement:**

	Highly Inaccurate	Somewhat Inaccurate	Neither Inaccurate or Accurate	Somewhat Accurate	Highly Accurate
Administrators and teachers collaborate towards making the school run effectively; there is little administrator-teacher tension.	☐ Highly Inaccurate	☐ Somewhat Inaccurate	☐ Neither Inaccurate or Accurate	☐ Somewhat Accurate	☐ Highly Accurate

IDENTIFYING LEADERSHIP AND ORGANIZATIONAL PROCESSES | 99

30. Select the button on the scale below that reflects the accuracy of the following statement:

The administrative team stresses teamwork and takes the lead in demonstrating how to work effectively as a team on school-related matters.

- ○ Highly Inaccurate
- ○ Somewhat Inaccurate
- ○ Neither Inaccurate or Accurate
- ○ Somewhat Accurate
- ○ Highly Accurate

31. Select the button on the scale below that reflects the accuracy of the following statement:

Parents promote community involvement by being involved with the school's teachers, administration, and school programs.

- ○ Highly Inaccurate
- ○ Somewhat Inaccurate
- ○ Neither Inaccurate or Accurate
- ○ Somewhat Accurate
- ○ Highly Accurate

32. Select the button on the scale below that reflects the accuracy of the following statement:

Discussion of issues in teaching and learning is a regular part of our school staff/in-service meetings.

- ○ Highly Inaccurate
- ○ Somewhat Inaccurate
- ○ Neither Inaccurate or Accurate
- ○ Somewhat Accurate
- ○ Highly Accurate

33. **Select the button on the scale below that reflects the accuracy of the following statement:**

Teachers can always find time during a regular school day to share teaching ideas or materials with at least two or three teachers.

Highly Inaccurate	Somewhat Inaccurate	Neither Inaccurate or Accurate	Somewhat Accurate	Highly Accurate
☐	☐	☐	☐	☐

34. **Select the button on the scale below that reflects the accuracy of the following statement:**

Teachers in the school are actively involved in determining school needs and strategies to improve instruction.

Highly Inaccurate	Somewhat Inaccurate	Neither Inaccurate or Accurate	Somewhat Accurate	Highly Accurate
☐	☐	☐	☐	☐

35. **Select the button on the scale below that reflects the accuracy of the following statement:**

Many of the students that I teach are not capable of learning the material I am supposed to teach.

Highly Inaccurate	Somewhat Inaccurate	Neither Inaccurate or Accurate	Somewhat Accurate	Highly Accurate
☐	☐	☐	☐	☐

36. **Select the button on the scale below that reflects the accuracy of the following statement:**

The attitudes and habits that my students bring to class greatly reduce their chances for academic success.

Highly Inaccurate	Somewhat Inaccurate	Neither Inaccurate or Accurate	Somewhat Accurate	Highly Accurate
☐	☐	☐	☐	☐

IDENTIFYING LEADERSHIP AND ORGANIZATIONAL PROCESSES | 101

37. Select the button on the scale below that reflects the accuracy of the following statement:

	Highly Inaccurate	Somewhat Inaccurate	Neither Inaccurate or Accurate	Somewhat Accurate	Highly Accurate
I am actively involved in improving my classroom teaching through pursuing alternative instructional strategies that work with different groups of students.	☐ Highly Inaccurate	☐ Somewhat Inaccurate	☐ Neither Inaccurate or Accurate	☐ Somewhat Accurate	☐ Highly Accurate

38. Select the button on the scale below that reflects the accuracy of the following statement:

	Highly Inaccurate	Somewhat Inaccurate	Neither Inaccurate or Accurate	Somewhat Accurate	Highly Accurate
Parents are involved on a regular basis in helping out with the school's program.	☐ Highly Inaccurate	☐ Somewhat Inaccurate	☐ Neither Inaccurate or Accurate	☐ Somewhat Accurate	☐ Highly Accurate

39. Select the button on the scale below that reflects the accuracy of the following statement:

	Highly Inaccurate	Somewhat Inaccurate	Neither Inaccurate or Accurate	Somewhat Accurate	Highly Accurate
Most of my students' parents support what I do in class.	☐ Highly Inaccurate	☐ Somewhat Inaccurate	☐ Neither Inaccurate or Accurate	☐ Somewhat Accurate	☐ Highly Accurate

40. Select the button on the scale below that reflects the accuracy of the following statement:

	Highly Inaccurate	Somewhat Inaccurate	Neither Inaccurate or Accurate	Somewhat Accurate	Highly Accurate
Teachers help and support each other.	☐ Highly Inaccurate	☐ Somewhat Inaccurate	☐ Neither Inaccurate or Accurate	☐ Somewhat Accurate	☐ Highly Accurate

41. Select the button on the scale below that reflects the accuracy of the following statement:

	Highly Inaccurate	Somewhat Inaccurate	Neither Inaccurate or Accurate	Somewhat Accurate	Highly Accurate
Teachers socialize with each other on a regular basis.	☐ Highly Inaccurate	☐ Somewhat Inaccurate	☐ Neither Inaccurate or Accurate	☐ Somewhat Accurate	☐ Highly Accurate

42. Select the button on the scale below that reflects the accuracy of the following statement:

	Highly Inaccurate	Somewhat Inaccurate	Neither Inaccurate or Accurate	Somewhat Accurate	Highly Accurate
Teachers willingly spend time after school with students who have individual needs.	☐ Highly Inaccurate	☐ Somewhat Inaccurate	☐ Neither Inaccurate or Accurate	☐ Somewhat Accurate	☐ Highly Accurate

43. Select the button on the scale below that reflects the accuracy of the following statement:

	Highly Inaccurate	Somewhat Inaccurate	Neither Inaccurate or Accurate	Somewhat Accurate	Highly Accurate
The administrative team treats teachers as equals.	☐ Highly Inaccurate	☐ Somewhat Inaccurate	☐ Neither Inaccurate or Accurate	☐ Somewhat Accurate	☐ Highly Accurate

44. Select the button on the scale below that reflects the accuracy of the following statement:

	Highly Inaccurate	Somewhat Inaccurate	Neither Inaccurate or Accurate	Somewhat Accurate	Highly Accurate
School is a nice place to be--I feel needed and wanted here.	☐ Highly Inaccurate	☐ Somewhat Inaccurate	☐ Neither Inaccurate or Accurate	☐ Somewhat Accurate	☐ Highly Accurate

45. Select the button on the scale below that reflects the accuracy of the following statement:

	Highly Inaccurate	Somewhat Inaccurate	Neither Inaccurate or Accurate	Somewhat Accurate	Highly Accurate
Teachers are proud of our school.	☐ Highly Inaccurate	☐ Somewhat Inaccurate	☐ Neither Inaccurate or Accurate	☐ Somewhat Accurate	☐ Highly Accurate

46. Select the button on the scale below that reflects the accuracy of the following statement:

My school has the money to provide resources to meet the needs of the middle grade students (socio-emotional, academic, physical).

Highly Inaccurate	Somewhat Inaccurate	Neither Inaccurate or Accurate	Somewhat Accurate	Highly Accurate
☐	☐	☐	☐	☐

47. Select the button on the scale below that reflects the accuracy of the following statement:

My students treat each other and the staff with respect. This is the reason there are few disciplinary problems and suspensions at my school.

Highly Inaccurate	Somewhat Inaccurate	Neither Inaccurate or Accurate	Somewhat Accurate	Highly Accurate
☐	☐	☐	☐	☐

References

Allaire, Y., & Firsirotu, M. E. (1984). Theories of organizational culture. *Organizational Studies, 5*(3), 193–226.

Argyris, C. (1954). *Organization of a bank: A study of the nature of organization and the fusion process.* New Haven, CT: Yale University Labor and Management Center.

Barth, R. (2001). Teacher leader. *Phi Delta Kappan, 82*(6), 443–449.

Bolman, L, & Deal, T. (1984). *Modern approaches to understanding and managing organizations.* San Francisco: Jossey-Bass.

Bossert, S. (1988). School effects. In N. Boyan (Ed.), *The hanbook of research on educational administration* (pp. 341–354). New York: Longman.

Bossert, S., Dwyer, D., Rowan, B., & Lee, G. (1982). The instructional management role of the principal. *Educational Administration Quarterly, 18*(3), 34–64.

Brown, T., Lemus, N., & Pickett, W. (1999). The three secrets of effective school leaders: Team building, school climate, and school vision. Retrieved December 12, 2007, from http://hdcs.fullerton.edu/faculty/orozco/stlec-3secrets.html

Creemers, B. (1994). *The effective classroom.* London, UK: Cassell.

Creemers, B. P. M., & Kyriakides, L. (2008). *The dynamics of educational effectiveness: A contribution to policy, practice and theory in contemporary schools.* London: Routledge.

Firestone, W. A., & Louis, K. S. (1999). Schools as cultures. In J. Murphy & K. S. Louis (Eds.). *Handbook of Research on Educational Administration* (pp. 297–322). San Francisco, CA: Jossey-Bass.

Fullan, M. (1991). *The new meaning of educational change.* New York: Teachers College, Columbia University.

Fullan, M. (2006). *The development of transformational leaders for educational decentralization.* Toronto, Canada: Michael Fullan.

Fuller, B., Wood, K., Rapaport, T., & Dornbusch, S. (1982). The organizational context of individual efficacy. *Review of Educational Research, 52*(1), 7–30.

Gomez, M. O., Marcoulides, G. A., & Heck, R. H. (2012). Examining culture and performance at different middle school level structures. *International Journal of Educational Management, 26*(2), 205–222.

Gronn, P. (2002). Distributed leadership as a unit of analysis. *Leadership Quarterly, 13,* 423–451.

Hall, G., & Hord, S. (2001). *Implementing change: Patterns, principles, and potholes.* Boston: Allyn & Bacon.

Hallinger, P., Bickman, L., & Davis, K. (1996). School context, principal leadership and student achievement. *Elementary School Journal, 96*(5), 498–518.

Hallinger, P. & Heck, R. H. (1996). Reassessing the principal's role in school effectiveness: A review of the empirical research, 1980–1995. *Educational Administration Quarterly, 32*(1), 5–44.

Harris, A. (2004). Distributed leadership and school improvement. *Educational Management Administration and Leadership, 32*(1), 11–24.

Heck, R. H. (2000). Examining the impact of school quality on school outcomes and improvement: A value-added approach. *Educational Administration Quarterly, 36*(4), 513–552.

Heck, R. (2007). Examining the relationship between teacher quality as an organizational property of schools and students' achievement and growth rates. *Educational Administration Quarterly, 43*(4), 399–432.

Heck, R. (2009). Teacher effectiveness and student achievement: Investigating a multilevel cross-classified model. *Journal of Educational Administration, 47*(2), 227–249.

Heck, R. H., & Hallinger, P. (2010, April). *Examining the effects of school leadership on the instructional learning environment, teacher effectiveness, and student math achievement.* Paper presented at the annual meeting of the American Educational Research Association, Denver, Colorado.

Heck, R. H., Larsen, T. J., & Marcoulides, G. A. (1990). Instructional leadership and school achievement: Validation of a causal model. *Educational Administration Quarterly, 26*(2), 94–125.

Heck, R. H., & Marcoulides, G. A. (1993, May). Principal leadership behaviors and school achievement. *NASSP Bulletin,* 20–28.

Heck, R. H., & Marcoulides, G. A. (1996). School culture and performance: Testing the invariance of an organizational model. *School Effectiveness and School Improvement, 7*(1), 76–96.

Heck, R. & Marcoulides, G. (1996). The assessment of leadership performance: A multilevel perspective. *Journal of Personnel Evaluation in Education, 10*(1), 11–28.

Heck, R. H., & Moriyama, K. (2010). Examining relationships among elementary schools' contexts, leadership, instructional practices, and added-year outcomes: A regression discontinuity approach. *School Effectiveness and School Improvement, 21*(4), 377–408.

Hofstede, G., Neuijen, B., Ohayv, D. D., & Sanders, G. (1990). Measuring organizational cultures: A qualitative and quantitative study across twenty cases. *Administrative Science Quarterly, 35,* 286–316.

Holt, C. R., & Smith, R. M. (2002). A relationship between school climate and student success.

Arkansas Educational Research & Policy Studies, 2, 52–64.
Hoy, W. K., & Feldman, J. A. (1999). Organizational health profiles for high schools. In H. J. Frieberg (Ed.), *School climate: Measuring, improving, and sustaining healthy learning environments* (pp. 84–102). London: Falmer Press.
Hoy, W. K. & Hannum, J. W. (1997). Middle school climate: an empirical assessment of organizational health and student achievement. *Educational Administration Quarterly, 33*(3), 290–311.
Hoy, W. K., Hannum, J. W., & Tschannen-Moran, M. (1998). Organizational climate and student achievement: A parsimonious and longitudinal view. *Journal of School Leadership, 8,* 336–359.
Hoy, W. K., Tarter, C. J., & Bliss, J. R. (1990). Organizational climate, school health, and effectiveness: A comparative analysis. *Educational Administration Quarterly, 26*(3), 260–279.
Ingersoll, R. (1994). Organizational control in secondary schools. *Harvard Review, 64*(2), 150–172.
Kuperminc, G. P., Leadbeater, B. J., Emmons, C., & Blatt, S. J. (1997). Perceived school climate and difficulties in the social adjustment of middle school students. *Applied Developmental Science, 1*(2), 76–88.
Kyriakides, L., Creemers, B., Antoniou, P., & Demetriou, D. (2009). A synthesis of studies searching for school factors: Implications for theory and research. *British Educational Research Journal.* Advance online publication. doi:10.1080/01411920903165603.
Lee, V. E., & Croninger, R. G. (1994). The relative importance of home and school in the development of literacy skills for middle-grade students. *American Journal of Education, 102*(3), 286–329.
Leithwood, K., Day, C., Sammons, P., Harris, A., & Hopkins, D. (2006). *Seven strong claims about successful school leadership.* Nottingham, England: National College of School Leadership.
Leithwood, K., & Jantzi, D. (1997). Explaining variation in teachers' perceptions of principals' leadership: A replication. *Journal of Educational Administration, 35*(4), 312–324.
Leithwood, K., Jantzi, D., Silins, H., & Dart, B. (1993). Using the appraisal of school leaders as an instrument of restructuring. *Peabody Journal of Education, 68*(2), 85–109.
Leithwood, K., Louis, K. S., Anderson, S. & Wahlsttom, K. (2004). Review of research: How leadership influences student learning. Wallace Foundation. Downloaded from http://www.wallacefoundation.org/NR/rdonlyres/E3BCCFA5-A88B-45D3-8E27-B973732283C9/0/RevieweofResearchLearningFromLeadership.pdf on December 19, 2007.
Leithwood, K., & Mascall, B. (2008). Collective leadership effects on student achievement. *Educational Administration Quarterly, 44*(4), 529–561.
Leithwood, K., Patten, S., & Jantzi, D. (2010). Testing a conceptualization of how school leadership influences student learning. *Educational Administration Quarterly, 46*(5), 671–706.
Lieberman, K. A., Saxl, E. R., & Miles, M. B. (2000). 'Teacher Leadership: Ideology and practice,' in A. Lieberman, E. R. Saxl, and M. B. Miles (Eds.) *The Jossey-Bass reader on educational leadership* (pp. 339–345). Chicago: Jossey-Bass.
Lumsden, L. (1998). *Teacher morale.* Eugene, OR: ERIC Clearinghouse on Educational Management. (ERIC Document Reproduction Service No. ED 422601).
Marcoulides, G. A., & Heck, R. H. (1993). Organizational culture and performance: Proposing and testing a model. *Organization Science, 4,* 209–225.
Marcoulides, G. A., & Heck, R. H. (2009). Educational applications of latent growth mixture models. In T. Teo & M. S. Khine (Eds.), *Structural equation modeling in educational research: Concepts and applications* (pp. 345–366). The Netherlands: Sense Publishers.

Marcoulides, G. A., Heck, R. A., & Papanastasiou, C. (2005). Student perceptions of culture and achievement: Testing the invariance of a model. *International Journal of Educational Management, 19*(2), 140–152.

Moran, T. E., & Volkwein, J. F. (1992). The cultural approach to the formation of organizational climate. *Human Relations, 45*(1), 19–47.

Mortimore, P. (1993). School effectiveness and the management of effective learning and teaching. *School Effectiveness and School Improvement, 4*, 290–310.

Ogawa, R., & Bossert, S. (1995). Leadership as an organizational quality. *Educational Administration Quarterly, 31*(2), 224–243.

Opdenakker, M. C., & Van Damme, J. (2007). Do school context, student composition and school leadership affect school practice and outcomes in secondary education? *British Educational Research Journal, 33*, 179–206. Retrieved from http://www.informaworld.com.

Owens, R. G. (1998). *Organizational behavior in education* (6th ed.). Boston, MA: Allyn & Bacon.

Reynolds, D., & Packer, A. (1992). School effectiveness and school improvement in the 1990s. In D. Reynolds & P. Cuttance (Eds.). *School effectiveness: Research, policy, and practice* (pp. 171–187). London: Cassell.

Robinson, V., Lloyd, C., & Rowe, K. (2008). The impact of leadership on student outcomes: An analysis of the differential effects of leadership types. *Educational Administration Quarterly, 44*(5), 564–588.

Saffold, G. S. (1988). Culture traits, strength, and organizational performance: Moving beyond "strong" culture. *Academy of Management Review, 13*(4), 546–558.

Sarason, S. (1982). *The culture of the school and the problem of change* (2nd ed.). Boston: Allyn & Bacon.

Scheerens, J., & Bosker, R. (1997). *The foundations of educational effectiveness.* New York: Pergamon.

Schein, E. H. (1990). Organizational culture. *American Psychologist, 45*(2), 109–119.

Supovitz, J., Sirinides, P., & May, H. (2010). How principals and peers influence teaching and learning. *Educational Administration Quarterly, 46*(1), 31–56.

Sweetland, S., & Hoy, W. K. (2000). School characteristics and educational outcomes: Toward an organizational model of student achievement in middle schools. *Educational Administration Quarterly, 36*(5), 703–729.

Taylor, D. L., & Tashakkori, A. (1995). Decision participation and school climate as predictors of job satisfaction and teacher's sense of efficacy. *Journal of Experimental Education, 63*(3), 217–227.

Teddlie, C., & Reynolds, D. (Eds.). (2000). *The international handbook of school effectiveness research.* London: Falmer Press.

Thompson, J. (1967). *Organizations in action.* New York: McGraw-Hill.

Trice, H. M. & Beyer, J. M. (1984). Studying organizational cultures through rites and ceremonials. *Academy of Management Review, 9*(4), 653–699.

Witziers, B., Bosker, R., & Kruger, M. (2003). Educational leadership and student achievement: The elusive search for an association. *Educational Administration Quarterly, 39*, 398–425.

Data-Informed Decision-Making ON High-Impact Strategies

An Instrument for Improving Principalship

JIANPING SHEN, VAN E. COOLEY, XIN MA, PATRICIA L. REEVES,
WALTER L. BURT, J. MARK RAINEY, & WENHUI YUAN

Introduction

Recent studies have isolated important sets of findings related to the role that leadership plays in shaping effective schools. One such set of findings is encapsulated in the results of a meta-analysis completed by Marzano, Waters, and McNulty (2005) that isolate principal responsibilities and behaviors associated with raising student achievement. Among those findings is the importance of monitoring both the conditions and processes that impact student achievement and the actual evidence of that achievement on a regular and systematic basis. In their 2005 report, Celio and Harvey offer a frame for monitoring school-level indicators of student achievement based on data typically available within the school environment, but this frame does not address a number of important school-level factors (Marzano, 2003) where data sources are not typically available and would need to be created. Further, studies of principals' practices using data to monitor both student success and the school conditions that correlate to the success reveal a very narrow range of actual data collection and use (Reeves & Burt, 2006).

Since a principal's ability to use data to monitor important school conditions is, itself, a condition that is associated with student and school success, a broader frame is needed to help principals achieve better accountability for the conditions in their schools that impinge upon student success. With the 2002 No Child Left

Behind Act (NCLB—Public Law 107–110) and, now, the Race to the Top (RTTT) provisions of the American Recovery and Reinvestment Act of 2009 (ARRA—Section 14005-6, Title XIV, Public Law 111-5) holding principals squarely accountable for both student outcomes and the school conditions, principals need better tools for monitoring their own work, especially the work of using data to monitor and inform the process of improving school-level conditions for raising student achievement.

In this study, we capitalize on the intersection of three streams of literature to develop an instrument that measures the extent to which principals engage in data-informed decision-making in relation to those high-impact strategies that are empirically associated with higher student achievement. The key words in the above sentence reveal the three important streams of literature: (a) data-informed decision-making in the age of accountability; (b) increasing evidence that what principals do makes a significant impact on the school and student achievement; and (c) high-impact strategies at the student, classroom, and school levels that are empirically associated with student achievement. Although much development has been made in the aforementioned three streams of literature, there has been no instrument that can be used to measure the extent to which principals engage in data-informed decision-making on those high-impact strategies that are empirically related to student achievement. This study fills the void.

In the following, we first review the three streams of literature, and make the connection among the three streams to point out the need for an instrument to measure important dimensions of a principal's work. We then discuss item development, sampling, and data collection. We report the results of structural equation modeling and Cronbach's alpha coefficients, among others, to demonstrate factorial validity and internal consistency of the instrument. Finally, we discuss the theoretical and practical implications of the developed instrument.

Literature Review

Data-Informed Decision-Making in the Context of Accountability

Using student assessment to make decisions about the quality of instruction for children has been part of the educational scene since the late 19th century. However, holding students, teachers, schools, and school districts accountable for student performance is a more contemporary invention (Evers & Walberg, 2002). Title I of the Elementary and Secondary Education Act (ESEA) of 1965 and the Coleman Report of 1966 initiated the federal policy shift from concerns about access to educational opportunity and distribution of resources, to a more pointed examination about student educational outcomes. Accountability for all students to demonstrate proficiency across a standardized core academic curriculum (Elmore, 2004) did not fully emerge, however, until the 2002 No Child Left Behind Act (NCLB—Public Law 107–110). This new act cemented federal educational accountability with specifications for holding all schools accountable for (a) a standards-based state curriculum, (b) teachers who are highly qualified in their teaching content and trained to utilize scientifically based, research-supported strategies, and (c) a series of Adequate Yearly Progress (AYP) benchmarks for raising all students to levels of proficiency in the core content areas.

With the advent of accountability, data have become an integral part of the systemic change (Shen & Ma, 2006) and "mountains of data" (Celio & Harvey, 2005) have been generated. Literature searches on the use of data for making decisions in educational settings yield a rich array of references and studies related to both the types of data available in school settings and the uses of data (both actual and recommended). With the accumulation of the vast amount of data in education, much of the discussion on how to use data for decision-making evolves from "data-driven," to "data-based," and (most currently) to "data-informed" (Cooley, Shen, Miller, Winograd, Rainey, & Yuan, 2006; Knapp, Swinnerton, Copland, & Monpas-Huber, 2006; Shen, Berry, Cooley, Kirby, Marx, & Whale, 2007; Shen & Cooley, 2008), with an understanding that data will "inform," rather than "drive," decision-making because there are rational, political, and moral elements in decision-making and "data" is only one important element in the process.

Some recently published empirical studies focus on (a) what data principals use and what decisions they make with the data (Shen, Cooley, Reeves, Burt, Ryan, Rainey & Yuan, 2010); (b) how individuals' organizational roles and the district reform history influence the construction of the meaning of data (Coburn & Talbert, 2006); (c) how district policies impact staff use of data (Kerr, Marsh, Ikemoto, Darilek, & Barney, 2006); (d) how the elements of data systems facilitate and inhibit effective use of data (Wayman & Stringfield, 2006); and (e) how school districts make choices in developing a formative assessment system (Sharkey & Murname, 2006).

Among others, there are two major weaknesses in the research and practice related to data-informed decision-making. First, as far as educational data are concerned, principals and teachers tend to focus on data *of* learning (e.g., ex post facto, standardized test data on student achievement), rather than data *for* learning (e.g., data on curricular and instructional practice) (Cooley, Shen, Miller, Winograd, Rainey & Yuan, 2006; Schmoker, 2004; Shen & Cooley, 2008). Second, there is a need to improve "leaders' expertise in accessing, generating, managing, interpreting, and acting on data" (Knapp et al., 2006, p. 39) and to improve leaders' awareness of a broader range of data sources and purposes. In this study, the researchers developed an instrument that will generate process data to indicate the extent to which principals engage in the use of data to inform decision-making on school-level high-impact strategies. Thus, this study addresses the two weaknesses and fills a void in the literature.

Principals' Impact on School Improvement

According to Leithwood, Louis, Anderson, and Wahlstrom (2004), leadership is found to be second only to classroom instruction among school-related factors that affect student learning, accounting for about 25% of total direct and indirect effects on student learning. The common core of basic leadership practices includes "setting directions," "developing people," and "redesigning the organization to develop one that supports the performance of administrators, teachers, and students." Through empirical research, we know much about the principalship (Cooley & Shen, 2000, 2003; Rodriguez-Campo, Rincones-Gomez, & Shen, 2005; Shen & Crawford, 2003; Shen, Cooley, & Wegenke, 2004; Shen, Kavanaugh, Wegenke, Rodriguez-Campos, Rincones-Gomez, Palmer, Crawford, Cooley, Poppink, VanderJagt, Hsieh, Ruhl-Smith, Keiser, & Portin, 2005), particularly the dimensions of principals' work that affect student learning. For example, researchers found that the impact of the principalship centers on a principal's role in shaping the school's instructional climate and instructional organization (Bossert, Dwyer, Rowan, & Lee, 1982; Goldring & Pasternak, 1994; Hallinger, Bickman, & Davis, 1996; Heck, Larson, & Marcoulides, 1990; Leithwood & Jantzi, 1999). Instructional climate includes, among others, the culture for school renewal (Sebring & Bryk, 2000; Smith, Guarino, Strom, & Adams, 2006), distributive and empowering leadership (Marks & Printy, 2003; Marks & Louis, 1997), high expectation for students (Cotton & Association for Supervision and Curriculum Development, 2003), and data-informed decision-making (Celio & Harvey, 2005; Shen et al., 2010). Research by Marcoulides and Heck (1993) and O'Donnell and White (2005) indicated that the principal's leadership in building the instructional climate and organizing the instructional program are significant predictors for academic achievement. Other studies by Heck and Marcoulides (1992) and Hallinger (1992) suggested that the principals' leadership appears to be exercised primarily through behaviors that shape the school-level instructional framework such as managing the instructional program and promoting a positive learning climate.

Subsequent studies conducted by Lee and Smith (1996), Louis, Marks, and Kruse (1996), Marks and Louis (1997), and Manthey (2006) also documented significant positive effects on achievement associated with principal leadership that shapes a strong professional community and collective responsibility for student learning. Principals' instructional leadership encompasses many factors such as promoting effective pedagogies, including, among others, (a) culturally relevant pedagogy (Boykin & Cunningham, 2001; Ladson-Billings, 1994, 1995a, 1995b, 1998; Dill & Boykin, 2000); (b) pedagogical content knowledge (Shulman, 1986, 1987; Grossman, 1990, 1994; Stein & Nelson, 2003); and (c) authentic learning (National Commission on Service Learning, 2002; Newmann, Marks, & Gamoran, 1996; Newmann & Associates, 1996; Resnick, 1994).

Some researchers have attempted to quantify the association between principal leadership, on one hand, and student achievement and other school outcomes, on the other. For example, Newmann, Rutter, and Smith (1989) found that measures of principal behaviors can have standardized regression coefficients up to 0.38 on teachers' sense of efficacy, community, and expectation, indicating small effects of principal behaviors. School organizational factors, many of which measure principal behaviors, account for about 10% to 38% of the total variance in teacher efficacy, community, and expectation (Newmann et al., 1989). Later, Barnett, McCormick, and Conners (2000) suggested that school leadership is characterized by a one-to-one relationship between the principal (leader) and the teacher (follower). Under this relationship, teacher-related outcomes (principal leadership and school culture), overall, show an intra-class correlation up to 25%. Although statistically significant, principal behaviors often show small effects on teacher-related outcomes such as school culture (Barnett et al., 2000). More recently, Marzano, Waters, and McNulty (2005) conducted a landmark meta-analysis of 70 empirical studies published in the last 25 years and found that the simple bivariate correlation between principal leadership and student achievement at the school level, corrected for attenuation, is .25. By definition, then, principal leadership accounts for about 6.25% of the variance in student achievement at the school level. In summary, various effect sizes from the above studies indicate a significant role for principals in improving schools and student achievement.

High-Impact Strategies for School Improvement

There is a rich body of literature on strategies for improving schools. It consists of, mainly, two streams of literature. The first stream includes large-scale meta-analyses such as those by Marzano et al. (2005) and Cotton (2003). These are quality syntheses of the literature on the relationship between principal leadership and school improvement, in general, and student achievement, in particular. These meta-analyses tend to distill a set of empirically supported strategies. However, since meta-analyses use original studies as data sources and, thus, have requirements for the kind of studies that are included in the meta-analyses, meta-analyses, by design, limit what studies are included. The second stream of literature includes those recent, influential studies that were not included in the meta-analyses. Such studies examine ideas such as the integration of transformational and shared instructional leadership (Marks & Printy, 2003), collective efficacy (Goddard, 2001; Goddard, Hoy, & Hoy, 2004; Manthey, 2006), collective responsibility (Lee & Smith, 1996), culturally relevant pedagogy (Boykin & Cunningham, 2001; Dill & Boykin, 2000; Ladson-Billings, 1994, 1995a, 1995b, 1998), instructional program coherence (Newmann, Smith, Allensworth, & Bryk, 2001), professional community (Louis, Marks, & Kruse, 1996; Marks & Louis, 1997), social trust (Sebring & Bryk, 2000), and organizational learning (Marks, Louis, & Printy, 2000). Table 1 summarizes the important aspects of principals' work that are related to school improvement, in general, and student achievement, in particular. The table also helps to illustrate the intersections between findings from the meta-analysis research and recent significant studies that expand upon the themes derived from meta-analysis.

From Table 1 we know many high-impact strategies to improve the school and student achievement. In the literature, some instruments have been developed to measure teachers' perceptions on certain aspects of the school culture and process that are related to the principalship, such as Short and Rinehart's (1992) School Participant Empowerment Scale which measures the level of teacher "decision making," "professional growth," and "autonomy," and the National Association of Secondary School Principals' School Climate Survey, which measures teachers' perceptions on, among others, "security and maintenance," "student behavioral values," and "instructional management." While such instruments offer some insights on how teachers view and interpret the work of principals, they do not specifically hone in on the principal's role to monitor and interpret the conditions for student success in the school. Further, these instruments do not collect data directly from principals; they are not built on a framework of those dimensions of principalship that are empirically associated with student achievement. There is an urgent need from the field to have an instrument that measures principals' actual work against high-impact strategies that are empirically associated with student achievement.

Focus of the Study

To connect the three streams of literature reviewed in the foregoing, the authors developed an instrument to help principals self-assess the extent to which they use data to engage in data-informed decision-making on high-impact strategies associated with student achievement. Based on a meta-analysis of 35 years of empirical research, Marzano (2003) developed a framework of 11 factors at the school, teacher, and student levels. All these factors are empirically related to higher student achievement. We selected Marzano's framework as the basis for building an instrument to help principals assess and expand their data-informed practices

TABLE 1. Principal Leadership Dimensions and Elements Empirically Associated With School Improvement and Student Achievement

Dimensions	Elements in Marzano's Balanced Leadership	Elements in Other Research
A. Inspirational agency for school renewal	• Affirmation • Change agent • Optimizer • Flexibility • Intellectual stimulation	• Self-efficacy (Smith, Guarino, Strom, & Adams, 2006), self-confidence, responsibility, and perseverance; rituals, ceremonies, and other symbolic actions (Cotton & Association for Supervision and Curriculum Development, 2003) • Influence of principal leadership on school process such as school policies and norms, the practices of teachers, and school goals (Hallinger & Heck, 1996) • The integration of transformational and shared instructional leadership (Marks & Printy, 2003) • Visibility (Witziers, Bosker, & Kruger, 2003) • Purposes and goals (Leithwood & Jantzi, 1999) • Encouraging teachers to take risks and try new teaching methods (Sebring & Bryk, 2000)
B. Orderly school operation	• Order • Communication • Discipline	• Safe and orderly school environment; positive and supportive school climate; communication and interaction; interpersonal support (Cotton & Association for Supervision and Curriculum Development, 2003) • Governance (Heck, 1992; Heck & Marcoulides, 1993) • Planning; structure and organization (Leithwood & Jantzi, 1999) • Minimizing classroom disruptions (Sebring & Bryk, 2000)
C. High, cohesive, and culturally relevant expectations for students	• Culture • Focus • Outreach • Ideals/beliefs	• Goals focused on high levels of student learning; high expectations of students; community outreach (Cotton & Association for Supervision and Curriculum Development, 2003) • Climate (Heck, 1992; O'Donnell & White, 2005) • Leadership of parents positively associated with student achievement (Pounder, 1995) • School mission, teacher expectation, school culture (Hallinger & Heck, 1996) • Defining and communicating mission; achievement orientation (O'Donnell & White, 2005; Witziers, Bosker, & Kruger, 2003) • Culture (Leithwood & Jantzi, 1999) • Collective efficacy (Goddard, 2001; Goddard, Hoy, & Hoy, 2004; Manthey, 2006) • Collective responsibility (Lee & Smith, 1996) • Culturally relevant pedagogy (Boykin & Cunningham, 2001; Dill & Boykin, 2000; Ladson-Billings, 1994, 1995a, 1995b, 1998)

continued

TABLE 1. (*continued*)

Dimensions	Elements in Marzano's Balanced Leadership	Elements in Other Research
D. Coherent curricular programs	• Curriculum, instruction, assessment • Knowledge of curriculum, instruction, and assessment	• Instructional organization (Hallinger & Heck, 1996; Heck, 1992; Heck & Marcoulides, 1993) • The integration of transformational and shared instructional leadership (Marks & Printy, 2003) • Supervising and evaluating the curriculum; coordinating and managing curriculum (Witziers, Bosker, & Kruger, 2003) • Instructional program coherence (Newmann, Smith, Allensworth, & Bryk, 2001)
E. Distributive and empowering leadership	• Input • Resources • Visibility • Contingent reward • Relationship	• Shared leadership and staff empowerment; visibility and accessibility; teacher autonomy; support for risk taking; professional opportunities and resources (Cotton & Association for Supervision and Curriculum Development, 2003) • Cultivating teacher leadership for school improvement; shared instructional leadership (Marks & Printy, 2003) • Promoting school improvement and professional development (Witziers, Bosker, & Kruger, 2003) • Teacher empowerment (Marks & Louis, 1997) • Professional community (Louis, Marks, & Kruse, 1996; Marks & Louis, 1997; Spillane, Shalveson, & Diamond, 2001) • Social trust (Sebring & Bryk, 2000)
F. Real-time and embedded instructional assessment	• Curriculum, instruction, assessment • Knowledge of curriculum, instruction, and assessment	• Instructional leadership; classroom observation and feedback to teachers (Cotton & Association for Supervision and Curriculum Development,, 2003) • Instructional organization (Hallinger & Heck 1996; Heck, 1992; Heck & Marcoulides, 1993) • The integration of transformational and shared instructional leadership (Marks & Printy, 2003) • Monitoring student progress (Witziers, Bosker, & Kruger, 2003) • Instructional program coherence (Newmann, Smith, Allensworth, & Bryk, 2001)
G. Data-informed decision-making	• Monitors/evaluates • Situational awareness	• The practice of teachers; student opportunity to learn; academic learning time (Hallinger & Heck 1996; Shen et al., 2010) • Supervising and evaluating the curriculum (Witziers, Bosker, & Kruger, 2003) • Information collection (Celio & Harvey, 2005; Leithwood & Jantzi, 1999; Shen et al., 2010) • Organizational learning (Mark, Louis, & Printy, 2000).

because (a) Marzano's 11 factors provide a broad evidence-based frame for monitoring school conditions for learning, and (b) these factors have high familiarity with building leaders due to the high visibility and popularity of Marzano's work in district and state-level school improvement programs.

Building on Marzano's meta-analysis, we developed and validated an instrument to measure the extent to which principals use data to engage in decision-making on the 11 factors. In so doing, we captured descriptors associated with each of the 11 factors right out of the meta-analysis work and used those descriptors in shaping the instrument items. The items guide principals to assess the degree to which they are focusing on or attending to conditions and processes that are important elements of the 11 factors. The items also elicit principal reflection on what evidence they are using to monitor or track these conditions and processes. As a result, the instrument provides a useful tool for principals to self-assess and improve their ways in which they attend to those 11 high-impact strategies in their work by using data sources that inform their decision making.

Method

The Sample

Through the Michigan Association of Secondary School Principals and Michigan Elementary and Middle School Principals Associations, we asked school principals to complete the designed instrument (Data-Informed Decision-Making on High-Impact Strategies) and assured them of the anonymity of their responses. We sent the on-line survey to the entire population of 3,061 school principles from these two associations, in an attempt to secure an adequate sample for our analysis. A total of 256 school principals responded, representing about 8.4% of the population.[1]

Although our sample size appeared reasonable, it was not a random sample. Nevertheless, we found that the sample was sufficiently similar to the population in main characteristics. For example, for the population, 59% were elementary school principals and 41% secondary school principals; for the sample, 61% were elementary school principals and 39% secondary school principals. For the population, 57% were male; for the sample, 52% were male. The other issue we wanted to address was whether our sample size was large enough to ensure a credible factor analysis, because small sample sizes tend to make solutions of factor analysis unstable (MacCallum, Widaman, Zhang, & Hong, 1999). These researchers have suggested a minimum sample size between 100 and 200 for factor analysis (with commonalities in the 0.5 range). Our sample size of 256 thus met this minimum standard.[2]

Marzano's (2003) Framework and Instrument Development

The following table (Table 2) illustrates Marzano's (2003) framework in his book entitled *What Works in Schools*, where, based on his meta-analysis, he provided the effect size of each high-impact strategy on student achievement.

As Table 2 illustrates, the instrument—Data-Informed Decision-making on High-impact Strategies—comprised of 42 items forming 11 scales. The items were developed, according to Marzano's (2003) 11-factor framework, by a team of researchers and experienced practitioners who isolated discreet behaviors associated with each of the 11 factors from a detailed description of Marzano's findings.

TABLE 2. Marzano's Framework as a Foundation for Instrument Development

School-level Factor
1. Guaranteed and viable curriculum (Items 1–4)
2. Challenging goals and effective feedback (Items 5–8)
3. Parent and community involvement (Items 9–12)
4. Safe and orderly environment (Items 13–16)
5. Collegiality and professionalism (Items 17–20)
Teacher-level Factor
6. Instructional strategies (Items 21–23)
7. Classroom management (Items 24–26)
8. Classroom curriculum design (Items 27–30)
Student-level Factor
9. Home environment (Items 31–34)
10. Learned intelligence (Items 35–38)
11. Student motivation (Items 39–42)

School principals were instructed to highlight an option that corresponded most closely to their response to each statement that describes a principal behavior or function associated with monitoring school conditions and processes associated with raising student achievement. Responsive options for each statement included "not at all," "not very much," "somewhat," and "to a very great extent" (with responses coded 1 to 4 from "not at all" to "to a very great extent"). With these response choices, school principals with a higher score would demonstrate more effort and attention in their work to a certain area or for a certain statement. Principals are expected to have some familiarity with the 11 factors due to the wide field exposure to Marzano's work. Additionally, the sample for this study has a heightened awareness of the 11 factors due to the fact that they are embedded in the state's school improvement framework. Please see Appendix 1 for the actual instrument.

The Analysis

We started with an item analysis to make sure that school principals were using the full range of provided responsive options. This task was performed by examining the frequencies on the responsive options for each statement. We then proceeded to examine factorial validity of the questionnaire. We performed a series of confirmatory factor analyses to examine (a) whether the 11-factor structure that we identified through theoretical review of research literature was present with our sample of school principals and (b) whether there was a higher-order factor structure highlighting principal leadership at school, teacher, and student levels. Essentially, a confirmatory factor analysis tests whether and, if so, how well a proposed model fits the observed variance/covariance matrix among items. Figures 1 to 4 schematically illustrate the measurement models on which we conducted the test for factorial validity.

Our expectation was to show that our data endorsed the 11-factor structure as evidence of our questionnaire as a sound representation or measurement of the construct we conceptualized as principals' data-informed decision-making on high-impact strategies. Procedurally, we compared the 11-factor model with three other models: the null model, the one-factor model, and the three-factor model. Assuming zero covariance among items, the null model contained no factor. However, assuming that all items load on a single factor, the one-factor model aimed to test the existence of a unitary concept of principals' data-informed decision-making on high-impact strategies. Comparison of a proposed model with the null and one-factor models is a routine procedure in instrument validation. In our study, we added one more model—a three-factor model. According to Marzano's framework, the items could fall into one of the three categories: school level, teacher level, and student level. Because of the clear principal leadership dimensions these items created, we were interested in seeing whether this three-factor model was compatible with the 11-factor model for the potential of simplifying the final factor structure of principals' data-informed decision-making on high-impact strategies.

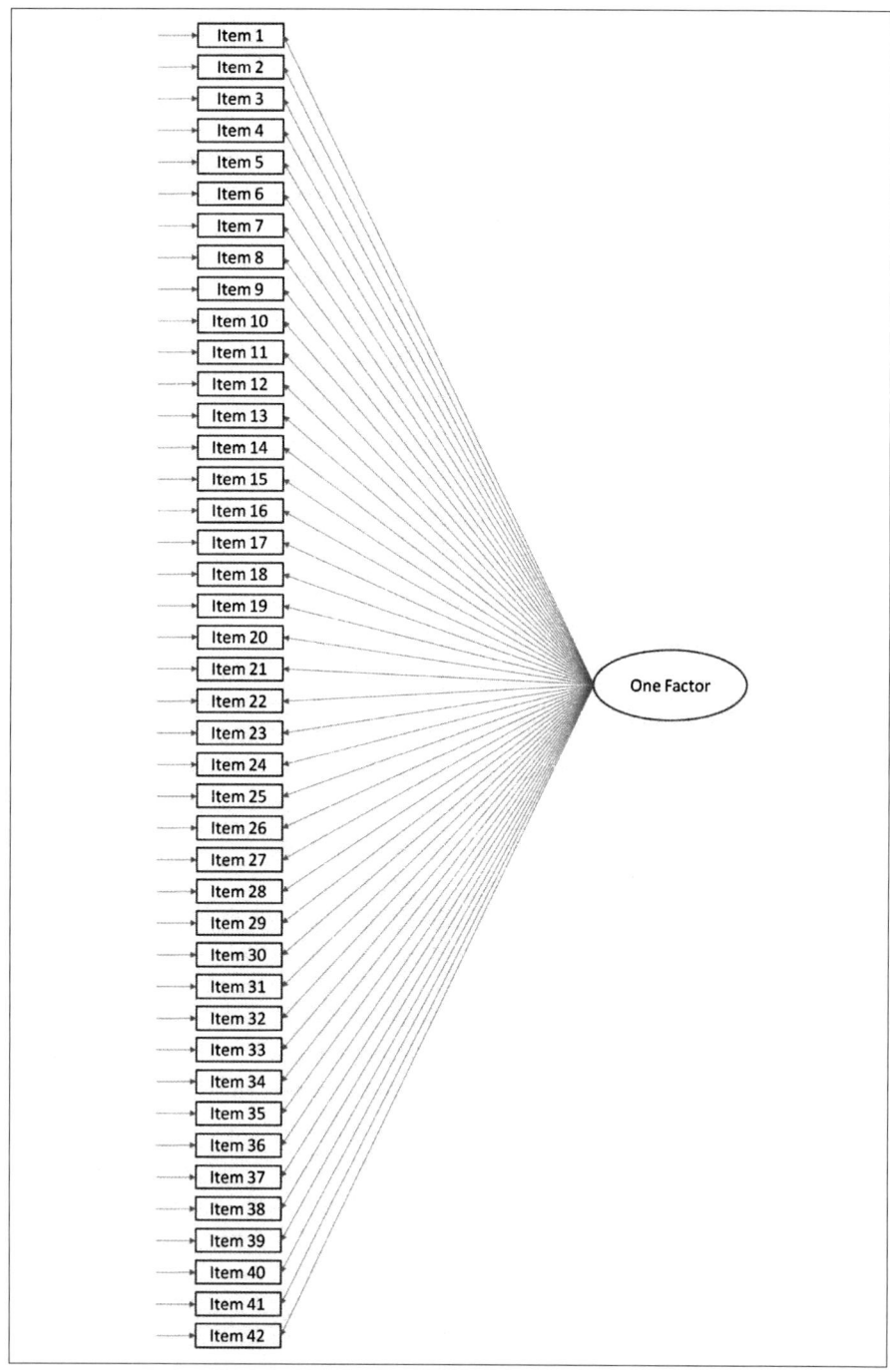

Figure 1. The One-Factor Model.

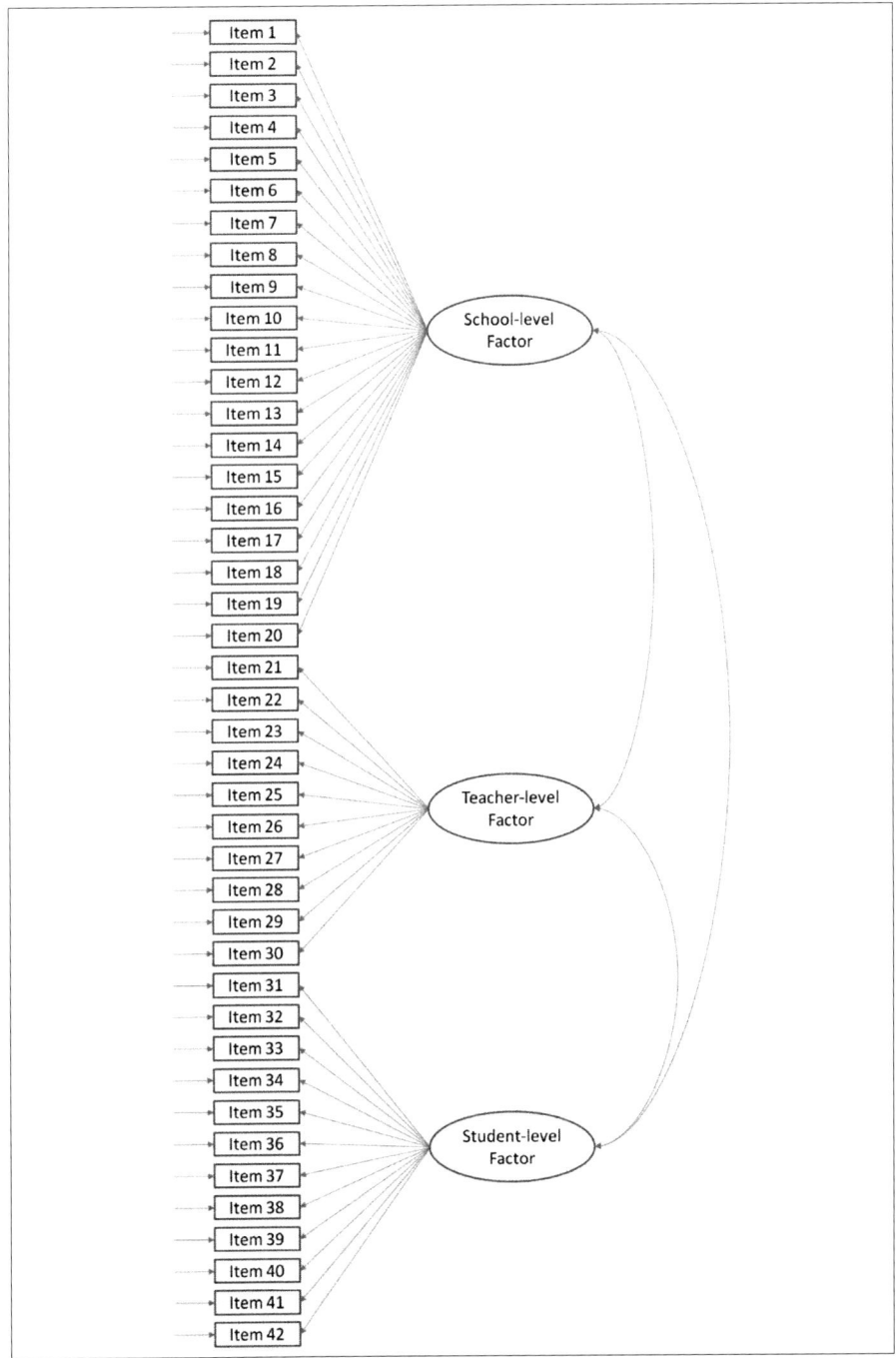

Figure 2. The Three-Factor Model.

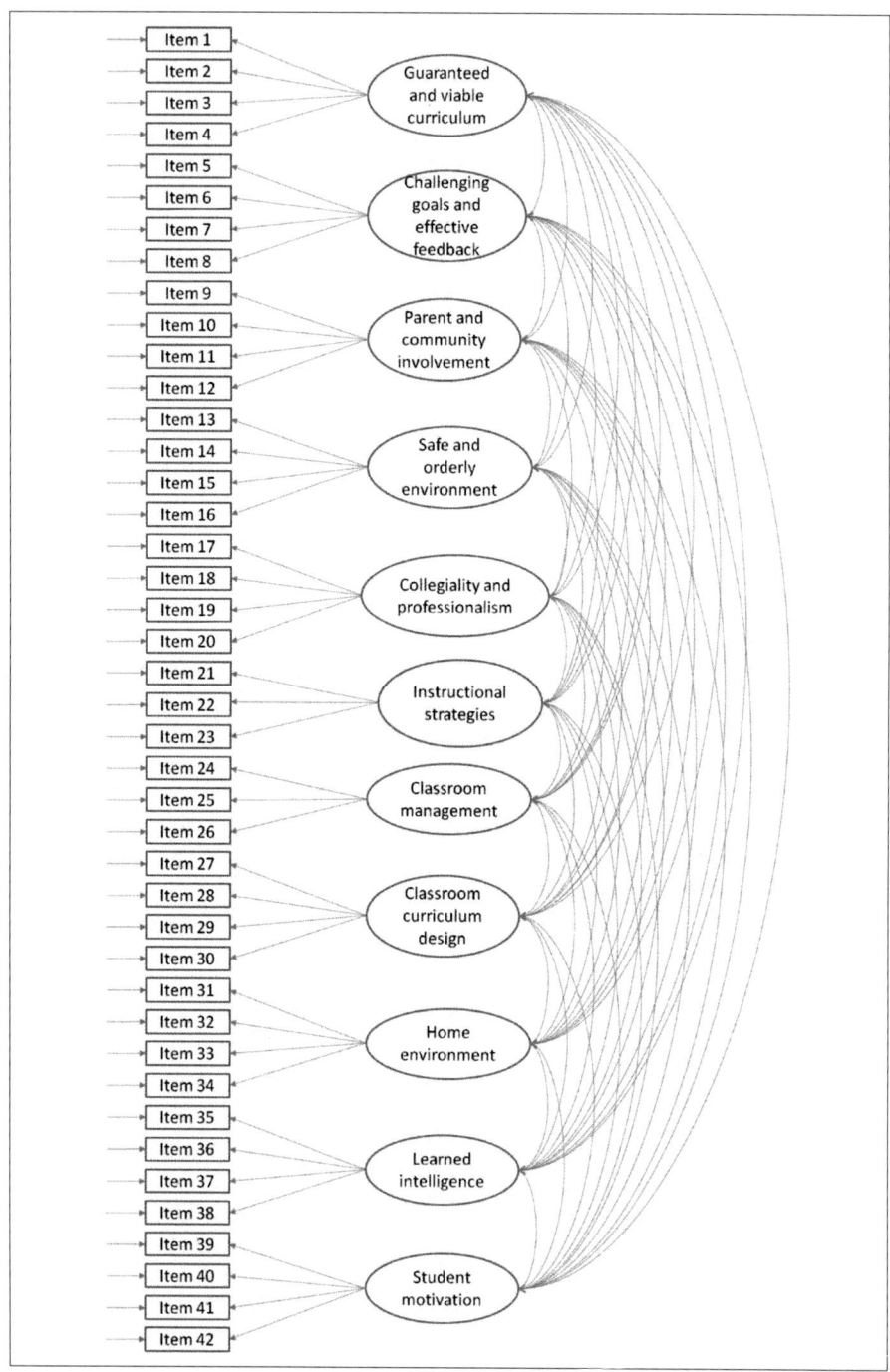

Figure 3. The 11-Factor Model.

DATA-INFORMED DECISION-MAKING ON HIGH-IMPACT STRATEGIES | 121

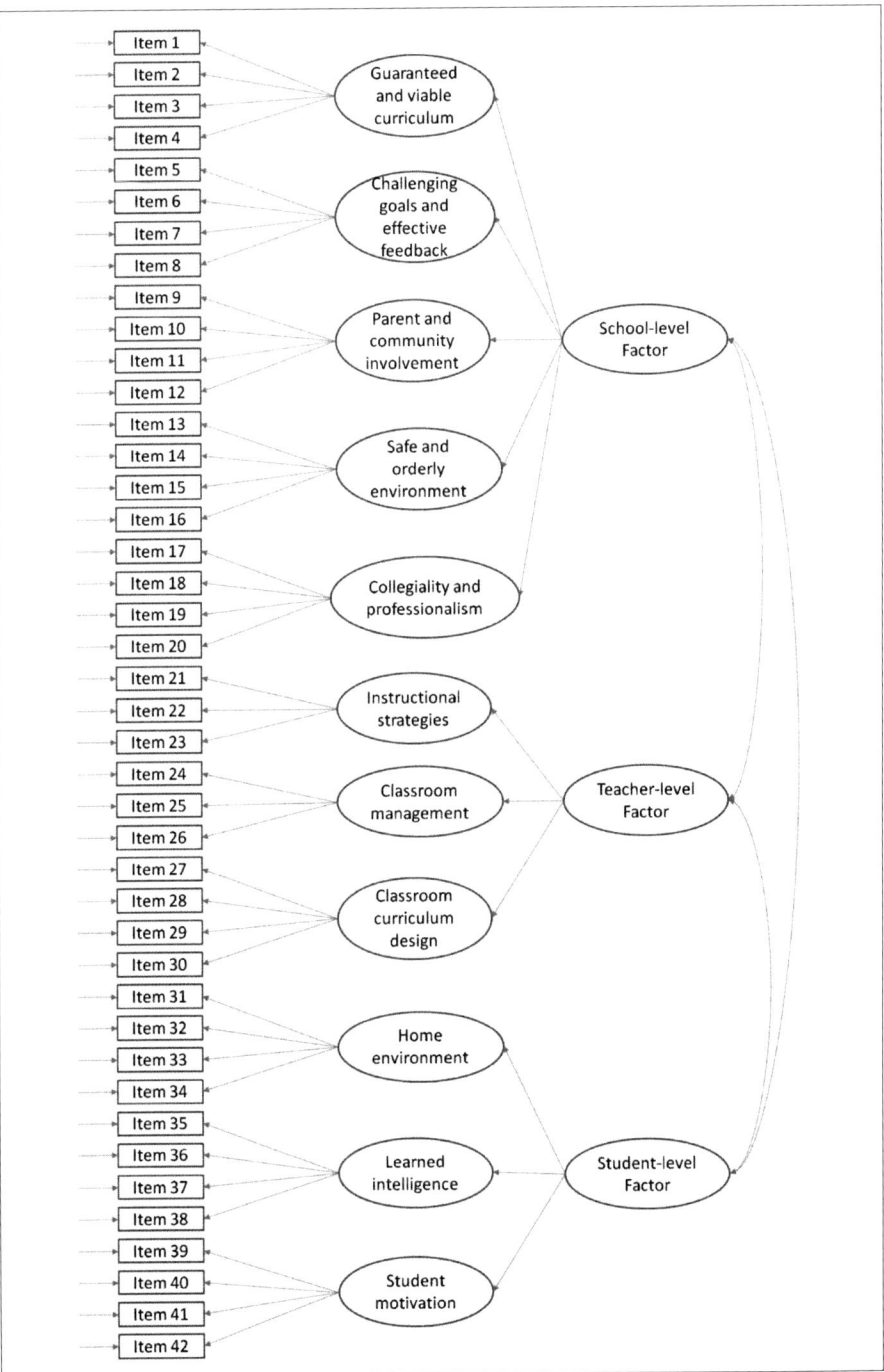

Figure 4. The 11-Factor Model with Three Higher-Order Factor.

Since Marzano organized the 11 factors under three categories (school, teacher, and student level factors), we also conducted a higher-order confirmatory factor analysis. In accordance with what Marzano's framework proposes, we specified that "guaranteed and viable curriculum," "challenging goals and effective feedback," "parent and community involvement," "safe and orderly environment," and "collegiality and professionalism" would load on a higher-order factor we considered as the school factor. We specified that "instructional strategies," "classroom management," and "classroom curriculum design" would load on a higher-order factor we considered as the teacher factor. Finally, we specified that "home environment," "learned intelligence," and "student motivation," would load on a higher-order factor we considered as the student factor.

The χ^2 statistic gives an indication of overall fit of the data to the model with a small χ^2 value indicating a good fit. As one of the absolute measures of fit that do not use an alternative model as the base for comparison, the χ^2 statistic provides only a rough idea about model-data-fit because it is sensitive to sample size, model size, and variable distribution. The standardized root mean square residual (SRMR) is a much better alternative absolute index. An SRMR value smaller than 0.08 is considered a good fit (see Hu & Bentler, 1999).

The comparative fit index (CFI) and the Tucker-Lewis index (TLI) can be considered as relative measures of fit because they use an alternative model as the base for comparison. CFI avoids the underestimation on the model-data-fit often occurring when a sample is small. TLI provides a measure of model-data-fit that is independent of sample size. Because both CFI and TLI measure the proportion of variance explained in relation to the null model, a value greater than 0.90 indicates a good fit in cases of both CFI and TLI (see Hu & Bentler, 1999). Finally, because the models in Table 3 are non-nested ones, information based estimates were also employed to evaluate goodness of fit, including the Akaike information criterion (AIC) and Bayesian information criterion (BIC). A best fitting model has the smallest estimate on both AIC and BIC.

With the scales empirically supported, we combined items relating to each scale in order to produce means and standard deviations for each scale. This task was performed by taking the average of valid responses within each scale for each school principal. This was a good opportunity for us to examine the distribution of the scale scores. Specifically, we examined two distribution indices: skewness, to make sure that scores were roughly symmetrical around the mean, and kurtosis, to make sure that the distributions were not overly peaked or overly flat. We also performed reliability analysis to investigate the internal consistency of each scale and the questionnaire as a whole. For this purpose, we used Cronbach's alpha as the measure of internal consistency.

Finally, we collected essential background information of school principals (and their schools) to perform data analysis to determine whether differences between principals with different background characteristics on a given scale were greater than we would expect by chance. This analysis took the form of analysis of variance (ANOVA). Our intention was to demonstrate that the scales would not discriminate against certain groups of school principals in any greater way than we would expect by chance.[3]

Results

Confirmatory Factor Analysis

We employed confirmatory factor analysis to examine how closely our data from the 42 specific items fit into the 11-factor structure of principals' data-informed decision-making on high-impact strategies. Table 3 presents estimates of indices that measure the extent to which a model fits the data at hand. Results indicated that the null model and one-factor model were poor fits to the data. Although the three-factor model represented an improvement in model-data-fit over the null and one-factor models, its indices fell seriously short of expected standards. At the same time, the 11-factor model showed a good fit across all indices. It had the smallest χ^2 statistic, had both CFI and TLI greater than 0.90, and had an SRMR value smaller than 0.08. In addition, the 11-factor model had the smallest estimates on both AIC and BIC. These confirmed that our model specification of each item of the questionnaire to load on the appropriate factor was supported by our data. In other words, data supported the model specification of all items proposed to measure, for example, "guaranteed and viable curriculum" to load on this factor (or construct).[4]

TABLE 3. Model-Data-Fit Indices

Model	χ^2	CFI	TLI	SRMR	AIC	BIC
Null model	9505.82	-	-	-	-	-
One factor	4088.35	0.62	0.60	0.10	17202.75	17481.06
Three factors	3253.14	0.72	0.70	0.08	16373.54	16661.79
Eleven factors	1519.68	0.91	0.90	0.05	14744.09	15204.62
Higher-order factors	1783.99	0.89	0.88	0.07	14926.40	15251.09

Note. CFI = comparative fit index; TLI = Tucker-Lewis index; SRMR = standardized root mean square residual; AIC = Akaike information criterion; BIC = Bayesian information criterion.

Higher-Order Factor Structure

Based on the factor structure of the 11-factor model, we examined the higher-order factors (Figure 4 as illustrated previously). The specification of higher-order factors did not improve the model-data-fit (see Table 3). In fact, all model-data-fit indices were consistently worse than those for the 11-factor model. The χ^2 statistic was 1783.99. CFI and TLI became 0.89 and 0.88, respectively. SRMR was 0.07. Additionally, AIC and BIC became 14926.40 and 15251.09, respectively. Therefore, there was no clear evidence of higher-order factor structure (pertaining to school, teacher, and student) that could be derived from the data collected from the questionnaire. We decided to maintain the 11-factor model as our final confirmatory factor analysis model.

Discrimination Analysis

Appendix 2 lists categorical background variables that we collected on school principals and their schools. ANOVA results indicated that none of these background variables was statistically significant among school principals in a systematic manner.[5] Specifically, there was no statistically significant gender difference in response to any of the 11 scales. Neither were there statistically significant racial-ethnic differences in response to any of the 11 scales. School principals with different administrative experiences responded differently to 1 out of 11 scales (safe and orderly environment): $F(4, 229) = 3.256, p = 0.013$. Principals of schools at different levels responded differently to 2 out of 11 scales (parent and community involvement as well as safe and orderly environment): $F(4, 229) = 3.189, p = 0.014$ and $F(4, 229) = 3.733, p = 0.006$.

Although the scale of safe and orderly environment appeared statistically significant twice, it seemed to us reasonable to expect that principles with different administrative experiences and in particular of different school levels (e.g., elementary, middle, and high schools) would view school safety and order differently. Overall, with 3 statistically significant results out of a total of 44 tests, results indicated that differences among principals of different background characteristics on a given scale were not much greater than we would expect by chance.

Scale Analysis

Table 4 presents means and standard deviations of each scale on the instrument. In general, there was greater response variation among school principals in the construct of home environment. This made sense to us in that the ability of school principals to track parents' behaviors and activities at home may vary depending on how large student enrollment is and other factors. Smaller variations occurred in terms of (a) guaranteed and viable curriculum, (b) challenging goals and effective feedback, and (c) safe and orderly environment. Such results were within our expectation, given that these administrative elements are often priorities of school principals. Distributional properties of each scale are presented in Appendix 3. In general, analytical results on skewness and kurtosis did not raise serious concerns about the data distribution of each scale on the questionnaire.[6]

TABLE 4. Descriptive Statistics for Scales

Scale	Mean	SD
Guaranteed and viable curriculum	3.24	0.71
Challenging goals and effective feedback	3.23	0.72
Parent and community involvement	2.93	0.81
Safe and orderly environment	3.26	0.75
Collegiality and professionalism	2.86	0.81
Instructional strategies	2.97	0.81
Classroom management	3.06	0.82
Classroom curriculum design	2.81	0.88
Home environment	2.36	0.94
Learned intelligence	2.71	0.82
Student motivation	2.50	0.85

Note. Measurement scale: 1 = not at all, 2 = not very much, 3 = somewhat, 4 = to a very great extent.

Reliability Analysis

Finally, we examined internal consistency of each scale on the questionnaire and the questionnaire as a whole. Results are presented in Table 5. Using Cronbach's alpha, we found that all scales were internally reliable with alpha coefficients ranging from 0.90 to 0.96, respectively. The instrument as a whole had an alpha coefficient of 0.98. This is a strong indication that this instrument has a high level of internal consistency.

TABLE 5. Reliability Statistics for Scales

Scale	Number of items	Alpha
Guaranteed and viable curriculum	4	0.91
Challenging goals and effective feedback	4	0.91
Parent and community involvement	4	0.92
Safe and orderly environment	4	0.92
Collegiality and professionalism	4	0.91
Instructional strategies	3	0.90
Classroom management	3	0.91
Classroom curriculum design	4	0.96
Home environment	4	0.96
Learned intelligence	4	0.90
Student motivation	4	0.94
Questionnaire as a whole	42	0.98

Discussion

Based on Marzano's (2003) framework in *What Works in Schools*, we developed and validated an instrument that measures the extent to which principals use data to engage in decisions on high-impact strategies that are empirically related to student achievement. As the analyses indicate, the instrument—Data-Informed Decision-Making on High-Impact Strategies: An Instrument for Improving Principalship—has good psychometric properties. The instrument reflects the intersection of three streams of literature on (a) the importance of data-informed decision-making, particularly the data *for* learning, (b) the role of principals in school effectiveness, and (c) high-impact strategies for raising student achievement. By offering principals a lens for viewing their work related to monitoring and assessing school factors associated with student achievement, the instrument reinforces the importance of the principal's monitoring role and the importance of using a broad range of data sources to carry out that role. The instrument also helps the principal stay focused on monitoring conditions and processes that are empirically associated with improving student outcomes. The instrument has theoretical and practical implications for the principalship, because it makes important connections between principals' use of data to improve their leadership (through monitoring and data-informed decision-making practices) and to address critical school-based factors associated with student learning at the same time.

Theoretically, the research confirms the factorial validity of the 11-factor model proposed by Marzano's (2003) meta-analysis of the last 35 years of empirical research on factors that are empirically related to student achievement. Our analyses do not, however, support a higher-order model with these 11 factors subsumed under school, classroom, and student levels. Essentially, our structural equation modeling analysis confirms the factorial validity of Marzano's 11-factor framework as a sound mental model to engage in conceptualizing and discussing the 11 factors for improving student achievement. As Senge (1990) reminds us of the importance of mental models, the framework of the 11 factors offers one valid way of conceptualizing the work on increasing student achievement from the principal's perspective.

Practically, our research provides principals with a useful tool to engage in improving student achievement. As established in the literature review for this study, the developed instrument connects three streams of the literature—those being the streams that suggest the importance of specific principal functions, the importance of monitoring, and the importance of using multiple forms of data to monitor conditions and processes empirically linked to raising student achievement. Therefore, the instrument helps principals (a) focus on those 11 high-impact strategies that are empirically associated with student achievement, (b) use data on their engagement with the 11 strategies for self-assessment and improvement, and (c) demonstrate their leadership in improving student achievement. In other words, the instrument helps principals make a connection between their leadership and raising student achievement (Elmore, 2000). With the collection and analysis of the data, the instrument will help overcome the challenge of implementation lag, drift, and abandonment (Schmoker, 2004) and engage in deep implementation of effective leadership strategies (Tucker & Codding, 2002; Reeves, 2004).

Given the theoretical and practical importance of developing instruments to guide principals' focus on evidence-based monitoring of achievement-linked school factors, further validation of this instrument is needed, particularly in the following two aspects. The first is to validate the instrument in other settings beyond the state of Michigan. The second is to inquire into the predictive validity of the instrument, after controlling demographic and other factors at the principal, teacher, and student levels. In order to protect the anonymity of our respondents, we did not collect principal or the school's identification information. The suggested further research will provide more data for psychometric properties of the instrument. Further research along such lines will be especially important in light of the RTTT (ARRA—Section 14005–6, Title XIV, Public Law 111–5) requirement that principals undergo annual performance reviews linked to student achievement and the school conditions that support improved student achievement.

Finally, we note that questions of the instrument were written in such a manner that would encourage self-reflection on critical issues of educational leadership on the part of school principals. As much as this function of the instrument is important and desirable, this format of questions may lead to the concern about response bias on the part of respondents. Although school principals did in general lean towards "somewhat" and "to a very great extent" as responsive options across all statements, all options had actually been used in their responses across all statements. For example, valid percentages ranged from 1% to 25% on the option of "not at all" across all questions (statements). Therefore, school principals did not seem to uniformly abandon certain options on any statement. This situation gives us confidence that the format of questions of the instrument did not present any serious threat to the validation of the instrument. Since reflective practice is also a leadership behavior empirically linked to leadership effectiveness at both the district and school level (Cotton & Association for Supervision and Curriculum Development, 2003), an instrument that focuses, at once, on significant leadership behaviors and, concurrently, on school conditions/processes through a reflective or self-assessment process can offer significant utility as part of a comprehensive professional performance review and development framework.

Acknowledgments

The development of this instrument was part of a grant funded by the Wallace Foundation. The items were developed based on Marzano's (2003), *What Works in Schools*. Alexandria, VA: Association for Supervision and Curriculum Development. Both the Wallace Foundation and Association for Supervision and Curriculum Development are acknowledged.

Notes

1. From a survey research perspective, we used Cochran's (1977) formulas to evaluate our response rate of 8.4%. With the alpha level set a priori at 0.05, a four-point scale, a level of acceptable error at 3%, and a standard deviation of the scale as 1.00 (see Bartlett, Kotrlik, & Higgins, 2001), the minimum sample size from a population of 3,061 is 246. Our actual sample size of 256 is, therefore, adequate from a survey research perspective.
2. Statistical research has shed little light on the issue of a minimum level of sample size for factor analysis in behavioral sciences (Guadagnoli & Velicer, 1988; MacCallum et al., 1999). In a review of 60 factor analyses published in four journals (*Educational and Psychological Measurement, Journal of Educational Psychology, Personality and Individual Differences,* and *Psychological Assessment*), Henson and Roberts (2006) reported a minimum sample size of 42. MacCallum et al. (1999) conducted a Monte Carlo analysis on sample size effects in which an excellent recovery of population factor structure is achieved with a minimum sam-

ple size of 60.
3. ANOVA is not a primary means to address the issue of invariance of the instrument across principals of different demographic characteristics. One strategy for future studies to investigate this issue is to perform multi-group confirmatory factor analysis as a way to demonstrate that the items measure the same number of constructs and with the same degree of precision across multiple group memberships.
4. According to Thompson (2004), both pattern and structure coefficients are helpful to appreciate a selected model. For the economics of space, these results are omitted but available from the authors.
5. For the concern of space, we reported only statistically significant ANOVA results. Full results are available from the authors.
6. In general, self-surveys among principals tend to show relatively positive behaviors. It would not surprise us if data from principals show some departure from a normal distribution. We would be concerned about a serious departure, which could indicate some problems in item construction. The near normal distribution of our data alleviated this concern considerably.

Appendix 1
Data-Informed Decision-Making on High-Impact Strategies: An Instrument for Improving Principalship

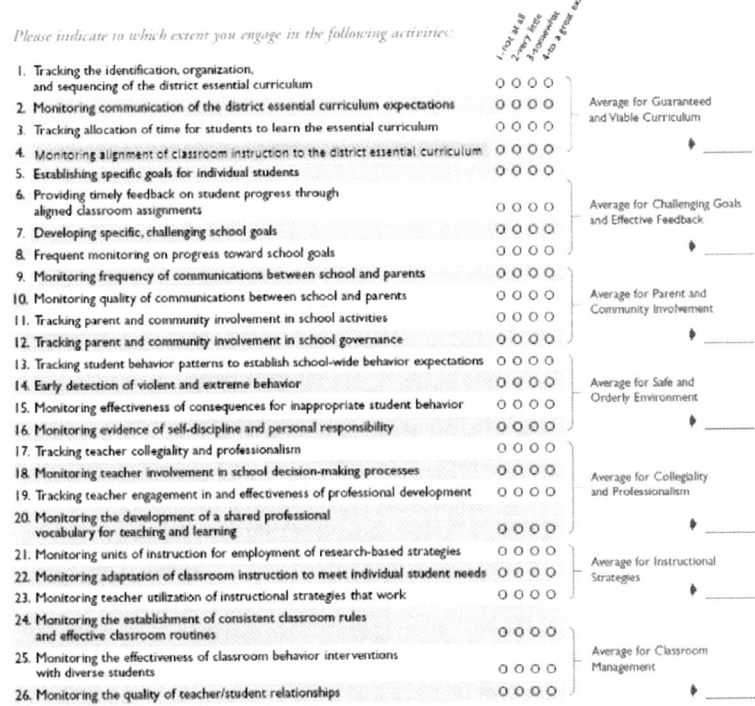

continued

Appendix 1. (*continued*)

#	Item	Rating	Group
27.	Tracking teacher clarity on the goals of instruction	○ ○ ○ ○	
28.	Monitoring the presentation of new content in multiple learning modes	○ ○ ○ ○	Average for Classroom Curriculum Design
29.	Tracking teacher organization of knowledge, skills, and content to facilitate learning	○ ○ ○ ○	
30.	Tracking engagement of students in complex tasks involving higher cognitive processes	○ ○ ○ ○	♦ _____
31.	Tracking parent communication with their children about school	○ ○ ○ ○	
32.	Tracking parent support for learning in the home environment	○ ○ ○ ○	Average for Home Environment
33.	Tracking evidence of parent supervision	○ ○ ○ ○	
34.	Tracking parent communicated expectations for their children	○ ○ ○ ○	♦ _____
35.	Tracking student experiences in and out of school	○ ○ ○ ○	
36.	Tracking student reading patterns for breadth and depth	○ ○ ○ ○	Average for Learned Intelligence
37.	Tracking student vocabulary development	○ ○ ○ ○	
38.	Monitoring direct instruction on vocabulary and phrases important to specific subject matter	○ ○ ○ ○	♦ _____
39.	Monitoring feedback to students on learning achievements	○ ○ ○ ○	
40.	Tracking learning activities for levels of student engagement	○ ○ ○ ○	Average for Student Motivation
41.	Tracking student opportunities to construct and work on long-term projects of their own design	○ ○ ○ ○	
42.	Tracking student understanding of personal motivation and efficacy	○ ○ ○ ○	♦ _____

Average for the Whole Instrument
♦ _____

Appendix 2
Characteristics of School Principals and Schools

Variable	Category
Gender	Male, female
Race-ethnicity	Euro-American (Caucasian), African-American, Hispanic, Asian, Native American, others
Years of experience	Less than 1 year, 1 to 5 years, 6 to 10 years, 11 to 15 years, more than 16 years
School level	Elementary school, middle school, high school, alternative school and others

Appendix 3
Distributional Properties of Scales

Scale	Skewness	Kurtosis
Guaranteed and viable curriculum	-0.67	-0.57
Challenging goals and effective feedback	-0.71	-0.24
Parent and community involvement	-0.67	-0.57
Safe and orderly environment	-0.71	-0.24
Collegiality and professionalism	-0.47	-0.52
Instructional strategies	-0.92	0.27
Classroom management	-0.38	-0.57
Classroom curriculum design	-0.53	-0.39
Home environment	-0.60	-0.33
Learned intelligence	-0.36	-0.68
Student motivation	0.17	-0.93
Standard errors (SE)	0.16	0.32

Note

This chapter was originally published as Shen, J., Cooley, V., Ma, X., Reeves, P., Burt, W., Rainey, J.M., & Yuan, W. (2012). Data-informed decision-making on high-impact strategies: Developing and validating an instrument for Principals. *Journal of Experimental Education, 80* (1), 1-25. Reprinted by permission of Taylor & Francis, http://www.tandfonline.com.

References

Barnett, K., McCormick, J., & Conners, R. (2000, December). *Leadership behaviour of secondary school principals, teacher outcomes and school culture*. Paper presented at the annual conference of the Australian Association for Research in Education, Sydney, Australia.

Bartlett, J. E., II, Kotrlik, J. W., & Higgins, C. C. (2001). Organizational research: Determining appropriate sample size in survey research. *Information Technology, Learning, and Performance Journal, 19*(1), 43–50.

Bossert, S., Dwyer, D., Rowan, B., & Lee, G. (1982). The instructional management role of the principal. *Educational Administration Quarterly, 18*(3), 34–64.

Boykin, A. W., & Cunningham, R. T. (2001). The effects of movement expressiveness in story content and learning context on the analogical reasoning performance of African American children. *Journal of Negro Education, 70*(1–2), 72–83.

Celio, M. B., & Harvey, J. (2005). *Buried treasure: Developing a management guide from mountains of school data.* New York: Wallace Foundation.

Coburn, C. E., Talbert, J. E. (2006). Conceptions of evidence use in school districts: Mapping the terrain. *American Journal of Education, 112,* 469–496.

Cochran, W. G. (1977). *Sampling techniques* (3rd ed.). New York: John Wiley & Sons.

Cooley, V. E., & Shen, J. (2000). Factors influencing applying for urban principalship. *Education and Urban Society, 32*(4), 443–454.

Cooley, V. E., & Shen, J. (2003). School accountability and professional job responsibilities: A perspective from secondary principals. *NASSP Bulletin, 87*(634), 10–25.

Cooley, V. E., Shen, J., Miller, D., Winograd, P. N., Rainey, J. M., & Yuan, W. (2006). Increasing leaders' capacity in data-based decision-making: State-level initiatives in Ohio, New Mexico, and Michigan. *Educational Horizons, 85,* 57–64.

Cotton, K., & Association for Supervision and Curriculum Development. (2003). *Principals and student achievement: What the research says.* Alexandria, VA: ASCD.

Dill, E. M., & Boykin, A. W. (2000). The comparative influence of individual, peer tutoring, and communal learning contexts on the text recall of African American children. *Journal of Black Psychology, 26*(1), 65–78.

Elmore, R. F. (2000). *Building a new structure for school leadership.* Washington, DC: Albert Shanker Institute.

Elmore, R. F. (2004). *School reform from the inside out: Policy, practice, and performance.* Cambridge, MA: Harvard Education Press.

Evers, W. M., & Walberg, H. J. (Eds.) (2002). *School accountability,* Stanford, CA: Stanford University, Hoover Institution Press.

Goddard, R. D. (2001). Collective efficacy: A neglected construct in the study of schools and student achievement. *Journal of Educational Psychology, 93,* 467–476.

Goddard, R. D., Hoy, W. K., & Hoy, A. W. (2004). Collective efficacy beliefs: Theoretical developments, empirical evidence, and future directions. *Educational Researcher, 33*(3), 1–13.

Goldring, E., & Pasternak, R. (1994). Principals' coordinating strategies and school effectiveness. *School Effectiveness and School Improvement, 5*(3), 239–253.

Grossman, P. L. (1990). *The making of a teacher: Teacher knowledge and teacher education.* New York: Teachers College Press.

Grossman, P. L. (1994). *Preparing teachers of substance: Prospects for joint work.* Occasional Paper No. 20, Seattle: Center for Educational Renewal, College of Education, University of Washington.

Guadagnoli, E., & Velicer, W. F. (1988). Relation of sample size to the stability of component patterns. *Psychological Bulletin, 103,* 265–275.

Hallinger, P. (1992). Changing norms of principal leadership in the United States. *Journal of Educational Administration, 30*(3), 35–48.

Hallinger, P., Bickman, L., & Davis, K. (1996). School context, principal leadership, and student reading achievement. *The Elementary School Journal, 96*, 527–549.

Hallinger, P., & Heck, R. H. (1996). Reassessing the principal's role in school effectiveness: A review of empirical research, 1980–1995. *Educational Administration Quarterly, 32*(1), 5–44.

Heck, R. H. (1992). Principals' instructional leadership and school performance: Implications for policy development. *Educational Evaluation and Policy Analysis, 14*(1), 21–34.

Heck, R. H., & Marcoulides, G. A. (1993). Principal leadership behaviors and school achievement. *NASSP Bulletin, 77*(553), 20–28.

Heck, R., Larson, T., & Marcoulides, G. (1990). Principal instructional leadership and school achievement: Validation of a causal model. *Educational Administration Quarterly, 26*, 94–125.

Heck, R., & Marcoulides, G. (1992). Principal assessment: Conceptual problem, methodological problem, or both? *Peabody Journal of Education, 68*(1), 124–144.

Henson, R. K., & Roberts, J. K. (2006). Use of exploratory factor analysis in published research: Common errors and some comment on improved practice. *Educational and Psychological Measurement, 66*, 393–416.

Hu, L. T., & Bentler, P. M. (1999). Cutoff criteria for fit indexes in covariance structure analysis: Conventional criteria versus new alternatives. *Structural Equation Modeling, 6*, 1–55.

Kerr, K. A., Marsh, J. A., Ikemoto, G. S., Darilek, H., & Barney, H. (2006). Strategies to promote data use for instructional improvement: Actions, outcomes, and lessons from three urban districts. *American Journal of Education, 112*, 496–520.

Knapp, M. S., Swinnerton, J. A., Copland, M. A., & Monpas-Huber, J. (2006). *Data-informed leadership in education*. Seattle: University of Washington, Center for the Study of Teaching and Policy.

Ladson-Billings, G. (1994). *The dreamkeepers: Successful teachers of African American children*. San Francisco: Jossey-Bass.

Ladson-Billings, G. (1995a). Toward a theory of culturally relevant pedagogy. *American Educational Research Journal, 32*, 465–491.

Ladson-Billings, G. (1995b). But that's just good teaching! The case for culturally relevant pedagogy. *Theory Into Practice, 34*, 159–165.

Ladson-Billings, G. (1998). Teaching in dangerous times: Culturally relevant approaches to teacher assessment. *The Journal of Negro Education, 67*, 255–267.

Lee, V., & Smith, J. B. (1996). Collective responsibility for learning and its effects on gains in achievement and engagement for early secondary school students. *American Journal of Education, 104*(2), 103–147.

Leithwood, K. A., & Jantzi, D. (1999). The relative effects of principal and teacher sources of leadership on student engagement with school. *Educational Administration Quarterly, 35 (Suppl.)* 679–706.

Leithwood, K., Louis, K. S., Anderson, S., & Wahlstrom, K. (2004). *How leadership influences student learning*. Minneapolis: University of Minnesota, Center for Applied Research and Educational Improvement. Retrieved on January 31, 2008, from http://www.wallace founResearchLearningFromLeadership.pdf.

Louis, K. S., Marks, H. M., & Kruse, S. D. (1996). Teachers' professional community in restructuring schools. *American Journal of Education, 33*(4), 757–798.

MacCallum, R. C., Widaman, K. F., Zhang, S., & Hong S. (1999). Sample size in factor analysis. *Psychological Methods, 4*, 84–99.

Manthey, G. (2006). Collective efficacy: Explaining school achievement. *Leadership, 35*(3), 23–24.

Marcoulides, G., & Heck, R. (1993). Organizational culture and performance: Proposing and testing a model. *Organization Science, 4*(2), 209–225.

Marks, H. M., & Louis, K. S. (1997). Does teacher empowerment affect the classroom? The implications of teacher empowerment for instructional practice and student academic performance. *Educational Evaluation and Policy Analysis, 19,* 245–275.

Marks, H. M., Louis K. S., & Printy, S. M. (2000). The capacity for organizational learning: Implications for pedagogy and student achievement. In K. Leithwood (Ed.), *Organizational learning and school improvement* (pp. 239–266). Greenwich, CT: JAI.

Marks, H. M., & Printy, S. M. (2003). Principal leadership and school performance: An integration of transformational and instructional leadership. *Educational Administration Quarterly, 39*(3), 370–397.

Marzano, R. J. (2003). *What works in schools.* Alexandria, VA: Association of Supervision and Curriculum Development.

Marzano, R. J., Waters, T., & McNulty, B. A. (2005). *School leadership that works.* Alexandria, VA: Association for Supervision and Curriculum Development.

National Commission on Service Learning. (2002). *Learning in deed: The power of service-learning for American schools.* Newton, MA: Author.

Newmann, F. M., & Associates. (1996). *Authentic achievement: Restructuring schools for intellectual quality.* San Francisco: Jossey-Bass.

Newmann, F. M., Marks, H. M., & Gamoran, A. (1996). Authentic pedagogy and student performance. *American Journal of Education, 104*(4), 280–312.

Newmann, F. M., Rutter, R. A., & Smith, M. S. (1989). Organizational factors that affect school sense of efficacy, community, and expectations. *Sociology of Education, 62,* 221–238.

Newmann, F. M., Smith, B., Allensworth, E., & Bryk, A. S. (2001). Instructional program coherence: What it is and why it should guide school improvement policy. *Educational Evaluation and Policy Analysis, 23,* 297–321.

O'Donnell, R. J., & White, G. P. (2005). Within the accountability era: Principal instructional leadership behaviors and student achievement. *NASSP Bulletin, 89*(645), 56–72.

Pounder, D. G. (1995). Leadership as an organization-wide phenomenon: Its impact on school performance. *Educational Administration Quarterly, 31*(4), 564–588.

Reeves, D. (2004). *Assessing educational leaders: Evaluating performance for improved individual and organizational results.* Thousand Oaks, CA: Corwin Press.

Reeves, P., & Burt, W. (2006). Challenges in data-based decision-making: Voices from principals. *Educational Horizons, 85*(1), 65–71.

Resnick, L. B. (1994). Performance puzzles: Using assessments as a means of defining standards. *American Journal of Education, 102,* 511–526.

Rodriguez-Campo, L., Rincones-Gomez, R., & Shen, J. (2005). Secondary principals' educational attainment, experience, and professional development. *International Journal of Leadership in Education, 8*(4), 309–319.

Schmoker, M. (2004). Tipping point: From feckless reform to substantive instructional improvement. *Phi Delta Kappan, 85,* 424–432.

Sebring, B., & Bryk, A. (2000). School leadership and the bottom line in Chicago. *Phi Delta Kappan, 81,* 440–443.

Senge, P. M. (1990). *The fifth discipline: The art and practice of the learning organization.* New York: Doubleday/Currency.

Sharkey, N. S., & Murnane, R. J. (2006). Tough choices in designing a formative assessment system. *American Journal of Education, 112,* 572–588.
Shen, J., Berry, J., Cooley, V., Kirby, B., Marx, G., & Whale, D. (2007). *Data-informed decision-making: A guidebook for data points and analyses in the context of Michigan School Improvement Framework.* Kalamazoo, MI: Michigan Coalition of Educational Leadership.
Shen, J., & Cooley, V. (2008). Critical issues in using data for decision-making. *International Journal of Leadership in Education, 11*(3), 319–329.
Shen, J., Cooley, V., Reeves, P., Burt, W., Ryan, L., Rainey, J. M., & Yuan, W. (2010). Using data for decision-making: Perspectives from 16 principals in Michigan, USA. *International Review of Education, 56,* 435–456.
Shen, J., Cooley, V., & Wegenke, G. (2004). Perspectives on factors influencing application of principalship: A comparative study of teachers, principals, and superintendents. *International Journal of Leadership in Education, 7*(1), 57–70.
Shen, J., & Crawford, C. S. (2003). The characteristic of the secondary principalship: An introduction to the special issue. *NASSP Bulletin, 87*(634), 2–8.
Shen, J., Kavanaugh, A., Wegenke, G., Rodriguez-Campos, L., Rincones-Gomez, R., Palmer, L. B., Crawford, C., Cooley, V. E., Poppink, S., VanderJagt, D., Hsieh, C., Ruhl-Smith, C. D., Keiser, N. M., & Portin, B. (2005). *School principals.* New York: Peter Lang.
Shen, J., & Ma, X. (2006). Does systemic change work? Curricular and instructional practice in the context of systemic change. *Leadership and Policy in Schools, 5*(3), 231–256.
Short, P. M., & Rinehart, J. S. (1992). School Participant Empowerment Scale: Assessment of level of empowerment within the school environment. *Educational and Psychological Measurement, 52,* 951–960.
Shulman, L. S. (1986). Those who understand: Knowledge growth in teaching. *Educational Researcher, 15,* 4–14.
Shulman, L. S. (1987). Knowledge and teaching: Foundations of the new reform. *Harvard Educational Review, 57*(1), 1–22.
Smith, W., Guarino, A., Strom, P., & Adams, O. (2006). Effective teaching and learning environments and principal self-efficacy. *Journal of Research for Educational Leaders, 3*(2), 4–23.
Spillane, J. P., Shalveson, R., & Diamond, J. B. (2001). Investigating school leadership practice: A distributed perspective. *Educational Researcher, 30*(3), 23–28.
Stein, M. K., & Nelson, B. S. (2003). Leadership content knowledge. *Educational Evaluation and Policy Analysis, 25*(4), 423–448.
Thompson, B. (2004). *Exploratory and confirmatory factor analysis: Understanding concepts and applications.* Washington, DC: American Psychological Association.
Tucker, M., & Codding, J. (2002). *The principal challenge: Leading and managing schools in an era of accountability.* San Francisco: Jossey-Bass.
Wayman, J. C., & Stringfield, S. (2006). Technology-supported involvement of entire faculties in examination of student data for instructional improvement. *American Journal of Education, 112,* 549–571.
Witziers, B., Bosker, R. J., & Kruger, M. L. (2003). Educational leadership and student achievement: The elusive search for an association. *Educational Administration Quarterly, 39*(3), 398–425.

• 6 •

Data-Informed Decision-Making

A Guidebook for Data Points and Analyses for School Improvement

JIANPING SHEN, VAN E. COOLEY,
GARY MARX, ELIZABETH KIRBY, & DAVID E. WHALE

Introduction

In this chapter, we introduce a tool entitled Data-Informed Decision-Making: A Guidebook for Data Points and Analyses for the School Improvement Team. With the advent of the accountability movement, data-informed decision-making becomes an important element inherent in the school improvement process. This tool was developed in partnership with school personnel and university faculty members during a state-wide educational leadership project in Michigan funded by the Wallace Foundation. The Michigan School Improvement Framework is similar to other frameworks proposed by other states and professional associations. The Michigan School Improvement Framework consists of five strands: (a) teaching for learning, (b) leadership, (c) personnel and professional development, (d) school and community relations, and (e) data and information management.

The guidebook was developed to address the data needs embedded in the Michigan School Improvement Framework and other similar school improvement frameworks. Two examples of data point and data analysis were developed for each benchmark within the Michigan framework. The importance of data-informed decision-making is self-evident. This tool is intended to provide concrete examples for principals and school improvement teams, and other educators. The tool has the following characteristics to meet the needs from the field: it is (a) more summative than formative, (b) decision-oriented, (c) need-based, and (d) caters to a wide audience. In the following sections, the authors discuss data-informed decision-making in the school improvement process, school improvement frameworks, the process with which the data-informed decision-making guidebook was developed, and the characteristics and utility of the guidebook.

Data-Informed Decision-Making

The Rise of Data-informed Decision-making

Over the past decade, school leaders have moved from analyzing inputs and resources to looking at outputs or student performance on standardized tests (Petersen, 2007). Knapp, Swinnerton, Copland, and Monpas-Huber (2006) suggested, leaders have always had data available to them and that effective leaders used data to guide them through decisions; however, data were not systematic, and often inadequate. The accountability movement has resulted in the development of systems to warehouse data and to make data more accessible.

The catalyst for the data-informed decision-making movement was the No Child Left Behind Act of 2001 which increased federal regulation and accountability in schools (Daily, 2009). Data-informed decision-making emerged from the desire to hold teachers and administrators more accountable for student learning. Like many initiatives, data-informed decision-making has been plagued by issues such as limited principal and teacher knowledge, time constraints, and the lack of a clear understanding by educators as to how to connect data with school improvement. Many educators fail to recognize that data goes beyond numbers and includes implications for curriculum, instruction, time-on-tasks, teacher and student relationships, and a myriad of other factors. Data-informed decision-making can be a powerful school improvement tool. The power rests with teacher and administrator expertise in utilizing data and their ability to make adjustments in program and practices that affect student learning.

The data movement has also resulted in confusion as to how data analysis process should be defined and the role of data in the decision-making process. The original and most frequently used terms are data-driven decision making and data-based decision making. There is growing consensus that data does not drive decisions. Knapp, Copland and Swinnerton (2007) contend that data inform, rather than drive decisions. They stress that decisions should not be totally based on data, but in combination with other factors that add clarity and understanding to the teaching and learning process. Data analysis gravitates from simply examining student standardized test scores to understanding why some students achieve and others do not.

The evolution of the data movement is not without challenge. Bernhardt (1998) observes that schools collect data, but leaders encounter barriers when they move to analysis and the utilization of data to make changes that impact student learning. The continued maturation of the data-informed decision making movement is a significant leap from past practice. As research and training continue, methodologies used by principals and teachers will become more sophisticated.

The Role of Data-informed Decision-making in School Improvement

Date-informed decision making must play a pivotal role in the school improvement process. With this said, it must be acknowledged that wide variances exist in teacher and administrator skills, attitudes, and beliefs in students' ability to learn. These skills and attitudes go beyond data analysis and include curriculum, instruction, student learning styles, an understanding of a student's culture, psychological and sociological factors, as well as an acknowledgement that the role of the teacher has changed. Teachers are now held accountable for student learning and expected to make adjustments when students fail to learn.

Principals and teachers typically focus on data *of* learning, rather than data *for* learning (Cooley et al., 2006; Schmoker, 2004; Shen & Cooley, 2008; Shen et al., 2010). Data of learning is a "passive activity" focusing on standardized test results instead of developing procedures to increase student achievement. Educators must value the "spirit of inquiry" and through the data analysis process identify factors that are promoting and inhibiting the learning process. Earl and Katz (2006) reported that data must propagate continuous inquiry and not just answer the question of the day. Inquiry involves looking beyond numbers to transform data into useful information used as a basis to make instructional and program adjustments.

Substantive school improvement requires that the use of data be meaningful, have a common and universally understood purpose, and is related to increasing student achievement. Knapp, Copland, and Swinnerton (2007) identified six purposes for using data: (a) diagnosis and clarification, (b) exploring alternatives, (c) justification for strategies or actions, (d) compliance, (e) guiding practice, and (f) as a management tool to determine how the organization is doing. These six purposes must be supported through a systematic analysis of the data. The most promising approach to data-informed decision-making is data intersections developed by Bernhardt (1998, 2004, 2010). Bernhardt advocates that teachers and administrators view data through multiple lenses, or data streams, that include (a) student learning or achievement data, (b) demographics, (c) perceptions, and (d) school process data, which provide useful informational tools for teachers and administrators to intervene and develop strategies to increase student learning. Through the use of data intersections, educators generate questions that focus on factors related to the learning process. From questions derived from the data, teachers and administrators develop strategies that address areas in need of improvement.

Michigan School Improvement Framework

This section addresses two key questions: (a) How does the Michigan School Improvement Framework (Michigan Framework) compare to other frameworks in current use across the country? and (b) Is it a valid choice to guide the development of tools for principals?

A sample of models for school improvement that are currently implemented by a selection of state departments of education and other governmental or accreditation agencies is analyzed and compared to the content of the Michigan School Improvement Framework. This analysis considers the validity of the Michigan Framework as a viable tool for use by school improvement practitioners.

What Is a Framework?

Croft (2007) defined a "framework" as "a set of tools, libraries, conventions, and best practices that attempt to abstract routine tasks into generic modules that can be reused" (What is a Framework section, para. 1). Frameworks allow people to focus on adapting established guidelines for effective practice to their particular problem or context rather than reinventing the wheel each time around. School improvement frameworks serve as a conceptual map to help guide practitioner thinking and action, and provide a common language or vocabulary that enhances communication within and across schools, districts, governmental agencies, and accreditation bodies.

Frameworks Developed by State Education Agencies

School improvement framework documents developed by state education agencies can be categorized in four groups based on their purpose and organization.

Documents identified as "frameworks" in the first group primarily address how a state education agency will meet the accountability requirements of the No Child Left Behind Act of 2001. Although these models make reference to services that are provided to local districts and schools, they are intended to establish procedural consistency for the state agency and thus lack specific guidance about what constitutes effective school improvement practice at the local district level.

The second group of documents includes surveys or checklists specifically designed to guide a process of need assessment or program review. Close examination of these instruments reveals they are associated with an organizing conceptual framework that is often more tacit than explicit. An example of this type of framework is the Patterns of Practice (POP) review process used in the District of Columbia. The POP Review examines practices based on nine standards: curriculum, assessment and evaluation, instruction, comprehensive and effective planning, school culture, professional development, leadership, organizational structure and resources, and parent and community involvement. The POP standards are based on 51 research-based indicators included in the *Handbook on Restructuring and Substantial School Improvement* (2007) created by the Center on Innovation and Improvement (CII), which was one of the national centers under the federal Comprehensive Centers Program. The handbook was approved by the U.S. Department of Education and is also used by the State of Virginia as the basis for providing training and technical assistance to local districts (District of Columbia Office of the State Superintendent of Instruction, n.d.).

New Mexico is another example of a state that uses a review process based on a tacit conceptual framework. The New Mexico Public Education Department, in collaboration with the Southwest Comprehensive Center, developed the Collaboration, Leadership, & Accountability for Student Success (CLASS) Assessment. CLASS describes characteristics of schools and districts at various levels of performance in three general categories: dynamic and distributed leadership; quality teaching and learning; and culture and collaborative relationships. Each category contains indicators that more fully describe the characteristics (New Mexico Public Education Department, 2009).

The third group of school improvement frameworks describes specific improvement processes or procedures for use by local districts and schools. Kentucky and Maryland are examples of states that use this approach. The Kentucky "Comprehensive School Improvement Planning Framework for Schools" (Kentucky Department of Education, 2004) includes references to "best practice" and "scientific research" related to the school improvement process, but local districts must request technical assistance from the department if they desire more detailed information. The Maryland School Improvement website (http://mdk12.0rg/) contains numerous tools and suggestions for how to implement school improvement practice using a data-based approach. The specific information provided for principals on the website comes close to outlining a theory of change or conceptual framework to guide people's thinking, but no formal model is presented.

The fourth and final group of documents includes models that explicitly identify a set of criteria for best practice constructed from a review of the literature and a process for stakeholder input. The Michigan School Improvement Framework is an example in this category along with frameworks developed in Ohio and Wisconsin, the two state models selected for direct comparison with the Michigan Framework in the analysis that concludes this section.

The Ohio Department of Education, in partnership with the Buckeye Association of School Administrators, created a leadership framework that identified six core areas of essential leadership practices: data and the decision-making process; focused goal setting process; instruction and the learning process; community engagement process; resource management process; and board or building level governance. These practices are incorporated in the Ohio Improvement Process (Ohio Department of Education, 2008).

The Wisconsin model is based on the *Characteristics of Successful Schools* (http://dpi.wi.gov/). The framework consists of the following seven characteristics supported by research: (a) vision; (b) leadership; (c) high academic standards; (d) standards of the heart; (e) family and community partnerships; (f) professional development; and (g) evidence of success.

Frameworks Developed by Research Institutions and Accreditation or Licensing Agencies

In addition to the Ohio and Wisconsin models described above, three nationally recognized frameworks that inform the school improvement process were selected for the purpose of analysis and direct comparison with the Michigan Framework. These included the Leading for Learning model, the Interstate School Leaders Licensure Consortium (ISLLC) Standards for School Leaders, and the AdvancED Accreditation Standards for Quality Schools.

Leading for Learning (Knapp et al., 2003) is a theoretical framework designed by the Center for the Study of Teaching and Policy, a national research consortium, with support from the Wallace Foundation. The model is based on an examination and synthesis of the research literature, concentrating on (a) instructional leadership, (b) school reform, (c) teacher learning and professional community, (d) teacher leadership organizational learning, (e) policy-practice connections, and (f) education in high-poverty, high-diversity settings. The framework also incorporated examples of leadership in action and educators' craft knowledge (Knapp et al., 2003, p. 5). This framework synthesized the findings of the literature review into five areas of leadership action focus on (a) learning, (b) building professional communities, (c) engaging external environments, (d) acting strategically and sharing leadership, and (e) creating coherence.

The Council of Chief State School Officers (CCSSO) recently updated the 1996 ISLLC Standards for School Leaders. The research base for this revision of the ISLLC framework contains 83 empirical studies as well as 47 examples of policy analyses, leadership texts, and other resources considered to be "craft knowledge" and "sources of authority" in the field (CCSSO, 2008, p. 7). Since 1996, 43 states have used the ISLLC document in its entirety or as a template for developing their own standards (CCSSO, 2008, p. 2).

The ISLLC framework, recently updated by the council of Chief State School Officers and adopted by the National Policy Board for Educational Administration in 2008, identified six standards: (a) shared vision; (b) school culture and instructional program conducive to student learning and staff professional growth; (c) management of the organization for a safe, efficient and effective learning environment; (d) collaborating with faculty and community and mobilizing community resources; (e) acting with integrity, fairness, and in an ethical manner; and (f) understanding, responding to and influencing the political, social, economic, legal and cultural context. Thirty-one "functions" are defined for these standards.

The AdvancED Accreditation Standards for Quality Schools were developed by the North Central Association Commission on Accreditation and School Improvement (NCA CASI) and the Southern Association of Colleges and Schools Council on Accreditation and School Improvement (SACS CASI) with research support from the National Study of School Evaluation (NSSE). The AdvancED Accreditation Process provides guidance and support with continuous improvement efforts to over 27,000 education institutions around the world (http://www.advanc-ed.org/). The seven AdvanceED standards, and accompanying 56 "indicators," are tied directly to the research on factors that impact student learning. These standards address (a) vision and purpose; (b) governance and leadership; (c) teaching and learning; (d) documenting and using results; (e) resource and support systems; and (f) stakeholder communications and relationships; and (g) commitment to continuous improvement.

How Does the Michigan Framework Compare to Other Models in Its Class?

A content analysis was conducted to determine how the five "Strands" in the Michigan Framework aligned with the AdvanceED and ISLLC Standards, Leading for Learning Action Areas, the Core Areas used in Ohio, and the Characteristics identified in the Wisconsin model. Because of differences in the terminology, organizing structure, and areas of emphasis within these frameworks it was often necessary to examine lower level descriptors to determine if a component was actually aligned. For example, both AdvanceED and ISLLC have standards that explicitly identify shared "vision," but the Michigan Framework lists "vision" as a Benchmark within the Leadership Strand. For purposes of this analysis, alignment means that similar wording was used to describe framework elements regardless of where the wording was located within the taxonomy established for the various models.

Table 1 summarizes the findings of the analysis. The table consists of the Michigan Framework Strands in the first row and a list of the models selected for comparison in the first column, creating a matrix of cells within the table itself. An "X" within a cell in the table indicates that the framework in that row contains a component that is comparable to the Strand from the Michigan Framework listed for that column.

TABLE 1. A Comparison Between Michigan School Improvement Framework and Others

Michigan Strands	Teaching for learning	Leadership	Personal and professional learning	School and community relations	Data and information management
Advance ED Standards	X	X	X	X	X
Leading for Learning Actions	X	X	X	X	X
ISLLC Standards	X	X	X	X	X
Ohio Core Areas	X	X		X	X
Wisconsin Characteristics	X	X	X	X	X

The Wisconsin model addressed teaching and learning from the perspective of academic standards and was listed as aligned because academic standards affect the teaching and learning processes. The Ohio framework included "Governance" as one of the core areas, and this was considered synonymous with leadership in the analysis. Both the Leading for Learning and ISLLC models integrated data and information management with other elements of their respective frameworks rather than list it as a separate component. Because data was intended to be used in similar ways, these models were considered aligned with the Michigan Framework for this area. The Ohio Department of Education addressed professional development as a key component of its school improvement process but it was not listed as one of the Core Areas in the School Improvement Framework document.

Only three elements from other models in the comparison group were not addressed within the Strands included in the Michigan Framework. The Leading for Learning model listed "creating coherence" as one of the action areas and ISLLC included two standards that apply to leadership action outside the realm of organizational improvement (ethics and activism). The fact that both of these frameworks target the actions of school leaders rather than a process of effective school improvement is a logical explanation for these omissions.

Although they use different terminology to describe key components, an examination of the models in the comparative group disclosed an emerging consensus about effective school improvement practices at the state, district, and school levels. The content analysis found an exceptionally high degree of alignment across the various models, leading to a conclusion that the Michigan Framework is a viable model to use as the basis for developing tools for principals.

The similarity among frameworks disclosed by this analysis is validated to some degree by a joint partnership agreement that was established between Michigan Department of Education (MDE) and the NCA CASI. Under the agreement, MDE recognizes and awards credit to NCA CASI accredited schools on the Michigan Report Card. NCA CASI recognizes and supports the MDE School Improvement Framework as evidence of meeting the NCA CASI requirement for school improvement (Michigan Department of Education, 2006). As a result of this agreement schools can use either the AdvanceEd or Michigan Framework as the guide for their school improvement work.

The Development and Characteristics of the Guidebook

The Development of the Guidebook

The tool—Data-Informed Decision-Making: A Guidebook for Data Points and Analyses for School Improvement—was developed out of a state-wide, inter-institutional grant project entitled State Action for Educational Leadership Project in Michigan. Partners of the project, funded by the Wallace Foundation, included Michigan Department of Education, four school districts (Benton Harbor, Flint, Grand Rapids, and Lansing), four state-level professional associations (Michigan Association of Supervision and Curriculum Development, Michigan Association of School Administrators, Michigan Association of Secondary School Principals, Michigan Elementary and Middle School Principals Association), and three universities (Central Michigan University, Eastern Michigan University, and Western Michigan University). Western Michigan University received the Wallace grant for the state-wide project. The purpose of the grant was to infuse the practice of data-informed decision-making into the Michigan K-12 system by providing guidance to both school districts and school leadership preparation programs. A combined approach for the project included (a) 16 schools in Benton Harbor, Flint, Grand Rapids, and Lansing, Michigan, serving as demonstration sites, (b) three universities and four professional associations incorporating data-informed decision-making into their respective certification and endorsement programs, and (c) Michigan Department of Education including the data-informed decision-making guidebook in the school improvement tool box (Marx, Berry, Kirby, Whale, Shen & Cooley, 2007, p. 3).

The Michigan School Improvement Framework (Michigan Department of Education, 2005) identifies five strands:

Strand I. Teaching for Learning: The school holds high expectations for all students, identifies essential curricular content, makes certain it is sequenced appropriately and is taught effectively in the available instructional times. Assessments used are aligned to curricular content and are used to guide instructional decisions and monitor student learning.

Strand II. Leadership: School leaders create a school environment where everyone contributes to a cumulative, purposeful and positive effect on student learning.

Strand III. Personnel & Professional Learning: The school has highly qualified personnel who continually acquire and use skills, knowledge, attitudes and beliefs necessary to create a culture with high levels of learning for all.

Strand IV. School & Community Relations: The school staff maintains purposeful, active, positive relationships with families of its students and with the community in which it operates to support student learning.

Strand V. Data & Information Management: Schools/districts have a system for managing data and information in order to inform decisions to improve student achievement.

For the data-informed decision-making guidebook, two examples of data types and analyses were suggested for each benchmark associated with the above strands. The examples in the guidebook could be used by both practitioners in the field to facilitate the school improvement process and by university faculty to deliver school leadership preparation programs. These examples are intended to assist school improvement teams who are grappling with state and federal mandates on standard-based reforms, assessment and evaluation, and accountability for student achievement. Wohlstetter, Datnow, and Park (2008, p. 239) noted that "building expertise and capacity at the school site for data-driven decision-making" is a necessary component for student success. In addition, the guidebook could also be used by faculty in educational leadership programs to examine their curriculum and embed data-informed decision-making into applicable coursework.

The approach to join schools, universities, and others in school improvement efforts has also been utilized by the Michigan Coalition of Essential Schools (n.d.), a collaboration of over 60 schools and four universities, through which the guidebook was developed. In this instance, school change is aligned with the Michigan School Improvement Framework (Michigan Department of Education, 2005) through the use of school-wide professional learning communities. Another project of note was conducted in Milwaukee, a group effort by the Joyce Foundation, the Milwaukee Public Schools, the Wisconsin Center for Education Research and the University of California at Los Angeles's National Center for Research on Evaluation, Standards, and Student Testing (Mason, 2002). The partnership used data to improve student achievement and performance in six urban schools. It found that "data must become an active part of school planning and improvement processes, and it must become infused and accepted into the school organization and culture" (Mason, 2002, p. 1).

The unyielding demands for accountability for student learning have resulted in a paradigm shift in how school principals and district leaders use data. School leaders today must demonstrate continuous school improvement to meet mandated state and federal requirements and the expectations of their local communities and stakeholders. Knowing how to gather, analyze, and apply data to improve instruction, guide professional development, and allocate resources prepares school leaders to achieve a vision for continuous school improvement and increased student achievement (American Association of School Administrators, n.d.; Stack, 2003; Learning Point Associates, 2004). This requires data-literate leaders who have the capacity and expertise needed to guide the school improvement process within the context of state standards and benchmarks. Data use is often relative to the individual skills and expertise of the building principal whose primary role and responsibility is providing instructional leadership for the school community.

The data-informed decision-making guidebook (Shen, et al., 2007) was created to support educators with concrete examples in ways to integrate data into the school improvement process. It is aligned with the Michigan School Improvement Framework (2005) and example data points and analyses were created based on the strands, standards, and benchmarks embedded in the framework. Data collection and mining is a dynamic process and the guidebook is intended to foster ideas and generate possible data analyses and displays for school improvement purposes. A "one size fits all" approach to data collection is not possible and school leaders need to sift through data systems to identify what types of data will best inform actions and results.

Characteristics of the Guidebook

The guidebook provides two illustrations for each of the benchmarks in the Michigan School Improvement Framework in terms of what data to use and how to analyze the data to inform decisions for school improvement. The 52 examples provided in the guidebook align with the 26 benchmarks in the Michigan School Improvement Framework (Michigan Department of Education, 2005). Please see in the appendix the data-informed decision-making guidebook in its entirety. The guidebook has the following four main characteristics:

First, the guidebook is more summative than formative. The data points and analysis in the guidebook are designed to be more summative than formative to provide school personnel with the kind of data needed to make decisions to improve student learning and evaluate the school improvement process. Unlike formative assessments, which are used to provide continual feedback throughout the school improvement process and guide strategies and adjustments as needed, summative assessments are likely to occur on a yearly basis as a means to assess the overall effectiveness of various aspects of the school improvement plan.

Second, it is decision-oriented. The examples of data and data analyses are such that a decision can be made after each analysis. The examples demonstrate how school leaders can engage in data-informed decision-making to facilitate the school improvement process in their schools or districts. Data showing success or pinpointing areas of weakness are equally important and inform school improvement teams in making informed decisions, targeting resources, identifying strategies, and continually monitoring the implementation and results of their actions.

Third, the guidebook is need-based. In a continuum from (a) an open-ended tool kit, to (b) an inquiry process, and to (c) a model of data points and analyses, this guidebook is intended to serve as (c), a model of practice for school leaders in the field. It is recognized that school leaders, and other constituents using state school improvement frameworks to guide their work, vary widely in terms of data literacy. The approach of providing concrete examples of the kinds of data that may be collected to measure standards was based on the premise that educators with varying degrees of data literacy would benefit from guideposts and support in their efforts to build capacity and strengthen school improvement initiatives. Similar to the guidebook produced by the North Central Regional Educational Laboratory (NCREL) and Learning Point Associates (2004), the examples provide foundational information on how to build processes to use and apply various forms of data, conduct data analyses, and produce meaningful results to inform decision making in practice (p. 1).

Fourth, it caters to a wide range of audiences. Skilled leaders are needed to transform school improvement practices and processes so that "the possibilities of wide-scale improvements and sustained student achievement are attainable" (American Institutes for Research, 2010, p. 9). The guidebook is designed to assist educators in various roles and capacities in developing data skills needed to lead school improvement efforts in the classroom, school, or district. It is designed to be flexible and may be modified to use as a curriculum guide for use in educational leadership programs in higher education and in professional education associations for professional development.

In summary, guides and tool-kits to assist school educators and stakeholders in collecting data are intended to support practitioners through examples so they may hone their data skills and meaningfully measure progress for school improvement (School Improvement Planning Processing Guide, 2005; Learning Point Associates, 2004). School improvement tools, such as the one featured in this chapter, contribute to the development of data-informed leadership, or "accountability literacy" (Knapp, Swinnerton, Copland, & Monpas-Huber, 2006) in which leaders develop the skills needed to use data to target student needs and leverage resources in ways that will yield greater gains in achievement. Changing the way things have always been done takes time and collaborative effort. The guidebook, produced by this joint project, exemplifies the kind of action and models that are needed to facilitate such change. Principals could engage the school improvement team to use the guidebook for school improvement.

Appendix
How to Use the Guidebook

The guidebook provides 52 examples for specific data points and analyses for 26 benchmarks organized under 12 standards and five benchmarks. Working with school personnel, we made sure that these data points and analyses were feasible in schools. Principals, school improvement teams, and other educators could use the guidebook as the first step in engaging in data-informed decision-making for school improvement. The guidebook constitutes a comprehensive examination of the most important aspects of school improvement, and its implementation by school improvement teams establishes a solid foundation on which to base improvement efforts. The individual context of each educational institution may require additional data points or data analysis methods, but the guidebook can serve to inform initial data analysis and examination and assists school improvement teams in their school improvement efforts.

Data-Informed Decision-Making
A Guidebook for Data Points and Analyses for School Improvement

Strand I. Teaching for Learning

Standards and Benchmarks	Type of Data	Type of Analysis
Standard 1: Curriculum		
Benchmark A: Curriculum alignment, reviewed, and monitored	District/school published curriculum guide	Conduct a content analysis of the district/school curriculum in key subject areas, tally the results on the extent to which the grade-level content expectations are addressed by the district/school curriculum; the higher percentage the grade-level content expectations are covered, the higher level of curriculum alignment.
	Scope and sequence documents from the written curriculum	Schematic and pictorial presentation of how the curriculum is aligned horizontally (across content areas at a grade level) and vertically (within a subject across the grade levels)
Benchmark B: Curriculum communicated	Schedules, agendas, and materials from professional development activities related to curriculum	Counts of professional development activities on communicating curriculum within the last five years; themes of the content of these activities such as focusing on sharing and discussing the grade-level and course curriculum
	Samples of communication with	Counts of communications with parents on curriculum

Standards and Benchmarks	Type of Data	Type of Analysis
	the parents related to curriculum	within the last five years; themes of the content of the communications such as announcement of the content schedule and suggested activities to help students to be successful
Standard 2: Instruction		
Benchmark A: Planning	Samples of lesson plans (over a significant period of time, e.g., one marking period)	For each key subject area, conduct a content analysis of the lesson plans to inquire into the extent to which grade-level content expectations are covered in one marking period; the higher the percentage, the more alignment between the adopted curriculum and the curriculum taught.
	Schedules, agendas, and materials from professional development activities related to instruction.	Counts of instruction-related opportunities/activities (such as team common planning time, learning community) to discuss the content and developmental appropriateness so as to improve teaching; themes of these activities such as common assessment and effective strategies for teaching a concept

Standards and Benchmarks	Type of Data	Type of Analysis
Benchmark B: Delivery	MEAP data at the item and theme levels	Conduct an analysis of student performance at the item and theme levels; if the content is covered in the lesson plans; the lower percentage of students get the items or themes correct, the greater the chance there is an issue of instructional delivery
	Classroom observation data	Use classroom observation instruments (such as the one based on What Works in Classrooms or the one designated by the school district) and tally the results to ascertain teachers' effectiveness in delivery
Standard 3: Assessment		
Benchmark A: Aligned to Curriculum and Instruction	Samples of assessment instruments	Conduct a content analysis of the instruments to test the alignment between curriculum/instruction and assessment, the higher percentage of the curriculum content covered in the assessment tools, the higher the content validity

Standards and Benchmarks	Type of Data	Type of Analysis
	Samples of assessment instruments	Tabulate the reliabilities and validities of the assessment instruments
Benchmark B: Data Report and Use	Schedule for reporting assessment results	Tabulate the time it takes to get the assessment results to the teachers, students, and parents
	Interview data and artifacts on data utilization	Synthesize the interview data and artifacts on data utilization to find out patterns related to how data inform curriculum and instruction
	List of sources of assessment data	Create a diagram to (a) illustrate the degree of coherence among various assessments, and to (b) identify other kinds of data that need to be collected or certain assessments that overlap and should be dropped

Strand II. Leadership

Standards and Benchmarks	Type of Data	Type of Analysis
Standard 1: Instructional Leadership		
Benchmark A. Educational Program	Annual School Report and School Improvement Plan	Conduct an analysis of the documents to compile evidence of the school leaders' knowledge of student and adult learning, curriculum, instruction, assessment, technology, and use of data to identify and respond to achievement gaps
	Documents related to planning, implementing, revising, and evaluating educational programs, such as an at-risk program (report cards, marking period grades, and dropout data, etc.)	Analyze the documents to determine the extent to which school leaders applied knowledge of the educational program to act as a catalyst for change with a focus on student results.
Benchmark B. Instructional Support	Records of classroom walkabouts, other observation strategies, and follow-up meetings with teachers	Analyze the records to identify how school leaders communicate expectations, monitor curriculum progress, identify gaps in curriculum and delivery, and enhance instruction.
	Records of intra- and inter-departmental, or grade-level meetings, preparation time, common preparation time, teacher professional days, in-service and faculty meeting agendas	Conduct an annual review of the records to identify how much time was allocated for teachers, grade level groups, or departments to collaboratively communicate about teaching and learning and examine best practices

Standards and Benchmarks	Type of Data	Type of Analysis
Standard 2: Shared Leadership		
Benchmark A. School Culture and Climate	Audit or survey data of school culture and climate (such as the NASSP School Climate Survey)	Conduct an analysis of school culture and climate survey results to assess the perception of various stakeholder groups that the staff has created a learning environment that is safe, orderly, inclusive, and equitable.
	School culture and climate survey results, school incident data (suspensions, expulsions, nature of disciplinary referrals, etc.)	Conduct annual audit of incident data and disciplinary referrals to determine the extent to which incidents and infractions result in subsequent disciplinary action. Conduct a discrepancy analysis between the perceptions of the school learning environment and actual incident data and disciplinary actions.
Benchmark B. Continuous Improvement	School Improvement Plans	Conduct a content analysis of three most recent, consecutive years of school improvement plans to look for evidence that the plans articulated a shared vision and mission, were results-focused, implemented and monitored, and that there is year-to-year continuation
	School mission statement, goals, action	Analyze the documents to locate evidence that (a) the

Standards and Benchmarks	Type of Data	Type of Analysis
	plan, and communication documents, e.g., Teacher Handbook, school newsletters, etc.	mission is clearly defined and integrated into all aspects of the school; (b) communication documents reflect and support school goals and mission as well as clarify the expectations and appropriate behavior of students; (c) the use of school resources is aligned with school goals and mission, with a focus on ensuring equity in student outcomes; and (d) professional development and support systems are linked to meeting school goals and mission.
Standard 3: Operational and Resource Management		
Benchmark A: Resource Allocation	Annual school budget	Conduct a line item analysis of the school budget by department, grade levels, or individuals with a particular focus on allocations for equipment, materials, and professional development to determine the degree to which fiscal resources provide equitable support for teaching and learning needs across the curriculum.
	School improvement plan, master schedule	Conduct a content analysis to learn how human

Standards and Benchmarks	Type of Data	Type of Analysis
	including common planning time assignments and room allocations	resources, time and space are allocated to support each of the improvement goals established by the school
Benchmark B: Operational Management	School policy handbooks for parents, students and staff	Conduct an annual audit of school policy handbooks to review the extent to which handbooks align with the requirements outlined in the Board Bylaws and Policies, Administrative Guidelines, and district Procedures and Forms (electronic versions are generally available for download).
	MDE School Infrastructure Database (SID) report, Assurance of compliance statements (SID and compliance data are usually collected by a central office administrator for each building and submitted to the Michigan Department of Education), similar school or district reports	Conduct an annual review of these reports to learn the degree to which the school meets all required state and federal regulations and building maintenance standards.

Strand III. Personnel and Professional Development

Standards and Benchmarks	Type of Data	Type of Analysis
Standard 1: Personnel Qualifications		
Benchmark A: Requirements	Teaching assignments, professional certificates, endorsements, and licenses for school staff.	Tally to show the percentage of professional staff that holds state-mandated levels of certification, licenses, and endorsements for the positions held and meet the Highly Qualified standards for NCLB.
	Copies of recruitment and selection materials and procedures for filling professional staff positions (job descriptions, reference checks, criminal background checks, etc.)	Analyze to determine how school leaders assure that all staff possess the qualifications, knowledge and skills needed to support student learning
Benchmark B: Skills, Knowledge and Dispositions	Teacher evaluation data related to content knowledge, communication skills, classroom management, and technology utilization for instruction; Student scores on state standardized tests	Conduct a gap analysis among various aggregate ratings on teacher evaluations with student scores on standardized tests and use a pattern analysis of the results to help identify professional development needs for the school
	In-service schedule for school; mentoring programs for new teachers; collaboration time built into teacher schedules.	Analyze the data to determine ways staff collaborate on student learning and support new teachers in the school

Standard and Benchmark	Type of Data	Type of Analysis
Standard 2: Professional Development		
Benchmark A: Collaboration	District professional development policies and records of professional development activities over the past school year.	Examine policies and resultant activities and products to determine the degree to which they demonstrate that teacher professional learning is conducted with colleagues across the school/district to improve staff practices and student achievement
	Professional development policies, sample records of professional development activities and sample teacher development plans over a three year period.	Conduct a content analysis for evidence that policy and practice emphasize sustained approaches to teacher learning that impact instruction in relation to student performance results
Benchmark B: Content and Pedagogy	Artifacts (agendas, handout material, etc.) from formal professional development activities over one school year and participant evaluation summaries for each activity	Code each activity by topic and create a frequency distribution to show the degree to which deeper content understanding is a goal for professional learning in the school. Analyze teacher evaluations to assess perceptions regarding how learning actually deepens content understanding.

		Interviews with a sample of new teachers, supervising teachers and other mentors, and administrators; survey feedback from teachers and supervisors in new teacher programs.	Conduct a qualitative analysis of interview data and an item analysis of survey results to learn the degree to which new teachers are supported in ways that help them succeed.
Benchmark C: Alignment		Professional development need assessment survey results, professional development sections from school improvement plan including a schedule of activities over one school year, school improvement goals	Create a graphic representation to examine the relationships among school improvement goals, student learning needs, teacher learning needs and professional development plans. Analyze the graphic to determine the degree to which these areas are aligned.
		Artifacts (descriptions, agendas, handout material, etc.) from professional development activities over one school year	Analyze the activities to determine the degree to which they provide opportunities for professional learning embedded in daily work, encourage colleagues to observe one another and provide feedback, or provide for guided practice in the classroom setting.

Strand IV. School and Community Relations

Standards and Benchmarks	Type of Data	Type of Analysis
Standard 1: Parent/Family Involvement		
Benchmark A: Communication	District and or school homework policy and samples of actual homework assigned to students in a particular content area over one marking period.	Conduct a content analysis to explore the degree to which homework policy and practice encourage parental involvement in ways that help the student be successful
	Samples of written forms of communication from teachers and the school sent to parents/families over one school year	Organize the samples by grade level and core curriculum content area and analyze the communications to assess the nature and amount of guidance provided for ways parents can be meaningfully involved in their child's education (establishing a quiet time and place for homework, asking about school, reading to or listening to a child read, visiting the library, etc.)
Benchmark B: Engagement	Lists of names and demographic information for parent representatives on committees such as school/district advisory groups, school improvement teams, Title I councils, and parent-teacher organizations.	Organize the data in a matrix by name and demographics and another matrix by name and advisory group. Analyze the matrices to learn about the scope of parental participation in decision making/governance groups and the degree to which the representatives reflect

		the diverse populations, neighborhoods and interest groups in the school community.
	Artifacts and oral history of events related to a recent policy decision made at the school/district level with direct implications for students and/or parents (attendance policy, dress code, curriculum adoption/change, etc.)	Conduct a case study analysis to inquire into the nature and extent of parental involvement in the decision making process and the degree to which the parent representatives communicated with other parents to obtain input and report results.
Standard 2: Community Involvement		
Benchmark A: Communication	School communication samples that targeted the community over the last year (public relations efforts, announcements, annual reports, etc.)	Organize the samples by month and form of communication (newspaper, newsletters, mail, phone messages, podcasts, radio/TV, World Wide Web, etc.) Analyze the data to assess the nature of the message(s), regularity of communication and the variety of communication tools utilized.
	School communication samples that targeted the community over the last year	Use content analysis to explore how the communication system addresses diversity issues and reaches out to people with a stake in quality education even though they do not have children in school.

Benchmark B: Engagement	Demographic information from school records and recent U.S. Census Bureau Fact Sheets http://www.census.gov/main/ www/cen2000.html	Conduct a need assessment based on characteristics and trends evident in the school community (trends in the numbers of single parent households, for example). Analyze the extent to which business, educational and community agencies are collaborating with the school to meet high priority needs.
	Printed materials, directories, lists, publications and documentary materials from the business community, local educational institutions and community agencies.	Inventory the data/information sources to determine the educational interests of the identified civic, cultural, economic, fraternal, governmental, patriotic, political, professional, religious, retired groups, and welfare or other community youth organizations and their potential for career awareness, resource sharing and/or extending learning opportunities for students. Conduct a gap analysis to inquire into the extent to which the school system is currently engaged in cooperative activities with identified groups and organizations or may not be taking advantage of potentially valuable resources for assisting in the education of children.

Strand V. Data and Information Management

Standards and Benchmarks	Type of Data	Type of Analysis
Standard 1: Data Management		
Benchmark A: Data Generation, Identification, and Collection.	Inventory of all types of data collected and used to develop the school improvement plan	Organize the data in a table by source: input (such as student demographics and community background), process (such as schooling activities), outcome (such as MEAP and other assessments), and perception (such as parental survey); analyze the table to assess the data collection process in general and the degree to which the school uses different types of data of high technical quality from multiple sources to inform decisions.
	Inventory of all types of data collected and used to develop the school improvement plan	Code each data type to identify how it was used (identify strengths and challenges, develop strategies, assess who is or is not learning and why, assess effectiveness of strategies, etc.) and display the results in a matrix. Examine how the school uses data in the planning process and integrates multiple sources to inform decision such as the interaction of race and outcome data to make decisions on whether certain groups of students tend to outperform or underperform

Benchmark B: Data Accessibility	Samples of routine reports to parents; Formative and summative reports made available to teachers and the time line for distribution of these reports during the school year.	Analyze the stream of information to determine the degree to which data are readily accessible to parents and teachers and allow them to monitor progress and make timely instructional decisions.
	Copies of policies, procedures, and protocols related to how parents, teachers and administrators request and receive data and information	Analyze the documents to assess how the school and district provide access to data when it is needed while maintaining security and ensuring it is available only to authorized users
Benchmark C: Data Support	Samples of reports from the school and district data management system provided to parents, teachers and administrators	Critically examine the reports to judge how well the data are organized, summarized and formatted to facilitate analysis and the extent to which the data show comparison across groups and over time.
	Agendas and other materials from school improvement committee meetings and faculty meetings held over one school year.	Conduct a content analysis of the historical materials to learn how and the degree to which opportunities were provided for the collaborative analysis of data.
Standard 2: Information Management		
Benchmark A: Analysis and Interpretation	Interviews and artifacts (meeting agendas, handout materials, minutes, etc.) needed to reconstruct the process	Use a case study method to analyze how well the data help staff make comparisons across groups and over time, and to assess the methods

	used to analyze the most recent MEAP data available to the school	used to examine the data, including aggregation and disaggregation.
	Interviews and artifacts (meeting agendas, handout materials, minutes, etc.) needed to reconstruct the process used to analyze the most recent MEAP data available to the school	Expand the case study above to explore what groups (parents, teachers, community members, etc.) participate in dialogue about the meaning of data, how people create meaning from the data, and how they decide what action is implied.
Benchmark B: Applications	School Annual Report, NCLB Report Card, and any similar reports or documents disseminated to the public	Review the documents to learn how the school shares what it has learned from data analysis and interpretation in ways that build support for the teaching and learning decisions that have been made based on the data
	School improvement plan and interviews with key members of the school improvement team focused on the use of data in the planning process	Analyze the school improvement planning process with an eye toward learning how information derived from data was used to evaluate program effects and determine action at the school and classroom levels

References

American Association of School Administrators. (n.d.). *Using data to improve schools: What's working.* Office of Educational Research and Improvement, U.S. Department of Education. Retrieved from http://aasa.files.cmsplus.com/PDFs/Publications/UsingDataToImprove Schools.pdf

American Institutes for Research. (2010, December). *What experience from the field tells us about school leadership and turnaround.* Naperville, IL: American Institutes for Research. Retrieved from http://www.learningpt.org/pdfs/leadership_turnaround_schools.pdf

Bernhardt, V. (1998). *Data analysis for comprehensive schoolwide improvement.* Larchmont, NY: Eye on Education.

Bernhardt, V. (2004). *Data analysis for continuous school improvement.* Larchmont, NY: Eye on Education.

Bernhardt, V. L. (2010). *Data, data everywhere: Bringing all the data together for continuous school improvement.* Larchmont, NY: Eye on Education.

Cooley, V. E., Shen, J., Miller, D., Winograd, P. N., Rainey, J. M., Yuan, W., & Ryan, L. (2006). Increasing leaders' capacity in data-based decision-making: State-level initiatives in Ohio, New Mexico, and Michigan. *Educational Horizons, 85*(1), 57–64.

Croft, J. (2007, June 12). Frameworks for designers. Retrieved from http://www.alistapart.com/

Council of Chief State School Officers (CCSSO). (2008). *Educational leadership policy standards: ISLLC 2008.* Washington, DC: Author. Retrieved from http://www.ccsso.org/

Daly, A. J. (2009). Rigid response in an age of accountability: The potential for leadership and trust. *Educational Research Quarterly, 45,* 168–216.

District of Columbia Office of the State Superintendent of Instruction. (n.d.). *Patterns of practice school review process.* Washington, DC: Author. Retrieved from www.taccweb.org/

Earl, L. & Katz, S. (2006). *Leading schools in a data-rich world: Harnessing data for school improvement.* Thousand Oaks, CA: Corwin Press.

Kentucky Department of Education. (2004, April). *Comprehensive school improvement planning framework for schools.* Frankfort, KY: Author. Retrieved from http://eric.ed.gov/

Knapp, M. S., Copland, M. A., Ford, B., Markholt, A., McLaughlin, M. W., Milliken, M., & Talbert, J. E. (2003). *Leading for learning sourcebook: Concepts and examples.* Seattle, WA: Center for the Study of Teaching and Policy, University of Washington. Retrieved from http://depts.washington.edu/

Knapp, M. S., Swinnerton, J. A., Copland, M. A., & Monpas-Huber, J. (2006). *Data-informed leadership in education.* Seattle, WA: Center for the Study of Teaching and Policy, University of Washington. Retrieved from http://depts.washington.edu/ctpmail/PDFs/DataInformed-Nov1.pdf

Knapp, M. S., Copland, M. A., & Swinnerton, J. A. (2007). Introduction: Evidence and decision-making. In P. Moss (Ed.), *Evidence and decision making* (106th Yearbook of the National Society for the Study of Education) (pp. 74–104). Malden, MA: Blackwell Publishing.

Learning Point Associates. (2004, December). *Guide to using data in school improvement efforts: A compilation of knowledge from data retreats and data use at Learning Point Associates.* Naperville, IL: Learning Point Associates. Retrieved from http://www.learningpt.org/pdfs/datause/guidebook.pdf

Marx, G. E., Berry, J., Kirby, B., Whale, D., Shen, J., & Cooley, V. (2007, February). *Data-based decision-making: Retooling school leadership curricula as part of a state-wide initiative in Michigan.* Paper presented at the meeting of the National Council of Professors of Educational Administration 18th Annual Conference-within-a-Conference, Las Vegas, NV.

Mason, S. (2002, April 1). *Turning data into knowledge: Lessons from six Milwaukee school districts. American Educational Research Association.* Lecture conducted from Joyce Foundation, Wisconsin Center for Education Research, New Orleans.

Michigan Coalition of Essential Schools. (n.d.). *Michigan coalition of essential schools.* Retrieved May 2, 2011, from http://www.michigances.org/history.htm

Michigan Department of Education. (2005). *School Improvement Framework.* Retrieved from http://www.michigan.gov/documents/SIF_4-01-05_130701_7.pdf

Michigan Department of Education. (2006, October 21). Announcement of joint agreement between MDE & NCA CASI. Current topics press release retrieved from http://www.michigan.gov/mde

New Mexico Public Education Department. (2009, September). *2009–2010 School and district improvement framework.* Santa Fe, NM: Author. Retrieved from http://www.ped.state.nm.us/

Ohio Department of Education. (2008, November). *The Ohio improvement process (OIP): Toward a unified state system of support.* Troy, OH: Author. Retrieved from http://education.ohio.gov/

Petersen, J. L. (2007). The brave new world of data-informed instruction. *Education Next, 7*(1), 36–42.

Schmoker, M. (2004). Tipping point: From faceless reform to substantive instructional improvement. *Phi Delta Kappan, 85,* 424–432.

School Improvement Planning Process Guide (3rd ed.). (2005, January). The Washington School Improvement Office and Office of Superintendent of Public Instruction. Retrieved from http://www.k12.wa.us/Improvement/publications/SIPGuide/SIPGuide.pdf

Shen, J., Berry, J., Cooley, V., Kirby, B., Marx, G., & Whale, D. (2007). *Data-informed decision-making: A guidebook for data points and analyses in the context of Michigan School Improvement Framework.* Kalamazoo, MI: Michigan Coalition of Educational Leadership.

Shen, J., & Cooley, V. (2008). Critical issues in using data for decision-making. *International Journal of Leadership in Education, 11*(3), 319–329.

Shen, J., Cooley, V., Reeves, P., Burt, W., Ryan, L., Rainey, J. M., & Yuan, W. (2010). Using data for decision-making: Perspectives from 16 principals in Michigan, USA. *International Review of Education, 56,* 435–456

Stack, C. (2003). *A passion for proof: Using data to accelerate student achievement.* Westerville, OH: National Middle School Association. Retrieved from http://www.scribd.com/doc/16451627/A-Passion-for-Proof-Using-Data-to-Accelerate-Student-Achievement

Walberg, H. J. (Ed.) (2007). Handbook on restructuring and substantial school improvement. Center on Innovation & Improvement, www.centerii.org: The Academic Development Institute. http://www.centerii.org/survey/downloads/Restructuring%20Handbook.pdf.

Wohlstetter, P., Datnow, A., & Park, V. (2008). Creating a system for data-driven decision-making: applying the principal-agent framework. *School Effectiveness and School Improvement, 19*(3), 239–259.

• 7 •

The Leadership Performance Planning Worksheet (LPPW)

A Development Tool for Early Career School Leaders

LYNN M. SCOTT

An Introduction to the LPPW

Skilled leaders are critical to the success of our nation's schools. Research (Hallinger and Heck 1998; Leithwood, Seashore, Anderson, & Wahlstrom, 2004; Louis, Leithwood, Wahlstrom, & Anderson, 2010) has provided compelling evidence for the link between educational leadership, as practiced by principals, and student learning. These and other studies have stimulated the growing consensus about the critical role that principals play in advancing student achievement goals in schools. While experienced principals typically have opportunities to develop within their profession over the course of their careers, new principals must face the numerous daily challenges of leading their schools while simultaneously learning how to be instructional leaders. While many new principals survive these initial years, others either perform at a capacity below the needs of their staff and students, or leave the profession.[1] To insure that there is sustained progress in school improvement and student achievement, there need to be developmental interventions early in principals' careers to maximize the impact leadership can have in schools.

This chapter presents the story of the development and successful applications of the Leadership Performance Planning Worksheet© (LPPW) as an effective developmental intervention. The LPPW© is a standards-based development tool, created by the NYC Leadership Academy (NYCLA),[2] a nonprofit organization that designs and implements innovative, standards-based leadership development programs for aspiring and current school leaders. The LPPW© is designed to strengthen leadership capacities in early career principals and to anchor school leader coaching and mentoring programs. The philosophy supporting this tool's design is that early-career principals should focus on developing mastery of a subset of key leader behaviors that have been found to develop instructional leadership capacity. In just a few short years, the LPPW© has proved to be an effective mentoring and coaching tool to accelerate purposeful, on-the-job development of instructional leadership behaviors and skills among early career principals. The chapter describes the development of the LPPW© and how it has proved to be an effective mentoring and coaching tool to accelerate the process of purposeful on-the-job development of instructional leadership behaviors and skills. It summarizes its reported value to the leadership development of early career principals, explains how the LPPW© was designed and provides an overview of pilot test results which analyzed its utility in school districts across 11 states. It also describes some emergent applications of the LPPW© among current users. In total, the chapter presents insights about the LPPW©'s utility to enhance the leadership proficiency of early career principals and for its potential to connect a school system's existing leadership development elements to strengthen its leadership continuum.

The LPPW© Was Created to Increase the Success and Retention of Early Career Principals

Often innovations emerge in an environment where problems can be fully explored and there is encouragement for the generation and testing of ideas. The LPPW© was created in such an environment when the Wallace Foundation began its education leadership initiative in 2000. The Wallace Foundation's strategic goal was to find ways to develop and support effective school leadership that could drive significant improvements in student learning. As one of the largest philanthropies supporting public education nationally, the Foundation sought to meet the challenges of inadequate leadership recruitment and preparation programs, difficult working conditions and harsh political climates. A tactic for achieving this goal centered on the importance of building the partnerships and networks to share broadly the knowledge and practices being developed by states and districts receiving Wallace grants. It was envisioned that ultimately the benefits from this learning community would be derived for states, districts, and students beyond the reach of the Wallace Foundation's direct funding. The Leadership Performance Planning Worksheet (LPPW©) was one of the success stories of this initiative

The LPPW© is an innovative development tool designed to strengthen critical leadership skills and behaviors in early-career school leaders. Used in conjunction with coaching or mentoring, it helps identify those development areas based on principals' challenges and anchors the creation of action plans to enhance their instructional leadership capacity. Since its introduction in 2008, principals, mentors and coaches who have used the LPPW© report that it helps maximize leaders' performance when combined with standards-based coaching and mentoring. Users report that the strengths of the tool lay in its focus on "Showstopper Behaviors"— the critical instructional leadership behaviors that early career principals should master to minimize their chances of failure. These behaviors also provide a developmental framework and a common language that permits principals to self-assess their leadership competencies and behaviors and identify key areas where they need leadership development and support. The behaviors also enrich the mentoring process by supporting objective conversations about challenges that principals are facing, improving mutual diagnosis of leadership development needs within the actual school content, and creating behaviorally based action plans for development.

Within the first three years of the LPPW©'s introduction, the New York City Leadership Academy (NYCLA) led the expansion of LPPW© users into 11 states, including urban, suburban, and rural school districts; has evaluated the LPPW© for its utility annually; and continually updates the tool based on data collection and other findings about its use. Moreover, state departments of education and school districts have collaborated with NYCLA to test applications of the LPPW© with other kinds of school leaders to include aspiring principals, assistant principals, experienced principals, teacher leaders, superintendents and assistant superintendents, Special Education Directors, and Career Development Directors. Within a short time, NYCLA has organized and maintained a growing learning community focused on the instructional leadership development needs of early career principals.

The Components of the LPPW© Focus on Instructional Leadership

The LPPW© comprises 39 critical leadership behaviors that have been identified through current theoretical models of instructional leadership, a synthesis of principal development and evaluation tools, and two years of pilot studies in urban, suburban, and rural school districts across the country. The behaviors are organized into the following eight dimensions:

> *1.0 Personal Behavior* (5 behaviors) addresses the principals' code of conduct and how they exemplify themselves in their leadership role. This dimension includes behaviors that cause principals to assess how their

expressed belief system guides their actions; how their personal and profession demeanor has an impact on others; how they demonstrate receptivity to different points of view; and the appropriateness of their responses to situations.

2.0 Resilience (5 behaviors) is a set of behaviors that directs attention to how principals respond to detractors from their leadership style. Detractors can come from external sources such as external disagreement or the level of ambiguity associated with an issue in the school, or from competing demands and conflicting directives. Principals are also asked to self-assess how they respond to internal detractors from their leadership style such as reacting constructively to disappoint or the ability to learn from mistakes and setbacks.

3.0 Communication (5 behaviors) represents the breadth and quality of a principal's communication. The five communication behaviors address the extent to which their communication reflects careful analysis and the ability to listen; how they directly communicate with students; the level of active communication with staff, families and the community; and how principals use rituals and routines as enablers of vision.

4.0 Student Performance (8 behaviors) addresses the behaviors that are intended to shape the outcomes principals are trying to achieve in their school. This dimension has the largest number of behaviors which are at the core of instructional leadership practice. They range from planning and goal setting behaviors, implementing effective instructional strategies, facilitating the analysis and alignment of effective instructional strategies, creating transparency in the process of reporting student achievement data and using it to make instructional leadership decisions.

5.0 Situational Problem Solving (4 behaviors) is the comprehensiveness and agility of a principal's problem solving techniques. The behaviors in this dimension include using evidence as a basis of decision making, clearly defining the structure of their decision-making, linking decisions to strategic priorities, and exercising professional judgment consistent with the values and beliefs of their school.

6.0 Learning (4 behaviors) is a dimension that is also central to the practice of instructional leadership. It centers on how principals facilitate and model a learning culture in the school. This dimension enables principals to assess their application of learning and change theories, how they apply research trends in education, and their approach to developing professional development plans.

THE LEADERSHIP PERFORMANCE PLANNING WORKSHEET (LPPW) | 173

7.0 Supervision of Staff (4 behaviors) addresses how principals exemplify direct leadership. This dimension includes how the principal encourages reflective practice, establishes a system for clear expectations and evaluation, and makes difficult decisions and responds to the outcomes of those decisions.

8.0 Management (4 behaviors) addresses how principals exemplify organizational leadership. Organizational leadership pertains to leadership behaviors that affect the organizational structure and processes of the school. The behaviors in this dimension cover time management in relation to school priorities, objective setting and planning, resource allocation, and creating structures within the school to ensure a safe and effective learning environment.

The LPPW© Is Designed for Purposeful, Active Use

The 39 behaviors are designed as a worksheet for principals to facilitate ongoing, developmental conversations with their mentors or coaches. Figure 1 displays a page from the LPPW©. The worksheet provides a description of the dimensions; the behaviors associated with the dimension that meet the standard of performance; an opportunity for the principal to self-assess his or her own behaviors against the standard; and a writing area to establish action planning notes. Principals are instructed to use the LPPW© to objectively discuss their leadership behaviors and the outcomes they generate in order to create a purposeful, evidence-based development strategy during their first year.

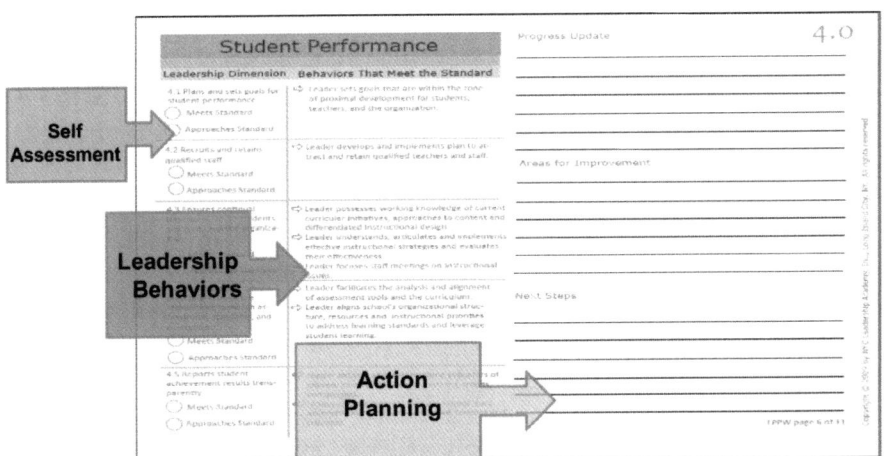

Figure 1. Sample Page from the Leadership Performance Planning Worksheet.

The behavioral standards listed for each worksheet dimension are grounded in principal development and evaluation tools created by the state departments of education in Delaware, Missouri, Kentucky, and New York City. They reflect a thorough review and synthesis of principal leadership standards used nationally, including Interstate school Leaders Licensure Consortium (ISLLC). The standards are written to allow principals to assess their actual behaviors in their school and community and to prepare for diagnostic or reflective conversations with their mentor or coach.

The purpose of the LPPW© is to efficiently develop new principals' capacities to the national principal leadership standards across these critical dimensions of instructional leadership. With this purpose in mind, the worksheet rating scale has two categories: 1. *Approaching the Standard*; and 2. *Meeting the Standard* to easily isolate the instructional leadership dimensions that need the most attention. To continue principals' engagement with the tool, each page provides write-in sections to prompt concrete action planning to include identifying areas for improvement, listing next steps to effect change, and progress updates on earlier development strategies. While the LPPW© design appears to be useful on its own to serve as a guide to critical instructional leadership behaviors, it is intended to be used with a mentor or coach to achieve efficient, robust development of critical instructional leadership behaviors. Sample pages of the LPPW© are at the Appendix.

The LPPW© Is Designed to Enhance the Mentoring and Coaching Process

Contemporary mentoring and coaching practices for leaders are grounded in the apprenticeship relationships within professions where experienced members socialize new members to the profession's norms and effective practices. Historically, the professions of law, medicine, and theology each integrated formal schooling with apprenticeships to accomplish the socialization and training of new members.[3] Today, mentoring and coaching is performed across many professions and organizational contexts and are responsible for numerous positive outcomes for protégés. For example, a 2008 multidisciplinary, meta-analysis of mentoring studies (Eby, Allen, Evans, Ng, & DuBois, 2008)[4] found that workplace mentoring relationships were related to higher levels of performance, inclination to help others, workplace situational satisfaction, higher levels of motivation and job involvement, and lower levels of psychological stress. Within the profession of principalship, mentors and coaches are expected to accelerate principals' acquisition of leadership skills and subsequent performance because they can convey their insights as experienced professionals in ways that are tailored to the novice principal's needs.

The potential that mentoring and coaching has for principals' development and performance has led to an expansion of programs across the country that are either organized by either school districts, departments of education, or professional associations (Villani, 2006). Yet, the Wallace Foundation reports that "most existing mentoring programs fall short of their potential" (Mintang, Mattis, & Spiro, 2007). Common problems include programs that become buddy systems or checklist exercises, insufficient focus on instructional leadership, and weak or non-existent training for mentors. The LPPW© is designed to ameliorate many of these problems by improving the focus, quality and outcomes of the mentor/coach-mentee relationship. The tool's instructions ask principals "to review the LPPW© with the coach/mentor early in the school year to identify the leadership dimensions [they] need to strengthen to improve student learning within the context of [their] school." Coaches and mentors are asked to explain to their school leader protégés that the LPPW© review process is an opportunity for growth and to create an environment that enables them to be reflective and open about strengths and weaknesses.

Effective mentoring and coaching is grounded in sound training. To address this need, the NYCLA trains mentors and coaches in the effective use of the LPPW© and in the practice of Facilitative Competency-Based (FCB) Coaching methods. The LPPW© training consists of a one day workshop designed to introduce mentors and coaches of current or aspiring leaders to the LPPW© and to facilitate practices that lay the foundation for the effective use of the tool. The training provides participants with the opportunity to explore in depth the LPPW© leadership dimensions and their behavioral standards, learn strategies for effectively using the LPPW© for the development of leadership capacity, and practice using the LPPW© for identifying entry points and activities for professional development for current and aspiring leaders.

NYCLA's Facilitative Competency-Based Coaching is standards-based coaching—an approach to school leadership development that enables the mentor/coach and mentee to work together on an agreed upon set of competencies (skills, knowledge and behaviors).[5] In practice, mentors and coaches foster a relationship that encourages the principal to engage in critical and targeted reflection on his/her leadership and its alignment to an articulated set of leadership competencies. The goal of FCB is to facilitate the paradigm or behavioral shifts necessary for the principal to strengthen his/her leadership capacity. Designed for coaches/mentors of school leaders, NYCLA typically provides 1.5 days of training for mentors/coaches which builds upon the coach/mentor's introduction to the LPPW©.[6] It covers a deep understanding of the coaching model and its key components. The training provides an understanding of the competency-based approach to school leadership development and creates an opportunity to practice key coaching skills of listening, questioning, feedback and diagnosis.

Facilitative Competency-Based Coaching, when used with the LPPW© is intended to engender transformational change in principals. This level of individual change refers to improvements in the ways that principals think about instructional leadership and school improvement. Transformational change also encompasses changing the behaviors principals perform as leaders, and their abilities to guide and motivate others to contribute to the goals of contributing to students' growth and achievement. FCB training has also been found to benefit mentor/coach programs. Administrators of mentoring programs report that the training programs and the use of the LPPW© have established a common perspective about early career principal development which has formed the foundation of learning community among their mentors and coaches.[7]

The LPPW© Helps Maximize the Performance of School Leaders and Their Mentors/Coaches

The use of the LPPW© has expanded to 11 states with over 1,100 principals and over 400 trained mentors using the tool. The size of this pool of users has resulted in learning how the LPPW© is being integrated in the broader context of leadership development systems in school districts and states. Administrators at the district and state levels report that the LPPW© helps them strengthen their existing leadership development programs. They have also cited that the LPPW© framework establishes a common language and coherence for their leadership development initiatives. Finally, these same administrators credit the LPPW© with the capability to connect the different elements of their leadership development continuum, ranging from principal preparation to on-the-job support to principal evaluation. What likely permits these stated system level benefits is the context free, standards-based language within the tool. Overall, users have confirmed that the LPPW© structures the processes and facilitates the outcomes that mentoring and coaching are intended to provide. Principals, mentors, and coaches have reported[8] that with regard to the LPPW©'s design:

- The leadership dimensions are relevant to their specific school site.
- Specific learning needs of principals are represented in the LPPW©.
- The LPPW© helps assess the school leader's skills and behaviors and identify areas that need improvement.
- The LPPW© facilitates discussions about instructional leadership and management skills.
- The LPPW© helps develop a plan to enhance leadership skills and behaviors.

Principals have consistently reported that the LPPW©, integrated with their mentoring/coaching, helped change how they perform as a school leader. Survey results from a majority of principals using the LPPW© during the first year of its administration[9] reported that the LPPW©:

- Caused them to think actively about being an instructional leader.
- Enabled them to begin a discussion about administration and management skills with their mentor/coach.
- Enabled them to begin a discussion about instructional leadership with their mentor/coach.
- Helped them understand what is required of effective instructional leadership.
- Enabled them to begin a course of action to achieve realistic goals.

Mentors and coaches have also reported anecdotally that the LPPW© offers them multiple points of entry to diagnose challenges facing principals and to begin and sustain conversations that lead to concrete actions that result in change. Some mentors and coaches use the LPPW© as a basis of general inquiry about their mentor's practice as an instructional leader. Other mentors use it as a diagnostic tool with their mentees to address specific problems or issues. Still other mentors and coaches have shared how the LPPW© dimensions and standards are the frameworks they consistently use when listening to their mentees, observing dynamics within the school, or when helping a mentee propose his or her own courses of action towards improvement.

The reports of the LPPW©'s utility and value are highly encouraging. The LPPW©'s strength appears to be in its orientation to early career principals' needs and in its simple design. The worksheet's listing of showstopper behaviors keeps developmental conversations and subsequent reflection focused on the most critical standards-based behaviors that early career principals must master. The LPPW©'s design is simple yet purposeful, enabling mentor and coaches to diagnose development needs and to structure purposeful developmental interactions. Overall, reports from users relay that the LPPW© has transformed the daunting task of crafting developmental interventions from complex instructional leadership taxonomies into a straightforward process to identify and meet the development needs of early career principals. Perhaps equally encouraging is the story of the LPPW©'s creation because it illustrates how, over a relatively short period of time, the right conditions and the right people can create a valuable innovation for many in the profession. The next section will describe how the LPPW© was designed and developed.

How Was the LPPW© Designed and Developed?

Typically when an innovation surfaces and is quickly adopted the reasoning for its creation and the actual work behind its success receive relatively little attention. Yet, the account of the LPPW©'s creation is important to provide because it illustrates how true collaboration among a small number of professionals can create something of value for the profession at large. The Wallace Foundation designed the context for the LPPW©'s design and development through the creation of "Leadership Issue Groups" (LIGs) in 2005. The LIGs were designed to bring together grant recipients and subject matter experts, over a three year period, to strengthen implementation of the work in the participating sites and publication of reports detailing lessons and actionable ideas that can inform and move the field. The groups were organized to focus on six critical issues:

1. *Governance*—redefining the roles and responsibilities of school boards and investigating ways to improve district governance structures
2. *Data Informed Decision-Making*—using data effectively to make better decisions
3. *Resource Allocation and Incentives*—developing methods, allocating resources and changing incentives to encourage effective leadership and teaching behaviors
4. *Roles and Responsibilities*—redefining the roles and responsibilities of school leaders to enhance student achievement outcomes
5. *High School Leadership*—identifying and fostering particular leadership skills and strategies needed to transform high school leadership and results
6. *Assessing Leadership Effectiveness*—developing ways to assess leadership behavior and improve results

The LIG formation and their periodic meetings established an incubator for ideas. Each issue group's participants had opportunities to share the progress of their ongoing work; design experimental approaches to address each issue; engage experts in the field to improve these experiments capture; analyze and publish what is being learned at each site and across sites; and engage additional Wallace Foundation partner organizations to improve the work and disseminate findings nationwide. The ensuing environment of innovative thinking and collaboration supported multiple rounds of discussions that led to the LPPW©'s design and subsequent pilot testing over the course of two years as part of the Assessing Leadership Effectiveness LIG.

Phase 1: The Idea Generation Process

Participants in the "Assessing Leadership Effectiveness LIG" represented eight states and 13 districts.[10] Each had been pursuing its own initiatives to improve principals' instructional leadership skills. During the first day's discussions, the group developed a consensus that there was a need for a tool to improve the performance of principals. Initially, discussions centered on tools that guided principals to exemplar levels of performance as well as tools that could remediate poor performance to acceptable levels of performance. Next, ideas emerged that ranged from developing a training program in performance feedback for supervisors to developing new protocols and processes for principals' performance reviews to developing new assessment instruments for teacher leaders and aspiring principals. As the discussion and idea generation progressed, group members agreed that any new tool that would be created needed to be centered on a professional development model that incorporated the expected knowledge, skills, and abilities principals needed on the job. The tool also needed to incorporate a core set of performance standards that were also adaptable to any state's existing standards for principal performance. Overall, the envisioned tool needed to be an integral component of an ongoing process that would develop the instructional leadership capacity of principals over a number of years.

The next topic of discussion during this first meeting centered on the targeted users of the developmental tool and participants agreed that early career principals could benefit most from a developmental tool. This sub-population of the profession was particularly vulnerable to setbacks and failure in an increasingly challenging job. The consensus of the group was that many new principals enter the profession where a sink or swim philosophy for development predominates and that this group was particularly overlooked for formal development assistance. Based on this initial round of discussions, ideas surface around the development of an intermediate assessment tool that could create awareness of deficiencies and opportunities to develop shortcomings before the end of their performance cycle. A sub-group consisting of representatives from Delaware, Kentucky, the NYC Leadership Academy, and Massachusetts pursued the development of this project.

Phase 2: Idea Refinement

Three months later, during the next round of LIG meetings, the sub-group refined these ideas. The objective to develop an assessment tool was revised because the amount of effort needed to establish its predictive validity and implement the assessment in multiple sites would be beyond the capabilities of the LIG. Instead, the sub-group decided to pursue the design of a new principal development inventory. The inventory would not be a stand-alone instrument but would be used in conjunction with ongoing coaching and mentoring to develop new principals' instructional leadership capacities. The specific design features included:

1. Inventory items would address core behaviors that develop the capacity to perform instructional leadership.
2. The items could be adaptable to different state standards.
3. The items could be adaptable to the wide variety of experience of new principals.
4. The sources for the inventory items would come from the tools currently in use in Delaware, Kentucky, at the NYC Leadership Academy, as well as the ISSLC Standards.

Moreover, the group agreed that mentors and coaches would need standardized KSA (Knowledge, Skill, and Ability) training in the proper use of the developmental inventory. To complete the project, the group agreed on the need for an assessment and feedback process that would support the use of the inventory during the life of the project.

Phase 3: Design Completion

During the next round of LIG meetings, in June 2006, and continuing throughout the life of the project, the NYC Leadership Academy assumed the leadership role in the sub-group and was responsible for the final design characteristics, the tool's content, and the specification of its use. While the focus of the tool remained to facilitate development of instructional leadership skills, the scope of these skills was reduced to what were called "showstoppers." Showstoppers were the short list of skills and behaviors that if not mastered first would very likely result in principals' serious performance deficiencies or eventual termination from their position. The sub-group however was faced with a trade-off when considering what items would be included in the tool. Attempts to comprehensively include critical instructional leadership behaviors and skills would produce a list that would be impractical for mentors and coaches to use, while an attempt to identify a manageable list that would meet the goals of the envisioned tool could possibly result in incorrect choices. The approach the participants took was to identify the behaviors and skills most critical to novice principals, particularly in their first two years. The approach was based on the notion that if given a long list of leadership capabilities that marked proficiency in the profession, the most critical should be developed first to perform in risky and demanding environments.[11] The LIG sub-group sought to identify no more than 50 instructional leadership behaviors and skills to establish a common language for development between novice principals and the mentors.

Next, the showstoppers needed to be anchored to established standards of performance. Tying the selected behaviors and skills to existing standards for performance would fully leverage the standards–based work that had already been completed and increase the likelihood of consistent development outcomes across different contexts of use. It made sense to the sub-group to create the LPPW© as a synthesis of items from existing assessment inventories and audit protocols. Recent work in instructional leadership standards, principal performance dimensions, and principal evaluation provided the LIG participants with a comprehensive source of behaviors and skills to screen and select no more than 50 showstoppers for the document.

The first tool reviewed was the NYCLA Performance Matrix. The Performance Matrix is aligned to national, state, and New York City Department of Education school leadership standards and identifies 45 behaviors organized into 12 leadership dimensions that reflect the attributes of transformational and instructional leaders. The Leadership Academy uses the performance standards to guide the selection of applicants to their program, establish the scope of their curriculum, make internship assignments, determine who will advance in their program, decide how to structure interventions, and how to design comprehensive evaluations of each aspiring principal participant. Relying on the NYC Leadership Academy staff's experience with developing and tracking the performance of the recent generation of New York City principals, the first set of showstopper behaviors was culled from this tool. Next Kentucky's "School Level Performance Descriptors for Kentucky's Standards and Indicators for School Improvement"[12] was reviewed for additional showstopper behaviors and skills that were not already covered in the NYCLA Performance Matrix. The Kentucky protocol defines the elements of whole school improvement, including leadership behaviors and skills, that every school can put into effect in order to produce desired learning results. The same review was performed with Delaware's Performance Appraisal System (DPAS II) for Administrators.[13] The design of DPAS II was driven by the Delaware Administrative Standards, which align with the ISLLC standards. DPAS II is grounded in research and an understanding of leader performance in high achieving schools. Additional documents reviewed included the Wallace Foundation's list of instructional leadership "driver behaviors"[14] and the ISLLC standards. These document reviews identified the tool's 39 behaviors.

Finally, the tool's design needed to motivate principals' continuous commitment to their leadership performance planning and development during their initial years in the position. In an attempt to encourage its sustained use, the LPPW© would include an area for principals to self-assess their current behaviors and skills against the standards of performance as well as areas for principals to make notes about development strategies and actions.

Testing the LPPW©'s Utility on a National Level

Pilot Test Design

After the LPPW©'s design completion, the next step was to organize a pilot test among interested states and districts in the larger LIG community. Test states and sites were identified and time was set aside for participants to review the tool and suggest revisions. Concurrent with the LPPW© vetting, the NYC Leadership Academy identified the coaching KSAs and coordinated the mentor/coach selection process with the test states and sites and designed and delivered the training program for each site's mentors/coaches. Finally the test sites and LIG designed the pilot test implementation plan.

The pilot test was designed to take place in eight sites across seven states. The original 2007/2008 pilot participants included:

- Springfield, Massachusetts
- Boston School Leadership Institute
- NYC Leadership Academy
- Delaware
- Kentucky
- Springfield, Illinois
- Missouri
- Arizona

The pilots were designed to provide answers to the following questions about development in a series of monthly and summative surveys:

- What LPPW© leadership performance dimensions were addressed during the mentoring/coaching process?
- Can targeted leadership performance planning using the LPPW© and coaching affect school leader learning?
- Can targeted leadership performance planning using the LPPW© and coaching affect school leaders' behavior?

As shown in Table 1, over 1000 professionals used the LPPW© during the pilot test. The pilot size fell into two categories—large scale oriented to piloting implementation strategies and small scale designed to test the feasibility of developing a mentoring/coaching program centered on the LPPW©. The NYCLA and the Missouri State Department of Education conducted the large scale pilots. NYCLA and Missouri already had large, fully established coaching and mentoring programs. The NYCLA coaching program was integral to the support provided to its recent graduates. Missouri's statewide Administrator Mentor Program was created in response to state requirements for all new school leaders to receive mentoring in their initial placement as a new administrator. The remaining sites wanted to investigate the LPPW©'s effectiveness and utility with the mentoring and professional development programs they currently had in place for early career principals and conducted smaller pilot tests.

The NYC Leadership Academy provided training to each site's mentors/coaches to ensure that there was a common base of knowledge about the effective use of the LPPW© and Facilitative Competency-Based Coaching methods before the pilots began.

TABLE 1. Participant Count for the 2008 LPPW Pilot Test

Pilot Location	#Principals	#Coaches	Total Participants
Springfield, MA	14	8	22
Boston, MA	15	4	19
New York City	478	44	522
Delaware	41	34	75
Kentucky	46	6	52
Springfield, IL	9	9	18
Missouri	334	114	448
Arizona	10	8	18
Grand Total	947	227	1,174

The pilot test lasted from January to April 2008. Data collection was integral to the study design to assess the LPPW©'s utility throughout the test period. Principals and their mentor/coaches received a monthly on-line survey at the end of the first three months to track how the LPPW© was being used during mentoring/coaching conversations. Monthly survey questions gathered the frequency and location of the mentoring/coaching sessions; queried the topics of discussions that occurred during the month's mentoring sessions; and asked which LPPW© leadership dimensions[15] were the topics of discussions. At the end of the last pilot month, participants received a summative survey that asked about the utility of the LPPW© performance standards about learning outcomes, and the perceived effectiveness of the mentoring/coaching process with the LPPW©. The results of survey analysis are presented in the next section.

LPPW© 2008 Pilot Test Results[16]

The LPPW© pilot test provided a relatively quick opportunity to learn about the utility of this new developmental tool. The study also provided the opportunity to learn about early career principals' on-the-job-development needs and to get a glimpse, albeit high level, at the nature of mentoring and coaching conversations. The pilot test participants never had an opportunity to acquire this kind of information about early career principals and mentoring. The systematic collection of these data would be an important addition to their program designs and revisions.

What Do Principals and Their Mentors/Coaches Talk About?

Conversations between principals and their mentors/coaches are typically confidential. Because of this reality, there have always been limits to fully understanding the challenges facing early career principals and the full value of a mentoring/coaching relationship. The pilot test surveys, however, provided an uncompromising insight into these developmental conversations. The monthly survey asked principals to identify the topics discussed in their mentor/coach meetings from a list of 13 options as shown in Figure 2.

The responses to this question are shown in Table 2. They indicate that principal-mentor/coach conversations tended to focus on immediate challenges facing the principal and the development of their leadership capacity. Discussions about attempts to solve specific problems in the school and feedback about administrative performance were among the top 5 topics discussed across the pilot sites. Discussions about developing leadership capacity, particularly reflective conversations about instructional leadership and conversations drawing upon the mentor's/coach's insights were also common across the pilot test sites. Conversation about specific development actions

> Mentoring/coaching meetings addressed during this past month. (Check all that apply)
>
> ☐ Discussions about my self-assessment generated by the worksheet
> ☐ Specific planning for ways to improve instructional leadership performance
> ☐ Attempt to solve specific problems in the school
> ☐ Updates on progress towards achieving instructional leadership performance goals
> ☐ Analyzing the causes for successful initiatives implemented in the school
> ☐ Analyzing the causes for unsuccessful initiatives that were attempted in the school
> ☐ Gaining insights about instructional leadership from the mentor/coach
> ☐ Feedback about instructional leadership performance
> ☐ Feedback about administrative/managerial performance
> ☐ Observation and critique of instructional leadership behaviors and style
> ☐ Reflective conversations about instructional leadership
> ☐ Supervision techniques
> ☐ Other

Figure 2. Monthly Survey Question to Identify the Topics Addressed During Mentoring/Coaching Meetings.

were also prevalent across sites, taking the form of specific planning for ways to improve leadership performance in New York City and Missouri, and discussing updates on progression towards achieving leadership performance goals across the remaining sites. The similarity of top topics across sites provides a glimpse at the areas where early career principals need assistance and how mentors and coaches are directly adding developmental assistance.

The monthly surveys also asked which critical leadership topics principals and their mentor/coaches concentrated on during their time together. In order to preserve the confidentiality of conversations, principals, mentors and coaches were asked to identify which of the LPPW© dimensions they focused on for performance planning. Figure 3 presents the top 5 leadership dimensions for Missouri and New York City respectively as reported in the April 2008 monthly survey. Despite the differences in school contexts between the two regions, it's noteworthy that principals

TABLE 2. Top 5 Discussion Topics During Mentoring/Coaching Meetings Collected During the April 2008 Survey

Top 5 Discussion Topics	NY City (N=108)	Missouri (N=146)
Attempts to solve specific problems in the school	70.4%	70.3%
Reflective conversations about instructional leadership	70.4%	52.0%
Gaining insights about leadership from the mentor coach	55.6%	46.6%
Specific planning for ways to improve leadership performance	55.6%	39.9%
Feedback about administrative performance	50.0%	41.9%

reported working on nearly the same leadership dimensions.

Top 5 Leadership Categories That Were The Focus Of Development In Missouri:	Top 5 Leadership Categories That Were The Focus Of Development In NY City:
• Situational Problem Solving • Supervision of Staff • Management • Student Learning • Personal Behavior	• Supervision of Staff • Student Learning • Situational Problem Solving • Communication • Resilience

Figure 3. Top 5 Leadership Dimensions That Were the Focus of Development in Missouri and NY City Collected From the April 2008 Survey.

What Are Principals' and Mentors'/Coaches' Opinions About the LPPW©'s Utility?

The pilot test summative survey included questions asking about the LPPW©'s utility to facilitate the mentor/coaching interactions directed at improving instructional leadership. Principals and mentors/coaches responded to five questions using a 5-point Likert response scale.[17] Tables 3 and 4 present the cross site response averages for each question for principals and mentor/coaches, respectively.

TABLE 3. Cross Site Principal Rating on the LPPW's Utility

Principals' Assessment—The LPPW provides sufficient information to…	Average Agreement Rating (4=Agree; 5=Strongly Agree), N=265
Cause me to think actively about being an instructional leader	4.19
Begin a discussion about administration and management skills with my mentor/coach	4.17
Begin a discussion about instructional leadership with my mentor/coach	4.16
Help me understand what is required of effective instructional leadership	4.09
Begin a course of action to achieve realistic goals	4.08

TABLE 4. Cross Site Mentor/Coach Ratings on the LPPW's Utility

Mentors'/Coaches' Assessment—The LPPW provides sufficient information to…	Average Agreement Rating (4=Agree; 5=Strongly Agree), N=162
Help the school leader understand what is required of effective instructional leaders	4.33
Begin a discussion about instructional leadership with the school leader	4.31
Begin a discussion about administration and management skills with the school leader	4.29
Cause the school leader to actively think about how to be an instructional leader	4.22
Help identify performance areas that need improvement	4.08

Principals and mentors/coaches provided ratings for every question that strongly suggests that the intended purpose of the LPPW© was realized. Each group of users agreed that the LPPW© causes principals to think actively about instructional leadership and what is required of effective leaders; begin discussions about instructional leadership, and management and leadership skills; and begin the process of performance improvement. These data suggest that the LPPW© promotes activities that are important features of the development process, namely cognitive readiness; interpersonal interaction directed at learning; and finally planning concrete actions to bring about change.

How Do the LPPW© Performance Standards Facilitate Leadership Development?

The pilot survey analysis also provided insights about the importance of including standards-based behaviors in the LPPW©. The tables below present these results comparing the data from the two largest and contextually different site administrations in New York City and Missouri.

Table 5 presents data from the summative survey that asked the extent to which principals agreed that the LPPW© performance standards facilitated productive *approaches to skill development*. The majority of respondents from both regions agreed that the standards facilitated self-assessment of current skills and behaviors; reflective conversations about being an instructional leader; productive dialog with their mentor/coach. The standards were also reported to facilitate the development of a plan to enhance their leadership skills and behaviors.

Tables 6 and 7 present results that explain how the standards guide the development of important leadership skills for New York City and Missouri respectively. New York City principals refer to the behavior standards to enhance their understanding of instructional leadership through active thinking and discussion with their mentor or coach. The LPPW© standards within the Management dimension also facilitate discussions about administration and management skills. The standards also cause principals to identify realistic development goals and the courses of action to achieve them. Missouri principals identify the same uses of the performance standards but with one exception—where a majority of the respondents agreed that the standards helped identify performance areas that needed further development.

Next, the summative survey asked about the possible ways that LPPW© use with a mentor or coach influenced behavior change. Behavior change is more likely to occur when principals recognize the instructional leadership behaviors they should perform, whether their current behaviors conform to these standards, and whether they are motivated to change the behaviors that are inconsistent with instructional leadership. Table 8 lists the percentage of principals, from Missouri and New York City, responding to the survey who agreed that mentoring or coaching with the LPPW© enabled principals to move towards productive behavior change.

TABLE 5. Survey Ratings About LPPW Performance Standards Facilitating Approaches to Skill Development

The Description of the Performance Standards Facilitates…	Missouri Principal % Agree to Strongly Agree (N=43)	NYC Principal % Agree to Strongly Agree (N=72)
Self-assessment of current skills and behaviors	97.7	86.1
The development of a plan to enhance leadership skills and behaviors	86	84.7
Productive dialog with my mentor/coach	93	88.8
Reflective conversations about being an instructional leader	93.1	91.6

TABLE 6. NY City Ratings About How LPPW Performance Standards Guide Development of Leadership Skills

The Description of the Performance Standards Facilitates…	NYC Principal % Agree to Strongly Agree (N=72)
Begin a discussion about administration and management skills	95.3
Cause me to begin a course of action to achieve realistic goals for leadership development	92.1
Cause me to actively think about how to be an instructional leader	92.0
Begin a discussion about instructional leadership	90.5
Help me understand what is required of effective instructional leaders	88.9

TABLE 7. Missouri Ratings About How LPPW Performance Standards Guide Development of Leadership Skills

The Description of the Performance Standards Facilitates…	Missouri Principal % Agree to Strongly Agree (N=43)
Help me understand what is required of effective instructional leaders	95.4
Cause me to actively think about how to be an instructional leader	95.3
Begin a discussion about instructional leadership	94.3
Begin a discussion about administration and management skills	94.3
Help identify performance areas that need further development	93.1

TABLE 8. Missouri and NY City Principals' Ratings About LPPW-Based Mentoring/Coaching Enabling Behavior Change

Using the LPPW with my mentor/coach…	Missouri Principal % Agree to Strongly Agree (N=43)	NYC Principal % Agree to Strongly Agree (N=72)
Enables me to identify the behaviors that I do perform which contribute to my performance as an instructional leader	93.0	90.5
Enables me to identify the behaviors that I should perform to enhance my performance as an instructional leader	86.1	87.3
Has motivated me to change how I perform my responsibilities as an instructional leader	65.2	79.3
Enables me to identify behaviors which I perform that interfere with my performance as an instructional leader	60.5	82.5

The results from this pilot test generated excitement among the LIG community at large. The pilot survey data produced persuasive evidence that the Leadership Performance Planning Worksheet was an effective coaching tool that structures productive conversations between principals and their mentors/coaches in service of developing instructional leadership capacity. Encouraged by the results, the NYC Leadership Academy decided to manage the expanded use, application, and evaluation of the LPPW© across the country. During the next year, work continued with seven of the eight original participants along with two new sites, Providence, Rhode Island, and Old Dominion University. The emerging network continued the original philosophy of the Wallace Foundation Leadership Issue Groups to expand learning by facilitating the sharing of effective practice across states and districts.

The LPPW© 2009 Pilot Test Results

The NYC Leadership Academy assumed responsibility for the 2009 pilot test. This second round of testing took into consideration that of the many "first adopters" were already expanding the application of the LPPW© in their leadership development programs. Sites were now expanding LPPW© use to aspiring principals, assistant principals, and experienced sitting principals in addition to early career principals. One site included other school administrators to include superintendents, assistant superintendents, special education directors, and career development directors. Over 740 school leaders and 238 mentors/coaches participated in this second round of pilot studies. The evaluation results for the LPPW© mirrored the 2008 results. In particular, most school leaders,[18] mentors, and coaches reported that the LPPW was most effective at facilitating reflection and discussion about instructional leadership and that similar leadership dimensions were the topics of discussion during mentoring/coaching sessions. It is noteworthy to report that the evaluation found that the prevalent leadership dimensions for mentoring and coaching were tied to the leader's position. Figure 4 displays the differentiation of development needs among four different types of school leaders.

The 2009 pilot test also surfaced that the LPPW©, in its current form, is designed best for the leadership challenges of aspiring principals, assistant principals, and sitting principals and has less utility for other school leaders. The test LPPW© applications with superintendents, assistant superintendents, special education directors, and career development directors produced lower ratings for the LPPW©'s general utility and specific ability to develop the leadership behaviors and skill demanded for their positions.

Top 3 Dimensions Listed

		First	Second	Third
Leaders were asked to list the three dimensions that they focused on most during their coaching or mentoring sessions.	Aspiring Leader	Personal Behavior	Communication	Student Learning
	Assistant Principal	Situational Problem Solving	Supervision of Staff	Management
	Principal*	Student Learning	Situational Problem Solving	Supervision of Staff
	Other School Administrator	Situational Problem Solving	Management	Supervision of Staff

*Does not include NYCLA principals because NYCLA principals were not asked to take the competencies that they targeted.

Figure 4. Top 3 LPPW Dimension Discussed During Mentoring/Coaching by Leader Role. 2009 Pilot Data.

The LPPW© Pilots Have Generated a Network of Users and AdditionalApplications

The positive outcomes of the 2008 and 2009 pilot tests have led to an expansion of users and important insights about the larger impact the LPPW© is having on principal leadership development programs. The NYC Leadership Academy reported that in 2010, there were 404 mentors and coaches using the LPPW© and 1121 school leaders, including teacher leaders and other administrators, using the LPPW© with mentoring and coaching to develop instructional leadership skills. User sites expanded to Florida, Fairfax County Virginia, Kansas, New York State, and in university programs in Illinois, Iowa, and Virginia. In total, school systems and universities in 11 states have incorporated the LPPW© into their leadership development programs. Potential and current LPPW© users explain that they are attracted to the tool's features of economy—through the emphasis on showstopper behaviors; precision—through the incorporation of performance based standards; and flexibility—through the range of leaders who have benefitted from using the LPPW© and the variety of ways leaders and their mentors/coaches can use the tool to facilitate instructional leadership development.

The breadth of LPPW© users and applications has surfaced the broader impact it is having on instructional leadership development programs. For example, the State of Missouri is providing evidence that the LPPW© is helping to structure aligned continuums of leadership development.

> Missouri's leadership development system is being designed to increase alignment between the core behaviors identified by the LPPW© and the content occurring in the seventeen preparatory institutions across the state that provide educational administration programs. The state will also increase alignment throughout aspiring principals' internship experience that links preparation to their initial practice. Their system will also increase the alignment needed in the evaluation mechanisms which assess the degree to which the leader is improving core leadership behavior addressed by the LPPW©. The alignment of the various components of the leadership system would provide a continuum of growth and development to Missouri's leaders. This continuum would especially be of assistance to those leaders working in schools and districts in most need of serious reform.

Another insight is that the LPPW© framework provides a common language for broader applications in states.

> For Kentucky, the LPPW© is central to the process of establishing a common language for on-going conversation and documentation in areas to include: (1) focusing on the critical leadership areas that principals need master in order to improve instruction in the context of the school's vision, mission, goals and challenges; (2) identifying one's own areas of strength and weakness and to record progress, and (3) discussing one's leadership behaviors and the outcomes they generate in order to create a purposeful, evidence based, growth and development strategy throughout a principal's career.
>
> Several Kentucky programs involving colleges and universities, school districts and schools have piloted the LPPW© with aspiring and sitting principals. Colleges and universities piloting the state's redesigned principal preparation program used the LPPW© to identify existing behaviors, knowledge and skills of aspiring candidates entering the redesigned program, at transition points and as an exit assessment to determine next steps in the candidates' professional growth for entry into the principalship. District instructional supervisors and instructional leadership teams are piloting the LPPW© to determine the behaviors, knowledge and skills of school leaders and instructional leadership teams and their capacity to improve student achievement and close achievement gaps. Schools in the School Administration Manager (SAM) Project* are piloting the LPPW© to determine principal growth needs for coaching teachers on improving classroom practice and providing highly effective teaching and learning for every student in every classroom every day.

LPPW© network members have also explained how the tool is being used to strengthen mentoring programs mandated by their states. Delaware is an example of a member employing this strategy.

Delaware, one of the recipients of the Race to the Top Grant, was one of the original users of the LPPW©. Administrator coaching is one of the pillars of their leadership development program. Delaware is creating a professional learning community of coaches, with the learning being both about current best practice in administration and about how to coach. Their coaches receive training provided by the NYC Leadership Academy that is grounded in the LPPW©. It emphasizes how to use the LPPW© with low inference data, listening skills (especially as opposed to coaching by telling war stories), and on developing skills and techniques used in coaching. Delaware's goals for integrating the LPPW© in their leadership development program are three-fold: (1) that coaches and mentors would use the LPPW© with their principals and assistant principals; (2) that principals and assistant principals use the LPPW© to analyze their work and for structuring their own professional development; and (3) that Department of Education decision makers recognize the LPPW© as a central organizing document for the work of coaching/mentoring new school administrators.

The successful LPPW© pilot results have also stimulated creation of new development programs within the network, such as in Rhode Island.

The Rhode Island Association of School Principals (RIASP), Rhode Island College and the Rhode Island Department of Education are jointly developing a coaching/mentoring program for new principals based on the design and current applications of the LPPW©. Their design, planned to develop exemplary school principals for the State of Rhode Island, includes providing regular coaching, a cohort model, expert speakers/trainers, and a dynamic professional development program. After reviewing the multi-state LPPW© pilot results, these institutions decided that the LPPW© should serve as an integral piece of this training. This program would require participation in four full-day workshops led by national experts on topics integral to school leadership and beginning the principalship, regular half-day cohort meetings, and regular one-on-one coaching meetings. Members of each cohort would participate in this program during their first three years in the principalship working with the same coach/mentor throughout the three years.

Moreover, some members in the user network, working closely with the NYC Leadership Academy, have generated a series of LPPW©-based tools to further enhance leadership development for school leaders. For example, the State of Missouri developed and tested an on-line version of the LPPW© and then collaborated with the NYC Leadership Academy to create the content for on-line coaching modules to support mentors and coaches state-wide. Recently, Missouri used the LPPW© as a framework for a new 360-degree feedback survey for principals.

The NYC Leadership Academy trains school districts, state education departments and others on how to use and customize the Leadership Performance Planning Worksheet to address their own unique educational context and specific needs. For more information, visit the NYC Leadership Academy website at http://www.nycleadership academy.org.

In all, the LPPW© is rapidly becoming established as a foundation for standards-based leadership development programs and tools. Past pilot tests, current usage, and the development of new applications and tools suggests that the LPPW© has the potential to anchor a school systems leadership continuum by connecting principal preparation programs, on the job support, and ultimately principal evaluation systems. The LPPW© framework provides the capability to identify leadership development needs within specific school district or regional contexts. The identification of these needs can inform the curricula and developmental experiences in principal preparation programs. In turn, the LPPW© and mentoring/coaching oriented to standards based instructional leadership behaviors can enable alignment between development programs and principals' evaluation systems.

Conclusion: The LPPW© Is Contributing to the Leadership Capacity of Early Career Principals

Schools need talented principals who can perform as effective instructional leaders. Yet early career principals face many challenges to quickly develop their capacity as effective leaders while facing the daily challenges in their schools. Their development needs are real and the consequences for their poor performance affect their students, their staff, and ultimately their career as a school leader. The goal of this chapter was to present the story of the development and successful applications of the Leadership Performance Planning Worksheet, a tool to address principals' development needs so they can improve student achievement in their schools. This account illustrates how true collaboration among a small number of professionals can create something of value for the profession at large. The LPPW©'s features and its reported value should encourage school leaders, mentors, and coaches to further explore this focused, standards-based approach to assist early career principals in successfully leading their schools. The description of the LPPW©'s design, development, and pilot tests presents the method behind the tool's creation and reactions from users in order to establish that the tool is consistent with the theory and current taxonomy of instructional leadership. Finally, the chapter described some of the new LPPW© applications that have emerged from current users to illustrate the broader impact the LPPW© has and is expected to have on leadership development programs for school leaders. In total, the LPPW© has engendered a productive dialog about early career principals' needs for leadership development through mentoring and coaching and a series of initiatives among LPPW© users to address these needs. Much has been accomplished in a short period of time. It is envisioned that the Leadership Performance Planning Worksheet and the work of those who use it will continue contributing to the development of our nation's instructional leaders.

Notes

1. Principal attrition studies conducted jointly by researchers at The University of Texas at Austin, Bank Street College, and the University Council for Education Administration (UCEA, 2008) found that only half of newly hired principals stay on the job for three years and 20 percent of newly hired principals at secondary schools with a high proportion of low-income students leave after a year.
2. Launched in 2003, the NYC Leadership Academy (http://www.nycleadershipacademy.org) develops and supports effective school leaders, with a focus on preparing principals to lead New York City's high-need schools. The NYC Leadership Academy provides the NYC-DOE and other school districts and state education departments across the country with strategic consulting and leadership advisory services.
3. The historical summaries of the emergence of these professions are found in *Education for the Professions of Medicine, Law, Theology, and Social Welfare* by E.C. Hughes, B. Thorne, A.M. DeBaggis, A. Gurin, and D. Williams (1973).
4. Eby, L.T., Allen, T.D., Evans, S.C., Ng, T., and DuBois, D. (2008).
5. As a standards-based approach, FCB Coaching can be applied to a variety of performance standards. This chapter only discusses its use with the LPPW© behavior standards.
6. Some school districts have elected for additional support for their mentoring/coaching programs after this initial training.
7. Based on written feedback in 2010 to the NYC Leadership Academy from then current LPPW© user states and districts.
8. Source: NYC Leadership Academy multi-site 2008 and 2009/2010 LPPW© user surveys.
9. Results are from the 2008 LPPW© summative evaluation.
10. Participating states included Delaware, Iowa, Kentucky, Missouri, Ohio, Rhode Island, Texas, and Wisconsin. Participating school districts included Appoquinimink, DE, Ceasar Rodney, DE, Atlanta, GA, Canton Public Schools, OH, Eugene School District 4J, OR, Portland Public Schools, OR, Jefferson County Public Schools, KY, New York City (represented by the NYC Leadership Academy, and New York City Region One), Providence, RI, Springfield Public Schools, IL, Springfield, MA, and St Louis, MO.
11. A 1970s Air Force study of combat pilot performance challenges in high risk environments and the subsequent development intervention stimulated the rationale behind the LPPW© showstopper behavior approach. The Air Force analysis showed that a pilot's chances of survival in combat dramatically increased after successfully completing 10 combat missions. Specialized training was created in 1975 to offer US pilots the opportunity to fly those 10 realistically simulated combat missions in a safe training environment to increase the likelihood of their success in the actual high risk environment. This approach to preparation is actually echoed every time we take a commercial airline flight. While airline flight crews receive extensive training for high risk–high consequence situations like in-flight emergencies passengers are presented with the most critical set of behaviors through briefings and brochures that will maximize the chances for survival in this novel high risk situation.
12. A copy of the Kentucky Standards and Indicators for School Improvement can be found at: www.education.ky.gov/KDE/HomePageRepositiry/Publications/KDE+Bookstore.htm.
13. Information about DPAS II can be found at: http://www.doe.k12.de.us/csa/dpasii/default.shtml.

14. The Wallace Foundation Driver Behaviors are a set of instructional leadership behaviors that serve as strategic levers for the larger array of skills needed to develop and implement key changes resulting in improved student achievement. They were identified by a panel of experts convened to better understand leadership effectiveness and how to best assess the performance of current and aspiring principals and superintendents.
15. This level of this measurement provided information about the usefulness of the LPPW framework without violating the confidentiality of the mentoring conversation that might occur if specific behaviors were identified in the survey. The survey also provided write-in blocks for participants to list dimensions or topics that were discussed but couldn't be categorized within the LPPW© framework.
16. The survey response rates varied each month and across each site. To present a balanced presentation of the survey responses, the analysis results are presented for the two largest pilots in New York City and the State of Missouri. Monthly survey results are presented from the end of the April 2008 survey.
17. The Likert response scale anchors were 1=Strongly Disagree; 2=Disagree; 3=Neither Agree nor Disagree; 4=Agree; 5=Strongly Disagree.
18. School leaders include aspiring principals, assistant principals, and sitting principals.

Appendix

Sample Pages from the Leadership Performance Planning Worksheet

NYC Leadership Academy
The Leadership Performance Planning Worksheet

LPPW

Dear School Leader,

Welcome to the Leadership Performance Planning Worksheet (LPPW), a tool designed to help early-career school leaders improve student progress through effective instructional leadership.

Developed by the NYC Leadership Academy in consultation with The Wallace Foundation and the state education departments of Delaware, Missouri and Kentucky, the LPPW reflects a thorough review and synthesis of principal leadership standards used nationally, including ISLLC. It is grounded in the belief that focused work on a subset of clearly defined school leadership competencies helps early-career school leaders promote student success. The LPPW contains eight leadership dimensions — (1) Personal Behavior, (2) Resilience, (3) Communication, (4) Student Performance, (5) Situational Problem Solving, (6) Learning, (7) Supervision of Staff, and (8) Management — and identifies core leadership behaviors critical to each. These core behaviors address the day-to-day challenges of school leadership and are responsive to a wide range of principal performance standards. The goal of the use of the LPPW is to ground the coaching (mentoring) relationship in concrete skill and knowledge development and set actionable goals.

School Leaders:

• Review the LPPW with your coach (mentor) early in the school year to identify the leadership dimensions you need to strengthen to improve student learning within the context of your school. You and your coach (mentor) should discuss your leadership behaviors and the outcomes they generate.

• Together with your coach (mentor), develop purposeful, evidence-based, leadership support and development strategies for your work together.

• Make the LPPW a living document by discussing and charting your leadership growth and progress regularly.

Coaches/Mentors:

• At the beginning of the school year, communicate to the school leaders you coach (mentor) that the LPPW review process is an opportunity for growth, and create an environment that enables them to be reflective and open about their strengths and weaknesses.

• Use the LPPW throughout the year to establish a common language for your coaching (mentoring) relationship and to focus your work together on concrete knowledge and skills development.

Copyright © 2010 by NYC Leadership Academy, Inc., Long Island City, NY. All rights reserved.

Communication

Progress Update   **3.0**

Leadership Dimension	Behaviors That Meet the Standard
3.1 Communicates in ways that reflect careful analysis and the ability to listen ◯ Meets Standard ◯ Approaches Standard	⇨ Leader's communication is clear and appropriate for each audience and matches media with message ⇨ Leader understands cultural patterns and adjusts his/her communication style accordingly. ⇨ Leader attends and responds to subtle nonverbal cues in others. ⇨ Leader consistently listens and checks for mutual understanding. ⇨ Leader does not avoid difficult issues; he/she deals with them honestly and directly by using low-inference data and providing examples. ⇨ Leader actively pursues disconfirming evidence when drawing conclusions.
3.2 Promotes the success of all students through consistently direct communication with students and by understanding and responding to their broader political, socio-economic and cultural contexts ◯ Meets Standard ◯ Approaches Standard	⇨ Leader interacts with student body on a consistent basis. ⇨ Leader models behavior for staff and encourages staff to engage in purposeful solicitation of students' ideas regarding successful classroom approaches to teaching and learning.
3.3 Collaborates with staff ◯ Meets Standard ◯ Approaches Standard	⇨ Leader knows all staff members and publicly acknowledges individual contributions. ⇨ Leader models, encourages, and reinforces efficacy in individuals to produce results and persevere even when internal and external difficulties interfere with the achievement of strategic goals. ⇨ Leader generates a sense of urgency by aligning the energy of others in pursuit of strategic goals.

Areas for Improvement

Next Steps

Communication

Progress Update   **3.0**

Leadership Dimension	Behaviors That Meet the Standard
3.4 Collaborates with families and community ◯ Meets Standard ◯ Approaches Standard	⇨ Leader establishes interactions with families and community members. ⇨ Leader develops clear process for gathering and transmitting information from and to families, with awareness of what families in the community do and do not have access to, in terms of electronic communication. ⇨ Leader is able to identify all stakeholders involved in the school. ⇨ Leader's presentations to parents and community members are organized and logical, include analysis, and are delivered in an engaging and dynamic style. ⇨ Leader provides clear, specific responses to questions. ⇨ Leader accords individuals consistent amounts of attention, time, and respect. ⇨ Leader demonstrates awareness of the public and political nature of his/her position, and applies explicit process for engaging public in controversial issues.
3.5 Appreciates rituals and routines as enablers of vision ◯ Meets Standard ◯ Approaches Standard	⇨ Leader develops consistent patterns of rituals and routines, and understands how they enable the leader's vision and strategic priorities. ⇨ Leader understands and honors the organization's existing culture of rituals and routines. ⇨ Leader has clearly established boundaries for behaviors that are considered fixed and immovable.

Areas for Improvement

Next Steps

THE LEADERSHIP PERFORMANCE PLANNING WORKSHEET (LPPW)

Student Performance

4.0

Leadership Dimension	Behaviors That Meet the Standard
4.1 Plans and sets goals for student performance ○ Meets Standard ○ Approaches Standard	⇨ Leader sets goals that are within the zone of proximal development for students, teachers, and the organization.
4.2 Recruits and retains qualified staff ○ Meets Standard ○ Approaches Standard	⇨ Leader develops and implements plan to attract and retain qualified teachers and staff.
4.3 Ensures continual improvement for students, teachers, and the organization ○ Meets Standard ○ Approaches Standard	⇨ Leader possesses working knowledge of current curricular initiatives, approaches to content, and differentiated instructional design including the options offered by technology. ⇨ Leader understands, articulates, and implements effective instructional strategies and evaluates their effectiveness. ⇨ Leader focuses staff meetings on instructional issues.
4.4 Demonstrates understanding of the relationship between assessment, standards, and curriculum ○ Meets Standard ○ Approaches Standard	⇨ Leader facilitates the analysis and alignment of assessment tools and the curriculum. ⇨ Leader aligns school's organizational structure, resources, and instructional provisions to address learning standards and leverage student learning.
4.5 Reports student achievement results transparently ○ Meets Standard ○ Approaches Standard	⇨ Leader gathers and uses multiple indicators of student success that reveal patterns, trends, and insights. ⇨ Leader creates systems to make school data accessible and understood by staff, families, and students.

Progress Update

Areas for Improvement

Next Steps

Student Performance

4.0

Leadership Dimension	Behaviors That Meet the Standard
4.6 Uses student performance data to make instructional leadership decisions ○ Meets Standard ○ Approaches Standard	⇨ Leader uses student performance data to guide decisions about instruction. ⇨ Leader provides staff with framework for looking at student work to identify instructional next steps for teachers and students.
4.7 Implements a systemic approach for struggling learners and special populations and critically reviews all approaches for effectiveness ○ Meets Standard ○ Approaches Standard	⇨ Leader monitors intervention strategies for effectiveness and adjusts them to accelerate learning. ⇨ Leader includes specialized knowledge and skills into general practice.
4.8 Continually reads and interprets the environment to identify patterns in student performance indicators ○ Meets Standard ○ Approaches Standard	⇨ Leader uses a multi-dimensional environmental analysis of student performance indicators. Diagnosis is ongoing.

Progress Update

Areas for Improvement

Next Steps

Author's Note

The NYC Leadership Academy trains school leaders, state education department personnel, and others on how to use and customize the Leadership Performance Planning Worksheet to address their own unique educational context and specific needs. For more information, visit the NYC Leadership Academy website at http://www.nycleadershipacademy.org.

References

Eby, L.T., Allen, T.D., Evans, S.C., Ng, T., and DuBois, D. (2008). Does Mentoring Matter? A Multidisciplinary Meta-Analysis Comparing Mentored and Non-Mentored Individuals. *Journal of Vocational Behavior, 72*(2), 254–267.

Hallinger, P., and Heck, R. (1998). Exploring the Principal's Contribution to School Effectiveness: 1980–1995. *School Effectiveness and School Improvement, 9*(2), 157–191.

Hughes, E.C., Thorne, B., DeBaggis, A.M., Gurin, A., and Williams, D. (1973). *Education for the Professions of Medicine, Law, Theology, and Social Welfare.* New York: McGraw-Hill.

Leithwood, K.K., Seashore, L.K., Anderson, S., and Wahlstrom, K. (2004). *How Leadership Influences Student Learning: A Review of Research for the Learning from Leadership Project.* New York: The Wallace Foundation.

Louis, K.S., Leithwood, K., Wahlstrom, K.L., and Anderson, S.E. (2010). *Learning from Leadership: Investigating the Links to Improved Student Learning: Final Report of Research to the Wallace Foundation. Duluth:* University of Minnesota, Center for Applied Research and Educational Improvement.

Mitgang, L.D., Mattis, M.C., and Spiro, J. (2007). *Getting Principal Mentoring Right: Lessons from the Field.* New York: The Wallace Foundation. Available at www.wallacefoundation.org

UCEA. (2008).*Implications from UCEA: The Revolving Door of the Principalship.* Austin: The University of Texas at Austin. Retrieved April 14, 2011, from www.ucea.org

Villani, S. (2006). *Mentoring and Induction Programs That Support New Principals.* Thousand Oaks, CA: Corwin Press.

• 8 •

The SAM Process

Changing Principals and Their Relationship with Teachers via Time/Task Analysis™ and TimeTrack™

MARK SHELLINGER
DIRECTOR, NATIONAL SAM INNOVATION PROJECT

"What would you do with fifty-five more days of instructional leadership time every year? As a principal, could you improve teaching and learning?" This is the question the National SAM Innovation Project asks every principal interested in beginning the process. After the first year of SAM work, the average principal has gained the equivalent of 27 extra days of instructional leadership time. After three years, the gain in time averages 55 days (Turnbull, Arcaira, & Sinclair, 2009, 2011; see results section, below).

Principals generally accept the notion that they are instructional leaders. Few school leaders argue with research correlating principal instructional leadership to improvements in teaching and student achievement. Leithwood, Louis, Anderson and Wahlstrom's (2004) landmark finding, that instructional leadership affects student achievement second only to the effects of teachers, is widely accepted yet generally ignored.

Why? Principals tend to do, and be, what they've seen. What they've experienced are principals who were administrative managers juggling dozens of activities and tasks to keep a school functioning. Their work can be described in two words: *interrupt driven*. A brief look at a principal's daily calendar makes it clear that tasks are rarely scheduled in advance. Instead, principals generally go with the flow as they deal with whatever comes at them throughout the day. Few principals would allow a teacher to dispense with lesson plans, but interrupt driven work is the norm for principals. For many in a school community, it is a leap of faith that a principal should, or even could, be a positive force in improving teaching and learning.

Figure 1 displays the School Administration Manger (SAM) Project logic model depicting the progression of project activities to project outcomes.

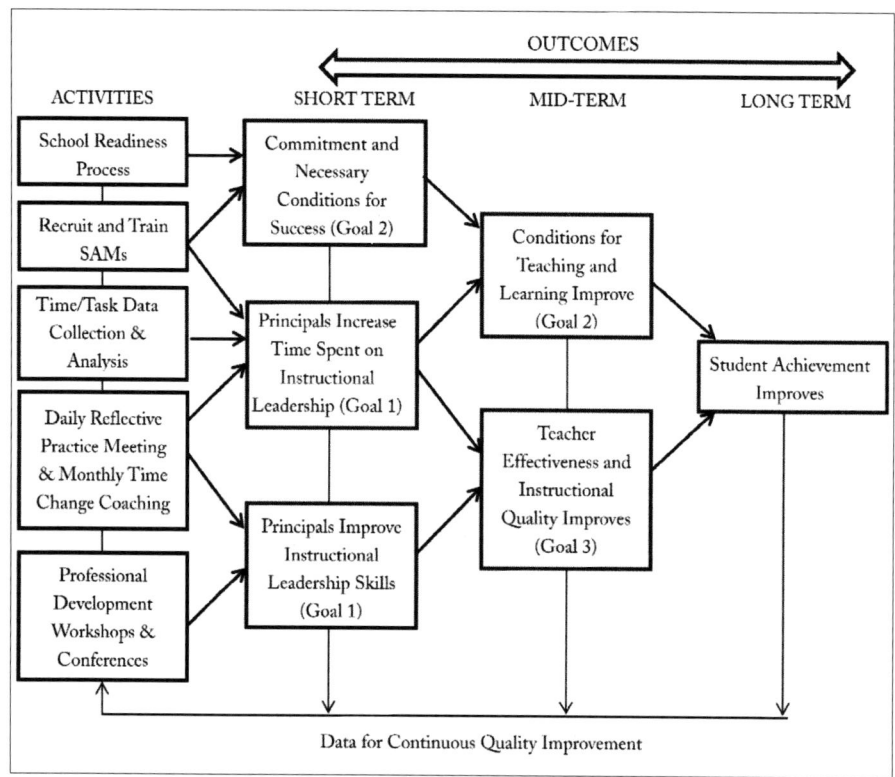

Figure 1. SAM Project Logic Model.

Principals' conflicting priorities of management and instructional leadership have implications for schools nationwide. Greater state and federal demands for improvement place ever-higher expectations on school leaders. As Walker (2009) observed, there has been a great deal of focus on school reform and the influence of the principal, yet few resources have been made available to assist the school leader; the resulting job is overwhelming.

The SAM process changes the status quo. It relies on the use of principal time data and a series of tools to refocus the principal's work and alter the expectations of teachers and parents. After a few months, SAM principals are spending the majority of the day in scheduled activities directly connected with improving teaching and learning. Relationships between principals and teachers improve and principals become closely connected to the work in each classroom. Accountability increases as instructional practices grow stronger.

The average US principal spends less than 32% of the day on teaching and learning (Turnbull et al., 2009). SAM principals spend the majority of their time improving teaching and learning by working with a SAM, School Administration Manager, a person trained in business skills or a current staff member. The SAM and principal schedule instructional leadership work in advance and begin distributing management duties. Many principals select two or three staff members to assist in this role. SAM coaches, trained by National SAM Innovation Project (NSIP), work with the principal and SAM to increase the time spent on instructional leadership and consider effectiveness. Reflective practice is a key element of this process and leads to a far more collegial relationship between administrators, teachers and parents.

History

The SAM process was initially funded by the Wallace Foundation as the Alternative School Administration Study (ASAS). As a former principal and superintendent, I was interested in determining how principals spent their time and if it would be possible to make instructional leadership the priority or the majority of time spent in a day. The initial study used a series of tools I created tied with coaching and professional development support. ASAS results were promising. All of the randomly selected principals increased instructional time and exceeded 60% of day/year. Additionally, rate of gain in student achievement significantly outpaced that of control schools (Shellinger, 2005).

The Wallace Foundation supported replication and development of the SAM professional development process until July 1, 2010. Extensive testing of the tools, and other SAM process elements, determined that when used separately they did not have an impact on change of principal practice. It was the use of the tools and coaching support, in an *integrated manner*, that consistently worked. The Foundation assisted with the creation of a non-profit, NSIP, to provide SAM implementation and support services for schools, districts and states through a fee-for-service structure. NSIP contracts with individual schools, districts and states to provide the SAM process. The tools Time/Task Analysis, TimeTrack, First Responders and the name SAM are trademark and copyright protected to ensure fidelity of use.

Tools

The National SAM Innovation Project uses a unique set of tools to track the principal's use of time and create systems to distribute management tasks. These tools help principals focus on collaborative work with teachers and parents to improve student learning.

The project developed and tested the *Time/Task Analysis* data collection system to quantify how principals spent time. Trained data collectors (retired principals and professors) "shadow" principals for five school days, and record data every five minutes following a strict protocol. Time/Task Analysis separates principal activities into three categories: primarily *instructional*, primarily *managerial*, and primarily *personal*. Use of the term "primarily" allows for categorization of activities that may overlap or be connected. After determining a category, the data collector then selects from a list of 25 management and instructional leadership descriptors. This gives the principal a detailed report on how time is currently spent during the school day.

Once collected and categorized, these data provide a baseline that is used for comparative purposes as the process is repeated every 12 months. Figure 2 is a sample Time/Task Analysis baseline report. Inter-rater reliability for the data collection system exceeds 90%.

Principals and SAMs use the baseline data to begin a daily process of scheduling their time using *TimeTrack* software, also developed for the project. This creates a lesson plan for the principal's work to improve instructional practice, increase parent engagement and improve the rate of student achievement.

Baseline

Management	72.6%
Instruction	23.6%
Personal	3.8%
Non Instruction	76.4%
Instruction	23.6%

High School - Principal

Management Descriptors	% of Time
Student Supervision	10.6%
Student Discipline	0.2%
Employee Supervision	4.3%
Employee Discipline	0.2%
Office Work Prep	39.8%
Building management	0.4%
Parents / Guardians	0.6%
Decision making groups, meetings	5.3%
District: meetings, Supervisors	6.0%
External: Officials, others	5.1%
Celebration	0.0%
Instructional Descriptors	**% of Time**
Student Supervision	0.4%
Work with students	0.2%
Employee Supervision	0.0%
Office Work/ Prep	4.7%
Observation, walk through	12.6%
Feedback to teacher	0.9%
Parents / guardians	0.0%
Decision making groups, meetings	1.7%
District: Meetings, supervision	1.7%
External: Officials, others	0.2%
Teaching / Modeling	0.0%
Professional Development	0.0%
Planning, Curriculum, assessment	1.3%
Celebration	0.0%

National SAM Innovation Project

Figure 2. Sample Time/Task Analysis Baseline Report.

TimeTrack becomes a running record of the principal's progress in increasing time spent on instructional leadership. It provides detailed reports on time spent each day, week, month and year on each of the 25 management and instructional descriptors. TimeTrack also provides the principal and SAM with detailed information concerning time spent with individual teachers and groups. This information is used during the *TimeTrack Daily Meeting* to consider if the amount of time spent is achieving the desired result in terms of change of teaching practice. If not, what else should the principal do?

The Time/Track Daily Meeting is initially a review of the principal's progress in increasing time spent on instructional leadership. The meeting also is a vehicle to mitigate management interruptions and develop new systems within the school.

Time Change Coaches, trained in a blended reflective practice process, borrowed from the business world and "blended coaching" (Bloom, Castagna, Moir, & Warren, 2005), help principals, SAMs and teachers change the use of time and continuously question the impact. *Professional Development* needs are identified by the Time Change Coach, principal and SAM. The project works to provide opportunities for SAMs and principals across the country to collaborate and learn from each other. Time/Task Analysis, or shadowing, is repeated annually.

Principals, SAMs and coaches use the annual Time/Task Analysis data as a summative evaluation on the overall increase in instructional leadership time. The coach asks the principal to assess the impact of the time change in order to connect with the desired result: change of teacher practice. This often leads the principal to consult with teachers. In the example above, teachers were appreciative of the time the principal was spending and suggested he consider starting a peer observation option where he would observe a teacher with several other teacher colleagues and then facilitate a conversation afterwards. This suggestion led to a voluntary program at the school and a dramatic increase in instructional time (see third year Time/Task Analysis data in Figure 3).

The Time/Task Analysis tool was developed and tested in Jefferson County Public Schools, Louisville, Kentucky. The objective was to develop a data collection system that would accomplish two goals:

1. Capture how a principal spends his/her work days.
2. Have a high degree of inter-rater reliability.

Developing clear definitions for the categories and descriptors was achieved through a series of focus group meetings with principals and university education leadership professors. A strict data collection protocol was established to mitigate the presence of the data collector. This required the principal to notify, prior to the collector's arrival, students, parents and staff of the purpose and restrictions. The pro-

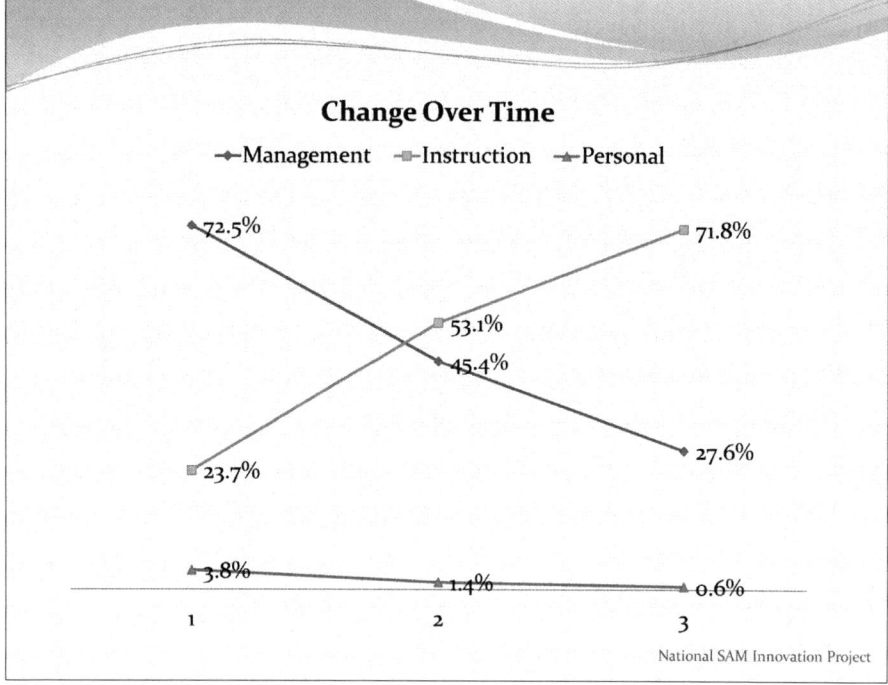

Figure 3. Change Over Three Years.

tocol requires the collector to be as "invisible" as possible, prohibiting direct eye contact or conversation with anyone during collection.

Data collectors must complete a series of certification steps to ensure inter-rater reliability including video based tests. Once certified, data collectors complete online refresher training, and another test, prior to assignment in the field to reach 95% inter-rater reliability.

The Time/Task Analysis tool has been administered over 3,000 times in 17 states and the District of Columbia. Principals consistently report that they find the data both believable and useful. The categories and descriptors have been aligned with all major systems of sorting principal behaviors and Vanderbilt Assessment of Leadership in Education (VAL-ED).

Results

An independent, external evaluation demonstrates that the SAM process works: the change of principal time spent on instructional leadership aimed at increasing teacher efficacy is statistically significant (Turnbull, Arcaira, & Sinclair, 2009). Joseph Murphy, a faculty member at Vanderbilt University, also commented that "the

SAM Project is the first time we can demonstrate a change of principal practice, increasing time spent on instructional leadership, in the history of educational leader preparation and development" (personal communication).

The 2009 external evaluation led to a follow-up study by Policy Studies Associates (PSA) with a larger group of participating SAM schools. The comprehensive study found that the average gain in instructional leadership time for participating principals was five hours and fifty-seven more minutes every week, the equivalent of twenty-seven extra days each year. By the end of the second year of SAM work, the gain increased to eight hours and thirty more minutes every week, the equivalent of thirty-eight extra days each year. By the end of the third year of participation the gain in instructional leadership time increased to twelve hours and twenty more minutes every week, the equivalent of fifty-five extra days each year.

The study also determined:

- The SAM process does what it is designed to do: increases principal time spent on instructional leadership.
- The increase in time is significant—adding the equivalent of more than one day per week in instructional leadership time.
- The increase of instructional time occurs at all levels: elementary, middle and high.
- The process works equally well in schools where a new staff member is hired to be the "SAM" and at schools where existing staff members take on the SAM duties.
- The longer the principal participates the greater the instructional time increase.

The researchers from Policy Studies Associates interviewed principals and SAMs across the country. From Turnbull et al.'s (2011, pp. 36–37) report, the following excerpt illustrates a principal's perception on what instructional leadership is, the need for increasing time on instructional leadership, and the tools that helped:

Reflecting on the comments of some of the principals and SAMs we visited, we can identify ways in which principals were trying to bring about potentially far-reaching school improvement, and how they found support for their efforts. Some principals already had strong leadership knowledge and skills; most told us that they wanted to learn to do better. We found examples of principals reflecting on their own practice and finding help in setting their own directions for new ways of working.

One principal who was new to the project was a veteran principal. Asked for a definition of instructional leadership, this principal took a deep breath and offered the following capsule vision extemporaneously:

Principal Model 1: The bottom line is, are the teachers moving the students forward? Instructional leadership, I think, needs to be centered on students—where they are and where they get to in a year's time. So instructional leadership is helping teachers use data to drive their instruction, helping them understand multiple forms of assessment...and then how you use those assessments to adjust the instruction. How you promote teacher dialogue and reflection. How you support them through professional development. How you make sure the professional development is happening in the classroom, which means multiple visits to classrooms....Then when you have teachers who need additional support it's adding more time in your visits and targeting in whatever the rubrics are....You have the professional learning communities that are occurring to support that, and you are always looking at the data and the problems of the kids.

This was a person who had a clear idea of what to do as an instructional leader and simply needed more hours in the day to do it. Adding a SAM to the building provided needed support. With a SAM who was eager to solve problems of all kinds in the running of the school, the principal was able to find some of those hours.

NSIP Scale and Sustainability

While the SAM professional development model uses standardized tools, processes, and procedures to manage and focus school leaders' time and effort, it also allows for tailored implementation to fit the specific needs and resources of each school. The National SAM Innovation Project has experienced steady controlled growth over the past eight years, developing a strong set of implementation and replication partners in seven states. The partners collaborate to protect program fidelity and provide a means for growth.

Sustaining SAM work is of critical importance to NSIP and its state level implementation partners. A fee-for-service structure was created with assistance from FSG Social Impact Advisors and the Non-profit Finance Fund. FY11 was the first year without grant support for the national and state SAM projects and served as a sink-or-swim fiscal test. Both the national and state organizations finished with positive fund balances, expanded SAM schools and improved services including significant upgrades to the online TimeTrack calendar tool. The fiscal model used by NSIP allows the cost for SAM schools to decrease each year as local capacity is established for each of the six implementation and support components are established.

Visit the NSIP website to learn how to get started with the SAM process: www.SamsConnect.com.

References

Bloom, G., Castagna, C.L., Moir, E.R., & Warren, B. (Eds.). (2005). *Blended coaching: Skills and strategies to support principal development.* Thousand Oaks, CA: Corwin.

Leithwood, K., Louis, K. S., Anderson, S., & Wahlstrom, K. (2004). *How leadership influences student learning.* Minneapolis, MN: University of Minnesota, Center for Applied Research and Educational Improvement.

Shellinger, M. (2005). *Alternative school administration study. Jefferson County Public Schools, Leading Education Achievement in Districts, a Wallace Foundation Initiative.* Retrieved from http://www.eric.ed.gov/ERICWebPortal/contentdelivery/servlet/ERICServlet?accno=ED490688

Turnbull, B., Arcaira, E., & Sinclair, B. (2009). *Evaluation of the National SAM Innovation Project.* Washington, DC: Policy Studies Associates.

Turnbull, B., Arcaira, E., & Sinclair, B. (2011). *Implementation of the National SAM Innovation Project: A comparison of project designs.* Washington, DC: Policy Studies Associates.

Walker, J. (2009). Super heroes or SAMs? A change in practice for a new kind of educational leader. *NCPEA Education Leadership Review, 10*(1), 67–73.

• 9 •
SREB's *High Schools That Work* School Improvement Model

JAMES E. BOTTOMS & PAULA E. EGELSON

The aim of *High Schools That Work* is to graduate students who are prepared for college or careers by creating a culture of high expectations, relevant school learning experiences, and a focus on continually improving high schools.

Introduction—Tools

As a part of the *High Schools That Work* school improvement model, the status and progress of participating high schools are examined by reviewing the results of student assessments in core academic areas and analyzing the results of teacher and student surveys focused on instruction and school culture. The two tools—*Using the HSTW Assessment to Improve Student Achievement and Readiness for College and Careers: A Guide and Workbook for* HSTW *Sites*, a workbook, and *Establishing Benchmarks for New and Maturing* HSTW *Sites*, a framework—found at the conclusion of this chapter can assist secondary school leadership teams in setting student achievement goals and benchmarking instructional practices and support for students.

The Context

High Schools That Work (*HSTW*) is a large-scale high school improvement effort that was developed by the Southern Regional Education Board (SREB). It focuses on how secondary students are educated and prepared for careers or college. This school improvement process includes state leaders, district personnel, community members, school administrators, teachers, students, and family members. The model can be replicated; its data can be used for continual improvement; the professional development opportunities are comprehensive; and technical assistance is available to participating schools.

HSTW was originally implemented in the Southeast as a program to strengthen the academic and career preparation of students enrolled in the general and vocational track in the late 1980s; it evolved into a comprehensive reform model in the 1990s that included both high schools and middle schools. In the early 21st century, the model has continued to expand with new resources and professional development opportunities. From the very beginning, the 10 Key Practices and Key Conditions were in place. The model involves changing school curricular efforts through policy at the state level and includes district and school educators participating in making those changes. The mission of *HSTW* has always been to advance best practices for the improvement of high schools, but also to inform state policy in this area.

HSTW Development Process—1985 to Today

In the 1980s state leaders across the Southeast were concerned about the lack of rigor of many high school courses. During this time period, the SREB Commission for Educational Quality addressed the substandard high school course options of general and vocational students by issuing a statement that academic skills must be of greatest concern for career, technical, and academic educators.

The SREB Commission for Educational Quality also created *Ten Recommendations for Improving Secondary Vocational Education* (1985). A group of state career and technical leaders approached SREB to take the lead in developing the ideas contained in the *Ten Recommendations* document and create an SREB-State Vocational Education Consortium. A plan emerged for a state network of high schools—called *High Schools That Work*—to build a partnership between SREB and the states. These efforts were unique because of the inclusion of policymakers and state departments of education in the school improvement process.

Phase I of *HSTW* Development—The *HSTW* Consortium of the 1980s started with six initial change strategies for high schools. They included site development workshops, technical assistance visits, summer staff development workshops, continual data collection, state accountability systems, and communication with policymakers.

Phase II of *HSTW* Development—The scaling up of *HSTW* began in 1992 with a six-year grant from the Wallace Foundation. This was an effective scale up of *HSTW* because of a clear set of goals, key practices, and conditions that made up a comprehensive framework for high schools; there was a set of services to assist schools in implementing the framework; there was a method for assessing student achievement; and there was a way of informing policymakers about progress.

Phase III of *HSTW* Development—The late 1990s was the beginning of Phase III *HSTW* development. At this time, *Making Middle Grades Work* (*MMGW*) was created to focus on improving instruction and grade transitions in the sixth, seventh, and eighth grades. The *MMGW* services are similar to what is provided with *HSTW*.

Phase IV of *HSTW* Development—At the beginning of the 21st century *HSTW* began a new phase of development. *Technology Centers That Work* (*TCTW*) was created, teaching techniques were embedded into reading and writing standards for all high school courses including career tech education, and the new rigorous career tech curriculum, *Preparation for Tomorrow*, was developed. The other big area of development was the creation of leadership materials and professional development to support principals as instructional leaders.

The number of *HSTW* sites increased from 60 in 1992 to over 700 in 1997, while the number of states increased from 13 in 1987 to 21 in 1997. Today there are more than 1,200 *HSTW* schools in 30 states.

The *HSTW* School Improvement Model

HSTW is a reform model that is teacher driven. Once 85% of a school faculty has agreed to use *HSTW* as a reform model, a contractual agreement is reached between SREB and the school. A Technical Assistance Visit (an internal and external evaluation) occurs at the school. The findings of the Technical Assistance Visit (TAV) form the School Improvement Plan for the school. Faculty members at the participating school are then a part of focus teams, which are issues-driven implementation groups. Focus group results pave the way for organizational and instructional change in the school. The *HSTW* model includes ten Key Practices that are best practices for high schools. Educators decide which one of these practices they want to focus on to improve their schools. Adaption of the model by schools is acceptable as long as high expectations are in place. Once the school needs have been established, SREB connects the school with the appropriate professional development. An SREB coach is assigned to the school to support the reform efforts and work with the school leadership team. *HSTW* assessments are administered to students, and surveys are administered to teachers and students to indicate progress and fidelity of implementation.

Ten Key Practices of SREB *HSTW* School Improvement Model and the Literature Base

The following are the SREB *HSTW* ten key practices that are foundational to the *HSTW* reform model. The practices are listed below with the accompanying literature base.

1. High Expectations: *Motivate more students to meet high expectations by integrating high expectations into classroom practices and providing frequent feedback. All students can learn in spite of their learning style.*
   Selected research that supports this key practice:
   - Schools that established high expectations for all students—and provided the support necessary to achieve these expectations—had higher rates of academic success than schools that had not established them (Edmonds, 1979; Rutter et al., 1979).
   - Rutter and his research team's (1979) findings of at-risk schools in London showed considerable differences in successful and unsuccessful schools' rates of student delinquency, unacceptable behavior, attendance, and academic success even after controlling for family risk factors. The successful schools placed emphasis on academics, clear expectations and regulations, high levels of student participation, and included a variety of resources for students.
   - Research showed that students who were perceived to be of low ability were given fewer opportunities to learn new material, asked less high-level questions, given shorter questions and less informative feedback, praised less and called on less frequently, and given less time to respond than students who were considered high in ability (Cotton, 1989).
   - Kathleen Cotton's (2003) review of principal essential traits and behaviors for school success research noted that one of the 26 was high expectations of students.
   - Idorenyin and Pitts (2005) found that teacher expectations played a critical role in the level of achievement of African American students in math.

2. Program of Study: *Require each student to complete an upgraded academic core and a concentration that leads to preparation for postsecondary studies and/or a career. This upgraded academic core includes four credits of college-*

preparatory English, four math credits, three science credits, three social studies credits, and a career or academic concentration.

Selected research that supports this key practice:

- McPartland and Schneider reported in 1996 that research supported the idea that students will learn more if they are offered a more demanding curriculum. They also analyzed the benefits of school reform approaches that could potentially offset higher rates of student failure with an academically strenuous curriculum.
- A study conducted of Missouri high school guidance programs (Lapan, Gysbers, and Sun, 1997) found that schools with more fully implemented guidance programs had students who reported higher grades, their school was better preparing them for their future, their school provided more college and career information, and their school had a more positive climate.
- Based on the review of the literature on Programs of Study (POS) combined with the observations concerning POS, there was cautious optimism about their positive impact (Lewis and Kosine, 2008).
- POS has the potential to enhance the effectiveness of Career Technical Education by aligning technical instruction with rigorous academic standards (Lewis and Kosine, 2008).

3. Academic Studies: *Teach more students the essential concepts of the college-preparatory curriculum by encouraging them to apply academic content and skills to real-world problems and projects. Align core academic areas to essential state and national standards that prepare youth for postsecondary studies and careers. Align student assignments, student work, and classroom assessments to at least the proficient-level standards as measured by a NAEP-like exam and state assessments. Embed reading and writing tasks into all courses and raise the awareness through Science, Technology, Engineering, Mathematics (STEM) initiatives that all teachers have the responsibility to show the broader aspect of math application beyond the math classroom.*

Selected research that supports this key practice:

- Two British secondary schools—one that used open-ended projects and one that used more traditional, direct instruction—found vast differences in mathematics understanding and standardized math achievement data. The study, conducted by Jo Boaler (1997), found that students at the project-based school did better than those at the more traditional school on math problems including analytical or conceptual thought and on those considered rote. In addition, three times as many students at the project-based school received the top grade achievable on the national examination in math.

- In a five-year study (Penuel et al., 2001), researchers at SRI International found that technology-using students in Challenge 2000 Multimedia Project classrooms outperformed non-technology-using students in communication skills, teamwork, and problem solving. Researchers found increased student engagement, greater responsibility for learning, increased peer collaboration skills, and greater achievement gains by students who had been labeled low achievers.
- Darling-Hammond and Friedlander (2008) studied five nonselective urban CA high schools that supported the success of low-income students of color where there had been positive student outcomes. Personalization (small learning environments, advisory systems, family connections) was key in these schools. Educators taught skills via the coursework that were relevant through the application of real world problems.

4. Career/Technical Studies: *Provide more students access to intellectually challenging career/technical studies in high-demand fields that incorporate reading and math and emphasize the higher-level academic and problem-skills needed in the workplace and in further education. Develop standards, conditions, and agreements for awarding postsecondary credit to high-demand career/technical fields to high school students. Require senior projects with academic, technical, and performance standards. Provide students opportunities to work toward a recognized employer certification. Develop a new, rigorous curriculum for the training of career tech teachers.*

Selected research that supports this key practice:

- There was a connection between rigorous high school coursework and success in post-secondary education (Adelman, 1999).
- Dual enrollment for career tech students was an approach for increasing academic rigor (Bailey, Hughes, and Karp, 2003).
- Luna and Fowler (2011) studied the College Plus program in Arizona, a dual enrollment program for at-risk students. Its purpose was to assist at-risk students in successfully graduat-

ing from high school and making a smooth transition to college by taking dual enrollment courses. College Plus students were compared to nonparticipating students and there were significant differences for College Plus students with regard to student retention, graduation, and college enrollment.

5. Work-based learning: *Enable students and their parents to choose from programs that integrate challenging high school studies and work-based learning and are planned by educators, employers and students.*
Selected research that supports this key practice:
- Students who participated in work-based learning showed an increase in completion of related coursework as well as an increase in attendance and graduation rates (Colley and Jamison, 1998).
- Research demonstrated that work-based learning was one of the best ways to improve outcomes for high school youth with disabilities (Hughes, Moore, and Bailey, 1999).
- Work-based learning during secondary school led to higher rates of adult employment success for all types of disability (Luecking and Fabian, 2000).
- Research showed that work-based learning helped with the clarification of secondary student career goals. The premise of work-based learning was that academic learning was more accessible and increased student engagement. There were higher attendance, higher completion of academic courses and higher graduation rates and college enrollment for students who participated in work-based learning than those who did not (Bragg, 2001).
- In studies and evaluations of work-based learning there was a positive association between secondary student participation in work-based learning and educational outcomes (attendance, course taking, and graduation) at the secondary level (Wonacott, 2002).
- Research indicated student attitudes about work-based learning were overall positive (Wonacott, 2002).

6. Teachers Working Together: *Provide teams of teachers the time and support to work together to help students succeed in challenging academic and career/technical studies. Encourage academic and career/technical teachers in*

engaging students regularly in reading books and articles, writing, making presentations, and using high-level reasoning and thinking skills. Support mathematics, science, and career/technical teachers working together to better align and integrate mathematics concepts and skills into assignments in science and career/technical classrooms. Support theme-based career academies and schools within school models.

Selected research that supports this key practice:

- Richard DuFour created the Professional Learning Communities that encouraged teachers to work together to utilize collective inquiry and create collaborative teams that focused on results and a commitment to continuous improvement (DuFour and Eaker, 1998).
- In 2006, RAND researcher Cassandra Guarino and associates analyzed federal Schools and Staffing Surveys. The research team discovered lower turnover rates among beginning teachers in schools with induction and mentoring programs that emphasized collegial support.
- Goddard, Goddard, and Tschannen-Moran (2007) found in schools with high levels of teacher collaboration (professional development, curriculum, instruction) student achievement outcomes were higher.
- Researcher Ken Futernick (2007) surveyed 2,000 current and former teachers in California and concluded that teachers felt greater satisfaction when they believed in their own efficacy, were involved in decision making, and had strong collegial relationships.
- School leaders who supported collaboration among teachers could improve teacher retention and teacher satisfaction, according to studies conducted by Susan Kardos and Susan Moore Johnson (2007). They found that new teachers seem more likely to stay in schools that had an integrated professional culture in which new teachers' needs were recognized and all teachers shared responsibility for student success.
- In the Darling-Hammond and Friedlander study (2008) where five California high schools for at-risk students were examined, teacher collaboration was intentional. The teams examined student progress, developed a more coherent curriculum, and teachers learned from one another.

7. **Students Actively Engaged:** *Engage students in academic and career/technical classrooms in rigorous and challenging proficient-level assignments, using research-based instructional strategies and technology. Students are engaged instructionally, socially, emotionally, and behaviorally.*
   Selected research that supports this key practice:
   - Benjamin Bloom found in 1980 that if two students were in the same classroom and one was actively engaged in the learning for 90 percent of the classroom hour while the other student was actively engaged for only 30 percent of the hour, there were quantitative as well as qualitative differences in the learning.
   - Student engagement appeared to be linked to various school reform initiatives and particular subject matters (Marks, 2000).
   - The National Research Council (NRC) concluded that high-need students strive to succeed when learning involves solving authentic problems, includes rigorous and challenging instruction with frequent assessment and feedback and draws upon peer collaboration (NRC, 2003).
   - McCombs and Miller's (2009) research on student motivation has been extensive. In several stages of her research, conducted with over 2,100 children and their 124 teachers in several states, specific instructional practices in three domains were found to be related to important motivational outcomes.

8. **Guidance:** *Involve students and their parents in a guidance and advisement system that develops positive relationships and ensures completion of an accelerated program of study with an academic or career/technical content. Involve parents in annual meetings with students and their mentors to review program and develop plans for the next year. Implement an advisor/advisee program for students.*
   Selected research that supports this practice:
   - Counselors who actively supported middle school students and their families in middle school in preparation for college enrollment (as opposed to sharing information) increased the chances of students enrolling in four-year colleges (McDonough, 1997; Plank and Jordan, 2001).
   - Lapan, Gysbers, and Petroski found in 2001 that in Missouri middle schools with comprehensive guidance programs students were more likely to report that they felt safer attending

their schools, having better relationships with teachers, their education was relevant and important to their futures, earning higher grades, and having fewer problems in school as opposed to students in middle schools without comprehensive programs.
- Improved school counseling has had a significant impact on college access for low-income rural and urban students and students of color (U.S. Department of Education, 2001; McDonough, 2004).

9. Extra Help: *Provide a structured system of extra help to assist students in completing accelerated programs of study with high-level academic and technical content. Support all students to become independent learners by building into their learning experiences opportunities to practice habits of successful learners such as study and literacy skills, time management and learning with others. Give students easy access to opportunities to meet course standards and graduate with peers. Support teachers in forming nurturing academic relationships with students aimed at improving students' work and achievement. Plan catch-up learning experiences for entering ninth-graders who are not prepared to succeed in college-preparatory courses. Work with postsecondary institutions to identify 11th graders not ready for postsecondary study and develop special courses for the senior year to prepare more students.*

Selected research that supports this key practice:
- Extra help for students supported the culture of high standards and the shared belief of school faculty that it was their primary responsibility to see that every student met standards (Smith and Shepard, 1989; Oakes, 1989).
- The need for extra help is found more extensively in high poverty high schools. There is a continuum of extra help for high school students from basic and intensive assistance (Balfanz, McPartland, and Shaw, 2002).
- Early identification and intervention programs (whole school reforms, attendance, behavioral and extra-help interventions) for at-risk middle school students discouraged student disengagement and increased graduation rates (Balfanz, Hertzog, and MacIver, 2007).

10. Culture of continuous improvement: *Use data to continuously improve school culture, organization, management, curriculum, and instruction to*

advance student learning. Create teacher focus teams or professional learning teams. Develop a strategic vision and plan for a school that includes a leadership team that makes the plan operational. Allow principals to make key school decisions.

Selected research that supports this practice:

- Lee, Smith, and Croninger (1995), in a report of extensive school restructuring, found professional learning communities to be critical in allowing staff to work together to change their pedagogy resulting in higher learning tasks and greater academic gains.
- The six steps for continuous school improvement included targeting and clarifying core beliefs, creating a shared vision of what those beliefs looked like in practice, gathering accurate data and using it in the analysis, identifying innovations to close gaps, developing and implementing an action plan, and including collaborative autonomy (Kline, Kuklis, and Zmuda, 2004).

HSTW's Key Conditions for Accelerating Student Achievement

The SREB *HSTW* Key Conditions assist state and district leaders, school administrators and teachers in working together to align resources, initiatives, and accountability efforts to support high schools in implementing a comprehensive school improvement design. The Conditions include:

- An organizational structure and process for ensuring that school administrators and teachers are continually involved in planning strategies to achieve the key practices.
- Each school needs a clear mission statement to prepare high school students for success in postsecondary education and the workplace.
- Leadership from the district and the school to improve curricula, instruction, and student achievement.
- Each school site should have a leadership team consisting of the principal, the assistant principal, and teacher leaders who support, encourage, and actively participate with the faculty in implementing the key practices.
- A district superintendent and school board members who support school administrators and teachers in carrying out key practices.

- A school superintendent and school board that will allow the high school to adopt a flexible schedule that enables students to earn more credits. The block schedule that *HSTW* recommends for challenged schools makes it possible for students to earn three credits in four years.

Vignette of a Successful *HSTW* School

To understand the *HSTW* process of school improvement, it is helpful to read about a school that has participated in the *HSTW* model with successful results. Warren Easton Charter School, a legendary high school in New Orleans, Louisiana, has weathered changes of many types, including Hurricane Katrina in 2005. As it implements the *HSTW* improvement model, Warren Easton is now receiving attention for the academic success of its 100 percent minority student body.

Opened in 1845, Warren Easton was the first public high school for boys in Louisiana. It is now a coed charter school enrolling approximately 850 students from throughout Orleans Parish Schools. The student population is more than 96 percent black, 3 percent Hispanic, and less than 1 percent Asian. Students come primarily from working-class families. The school was closed during the 2005–2006 school year after Hurricane Katrina caused families to evacuate the city. It reopened for the 2006–2007 school year as a charter school with a board, operating through the Warren Easton Charter Foundation.

Warren Easton's school improvement efforts have paid off in higher achievement scores, an attendance rate of more than 96 percent, a graduation rate of 98 percent, and a dropout rate of less than 1 percent in 2010. (Graduation rates reported here reflect the percentage of enrolling seniors who earn a regular diploma at the end of the school year.) The school has enjoyed continuous improvement for the past three years. It received a baseline School Performance Score from the state of 76.6 percent in 2007–2008, climbing to 91 percent in 2008–2009, and improving to 92.6 percent in 2009–2010. The 2010 score incorporated 2010 test scores plus 2009 attendance and dropout figures.

In its new role as a charter school, Warren Easton has stepped up its efforts to raise student achievement. "We were already implementing some of the *HSTW* Key Practices before the hurricane," said Principal Alexina Medley. When the school reopened after Katrina, it began a concerted effort to implement the *HSTW* design, embracing the Key Practices and receiving coaching from an *HSTW* school improvement consultant. The school received a Site Development Workshop in August 2008 and Technical Assistance Visit in October 2008.

A definite strength for the school was the fact that key school leaders, two administrator assistants and *HSTW* school improvement coordinator—all dedicated to the *HSTW* Goals, Conditions, and Key Practices—remained with the school after Hurricane Katrina. Supporting the school's reform, district curriculum content specialists chart the school's progress and provide assistance in carrying out the model.

Every student expecting to receive a diploma from Warren Easton Charter School must complete a challenging academic core of four English/language arts, four mathematics, four science and four social studies courses. Medley says, "We tell our students, 'If you want to graduate from Warren Easton, this is what you will need to do.'"

TABLE 1. Students Completing the *HSTW*-Recommended Curriculum and Meeting the Readiness Goals: Warren Easton and Other All-Minority Schools in Louisiana

	Warren Easton	All-Minority Schools
Four College Prep English Courses	96%	40%
Four College Prep Math Courses	89	66
Three Science Courses	100	67

Source: 2010 *HSTW* Assessment

The 2010 *HSTW* Assessment showed that Warren Easton students reported completing the *HSTW*-recommended academic curriculum to a much higher degree than students from the eight other all-minority *HSTW* sites in Louisiana (Table 1). High percentages of Warren Easton students see the importance of high school studies to their future aspirations. Every student participating in the 2010 *HSTW* Assessment said it is very important to graduate from high school, 94 percent said it is very important to attend all their classes, and 93 percent said it is very important to continue their education beyond school.

To help students meet higher standards, Warren Easton has established an extra-help program that includes credit recovery, seat-time recovery, academic catch-up led by an assistant principal on Saturdays, and tutoring before and after school and on Saturdays. Two interventionists—one for math and science and the other for English/language arts and social studies—monitor students' progress in the program and help with remediation in the classroom. Students are monitored for absences, tardiness and disciplinary occurrences. "We believe a student should be out of school only if there is no other choice," Medley said. "We want to help every student remain in school."

Teachers are organized into small learning communities for curriculum and instruction, classroom management, and technology. The school is moving in the direction of teacher peer observation of rigor and student engagement in the classroom. Teachers are encouraged to blend academic and real-life content in their classes. The school reading coach supports teachers with strategies to improve reading and writing in the content areas and ways to implement the school plan of literacy across the curriculum. Teachers are also working to improve numeracy across the curriculum.

When asked how other schools might improve performance and keep more students in school until graduation, Medley said, "Find ways for teachers to work together in the best configuration for your school. That is paramount in getting them to work together.... Our goal is excellence, and our striving to reach this goal must be a cooperative effort."

Evaluation Findings for *HSTW*

The following *HSTW* research studies are presented in chronological order. They were chosen because they represent a cross-section of *HSTW* studies. Some of the studies were externally driven and others were initiated internally. *High Schools That Work* schools assess their 12th grade students in science, mathematics, and reading, using National Assessment of Educational Progress (NAEP) proficiency standards. The schools are also asked to collect data on student course-taking patterns, student behaviors, and attitudes, and teacher attitudes and characteristics. There is follow-up with graduates one year later to find out how well their high school experiences prepared them for postsecondary education and work. The assessments and student assessment data are used to prepare an annual site progress report for each school to measure accomplishments and note ongoing challenges.

- In 1999, American Institutes for Research (AIR) stated that *HSTW* was a national school reform effort that helped raise student achievement. AIR also designated *HSTW* as strong in providing professional development and technical assistance to schools.
- In the late 1990s, with funds from the United States Department of Education/Office of Adult and Vocational Education, SREB was able to assist 25 urban New American High Schools in implementing the *HSTW* design over a 12-month period. When these schools were compared with other schools that had not received such assistance in 2000, *HSTW* schools showed greater gains in reading, mathematics,

and science achievement than the comparison schools (Kaufman, Bradby, and Teitelbaum, 2002).
- *High Schools That Work* Follow-up Study of 2004 Graduates: Transitioning to College and Careers from an *HSTW* High School. This survey focused on what students had accomplished over the past 12 months and helped determine how well high schools were preparing students for college or careers. There were 6,535 students from 423 high schools that returned completed surveys. Sixty-six percent of graduates were currently enrolled in college; 59% were currently employed; and 3% were currently in the military. Of the students currently enrolled in college, 25% were enrolled in remedial courses. If students had taken a rigorous course of high school study, they were not in remedial classes. When asked what their high schools should do differently, graduates replied that mathematics should have been emphasized more and there should have been more course counseling for students.
- CSRQ (Comprehensive School Reform Quality) Center of the American Institutes for Research (2006) scored *HSTW's* highest rating on materials and training for school improvement. The report summarized that:

1. *HSTW* was developed on a solid foundation that linked the model's design to a research base for the model's core components;
2. There was moderately strong evidence that there were services and support to implement the model; and
3. There were formal processes for understanding the workings of the model, setting aside school resources such as materials and time, and using benchmarks for implementation.

The Center did not, however, rate *HSTW* in 2006 on positive effects in student achievement. None of the 48 studies used the research methodology preferred by the Institute of Education Science, namely an experimental or quasi-experimental design. (Such a design would involve at least 20 *HSTW* high schools and 20 control schools and the cost would be beyond the resources of SREB.)

- This study focused on *HSTW* as a model to advance reform efforts. Case studies of five reform models were developed by the Consortium for Policy Research in Education (CPRE) of the University of

Pennsylvania in 2006. For the *HSTW* model, three high schools were studied for a total of three years. Researchers concluded that *HSTW* impacted changes in school structure and organization. They said, *HSTW* is "ultimately about empowering teachers to full responsibility for the success of all students and giving them access to the resources they need to do so." The researchers found that implementation of *HSTW* could be adapted; district leaders stated that the Technical Assistance Reports were of great value. The report concluded that "for teachers and administrators who come to a general consensus about a vision for change for their schools and are willing to invest time and effort to realize that vision, *HSTW* offers a participatory structure and wealth of professional expertise that can significantly advance reform efforts. Under the right conditions, the *HSTW* design can empower teachers; develop a deep commitment to reform; and support instructional improvements, collaboration and teacher-student relationships."

- Educational Testing Service (Young and Cline, 2009) studied the *HSTW* indices created to measure the implementation of *HSTW* Key Practices. It found the indices predictive of achievement scores on the *HSTW* assessments in reading, mathematics, and science. The single most critical predictor was the degree of student completion on the *HSTW*-recommended curricula. Students who completed the recommended curricula had significantly higher scores on all three sections of the 2006 *HSTW* Assessment than those who did not.

- In 2009, 49 high schools in Arkansas participated in *HSTW*. To determine the level of implementation success at these schools, the *HSTW* assessment results (mathematics, reading, and science) and the implementation of *HSTW*'s Key Practices that aid in students' learning were gleaned from student and teacher surveys and analyzed. Schools that were high implementers had students who had higher state achievement results and state report card results than schools that were designated as medium and low implementers.

Conclusion

HSTW is a school reform approach that originally was implemented in the Southeast as a program to strengthen the academic and career preparation of high school students enrolled in the general and vocational track and has evolved over the past 25 years into a model that includes continual learning of all students in preparation for a career or college. Critical to the *HSTW* reform process are the *Ten Key Practices*, the *Key Conditions for Accelerating Student Achievement*, and supporting tools and publications such as *Using the* HSTW *Assessment to Improve Student Achievement and Readiness for College and Careers: A Guide and Workbook for* HSTW *Sites* and *Establishing Benchmarks for New and Maturing* HSTW *sites*.

Resources

The following are a sample of SREB professional development opportunities associated with *HSTW*.

(a) SREB National Webinar Series for *High Schools That Work and Making Middle Grades Work*—October to April. SREB offers several National Webinars focused on the critical literacy and mathematics skills students need to get ready for high school and transition successfully to postsecondary studies and careers. Webinars in 2012 will address the new Common Core State Standards (CCSS) and their impact on current school and instructional practices.

(b) SREB Annual National *High Schools That Work* Summer Conference. SREB's annual *High Schools That Work* Staff Development Conference supplies state, district, school, and teacher leaders with new strategies for designing schools that provide more students with relevant, meaningful educational experiences, so more students graduate and they graduate prepared for college and careers in the 21st-century economy.

The following are examples of SREB publications associated with *HSTW*.

(a) SREB. (2002). HSTW *technical assistance guide for team members: Improving the reading, mathematics and science competencies of career/technical students*. Atlanta, GA: Author.

This guide explains what is expected of technical assistance team members and how these visits help schools make significant strides in raising expectations for student performance, revising what and how students are taught, changing how schools relate to students and how students relate to one another, and using data to drive continuous school improvement.

(b) Bottoms, G. (2001). *What school principals need to know about curriculum and instruction.* Atlanta, GA: SREB.

Increasingly, schools and school leaders are being held accountable for the achievement of all students, not just the best students as in the past. This publication provides guidelines for school leaders to understand and prepare for their changing role.

(c) Bottoms, G., & Phillips, I. (2010). *Skills for a lifetime: Teaching students the habits of success.* Atlanta, GA: SREB.

Based on more than two decades of SREB research and experience, this book outlines the specific tools for building the major characteristics—or habits of success—that all students need in high school, postsecondary studies, advanced training and careers. With creative teacher tools, lesson ideas and guidance from educators with proven success in this effort, the book offers schools and districts a comprehensive framework for helping more students become independent, successful learners.

(d) SREB. (2003). *Literacy across the curriculum: Setting and implementing goals for grades six through 12.* Atlanta, GA: Author.

This volume is essential for state, district and school leaders who plan to implement school-wide literacy programs. It provides concrete, research-based steps not only to raise reading and writing achievement but also to help students learn more in every class by using literacy skills.

Appendices

Although SREB's Leadership professional development modules that support *HSTW* school activities and the rigorous Career Tech Education professional development modules are good examples of tools principals can use, two *High Schools That Work* tools and publications were selected to be highlighted in this chapter. They provide planning tools (a workbook and a framework) to track continuous school improvement and student achievement based on the outcomes of *High Schools That Work* assessments and surveys. These assessments are based on the *HSTW* Key Practices. Principals can use these tools with leadership teams to set student achievement goals and benchmark appropriate instructional practices and support for students.

Appendix A. Using the HSTW *Assessment to Improve Student Achievement and Readiness for College and Careers: A Guide and Workbook for* HSTW *Sites*

This guide and accompanying workbook explain the *High Schools That Work* Assessment and enable schools to see where they stand in their efforts to achieve continuous school improvement. The guide provides detailed information about the assessment and the data report schools receive. The workbook allows schools to document their progress by responding to a series of questions, which are largely derived from the student and teacher survey sections of the *HSTW* assessment.

Workbook Excerpt

Schools can use this workbook to explore their *HSTW* Assessment Reports and use the data to guide their actions to improve student achievement. Complete this document as a school team and discuss actions that your school can take to increase student achievement. As the leadership team members read the questions, they should keep in mind the indices related to instructional effectiveness and student achievement that are connected to the Key Practices.

These indices include: emphasis on high expectations, emphasis on literacy across the curriculum, emphasis on numeracy across the curriculum, emphasis on challenging and engaging science curriculum and instruction, completion of the *HSTW*-recommended curriculum, emphasis on integrating academic content and skills into career/technical courses, emphasis on career/technical studies, emphasis on providing quality work-based experiences, emphasis on providing timely guidance to students, perceived importance of high school studies, and emphasis on providing quality extra help. How did we do?

1. Who participated in the assessment from your school: a random sample, career tech students, all seniors? How many completed the survey and subject tests?
2. What is your "high-scoring site" school category and what does that represent?
3. For which three categories of indicators did the highest percentages of your students report an intensive emphasis?
4. For which three categories of indicators did the lowest percentages of your students report an intensive emphasis?
5. What are the two or three positive things that stand out?
6. What are the two or three challenges that stand out?
7. For which indicators do the results strike you as surprising? Why?

8. For which indicators are the results what you expected? Why?
9. What value does this data provide?
10. How can we use this information?

Appendix B. *Establishing Benchmarks for New and Maturing* HSTW *Sites*

High Schools That Work expects schools to show continuous progress in implementing proven classroom practices and improving student achievement. Schools can use this document to verify improvement in student achievement and progress toward implementing the HSTW improvement framework.

Setting Interim Benchmarks to Meet the 10-Year Goal Excerpt

To achieve a 10-year goal, schools should establish interim benchmarks on key indicators regarding changes to be made in school and classroom practices. While this document has been laid out as a 10-year plan, schools are encouraged to use a six-year plan. The goals set for 10 years would then become the goals set for six years. After setting goals, schools must also be sure to determine actions school leaders and teachers must take to meet those target goals. To determine interim benchmarks:

- Subtract your school's baseline percentage from the 10-year (or six-year) goal.
- Divide that total by five (or three) to get the change needed each year.
- Determine the goal for your next assessment year by adding one-fifth of the difference between the baseline and the target 10-year goal, or by adding one-third of the difference between the baseline and the target six-year goal.
- Repeat the process for the remaining intermediate years.

The following example uses 2012 as the baseline year with 2022 as the 10-year goal.

High Expectations	Baseline	+2 Years	+4 Years	+6 Years	+8 Years	10-Year Goal
Students say they read 10 or more books (or their equivalent) for language arts courses.	35%	45%	55%	65%	75%	85%

~ Difference between baseline (2010)
   and 10-year goal (2020)   85%-35% 50%
~ Change needed every two years: 50% divided by 5=10%
~ Benchmark for 2014:   35%+10%=45%
~ Benchmark for 2016:   45%+10%=55%
~ Benchmark for 2018:   55%+10%=65%
~ Benchmark for 2020:   65%+10%=75%
~ Benchmark for 2022:   75%+10%=85%

Meeting *HSTW* Readiness Goals

Raise the reading, mathematics, science, communication, problem-solving and technical achievement of more students to meet readiness standards for college and careers.

Indicators—Meeting *HSTW* Readiness Goals	Baseline	+2 years	+4 years	+6 years	+8 years	10-Year goal
The percentage of students meeting the readiness goal.						85%
The percentage of students meeting the mathematics goal.						85%
The percentage of students meeting the science goal.						85%
The percentage of students graduating from high school on time.						90%

References

Adelman, C. (1999). Answers in the toolbox: Academic intensity, attendance patterns, bachelors' degree attainment. Washington, DC: Department of Education, OERI.

American Institutes for Research. (1999). An educators' guide to schoolwide reform. Arlington, VA: Educational Research Service.

Bailey, T., Hughes, K., & Karp, M. (2002). Dual enrollment programs: Easing transitions from high school to college. *CCRC Brief.* Washington, DC: Office of Vocational Education, United States Department of Education.

Balfanz, R., Hertzog, L., & MacIver, D. (2007). Preventing student disengagement and keeping students on the graduation path in urban middle schools-grade schools: Early identification and effective interventions. *Educational Psychologist, 42*(4), 223–235.

Balfanz, R., McPartland, J., & Shaw, A. (2002, April). *Re-conceptualizing extra help for high school students in a high standards era.* Baltimore, MD: Center for Social Organization of Schools, Johns Hopkins University.

Bloom, B. (1980, Summer). The new direction in educational research: Alterable variables. *The Journal of Negro Education, 49*(3), 337–349.

Boaler, J. (1997). Participation, knowledge and beliefs: A community perspective on mathematics learning. *Educational Studies in Mathematics, 40*(3), 259–281.

Bragg, D. (2001). Promising outcomes for tech prep participants in eight local consortia: A summary of initial results. Minneapolis, MN: National Research Center for Career and Technical Education, University of Minnesota.

Colley, D. A., & Jamison, D. (1998). Post-school results for youth with disabilities: Key indicators and policy implications. *Career Development for Exceptional Individuals, 21*(2), 145–160.

Comprehensive School Reform Quality Center. (2006). CSRQ Center report on middle and high school CSR models. Retrieved January 31, 2012, from www.csrq.org/MSHSreport.asp

Cotton, K. (1989, November). *Expectations and student outcomes. School Improvement Research Series.* Portland, OR: NWREL.

Cotton, K. (2003). *Principals and student achievement: What the research says.* Arlington, VA: Association for Supervision and Curriculum Development.

Darling-Hammond, L., & Friedlander, D. (2008, May). Creating excellent and equitable schools. *Educational Leadership, 65*(8), 14–21.

DuFour, R., & Eaker, R. (1998). *Professional learning communities at work: Best practices.* Bloomington, IN: Solution Tree Press.

Edmonds, R. (1979, October). Effective schools for the urban poor. *Educational Leadership, 37*(1), 22–23.

Futernick, K. (2007). *A possible dream: Retaining California teachers so all students learn.* Sacramento: California State University.

U.S. Department of Education, National Center for Education Statistics. (2001). *Paving the way to postsecondary education: K-12 intervention program for underrepresented youth.* Washington, D.C.: Author.

Goddard, Y., Goddard, R., & Tschannen-Moran, M. (2007). A theoretical and empirical investigation of teacher collaboration for school improvement and student achievement in public elementary schools. *Teachers College Record, 109*(4), 877–896.

Guarino, C., Santibanez, L., & Dailey, G. (2006, Summer). Teacher recruitment and retention: A review of recent empirical literature. *Review of Educational Research, 76*(2), 173–208.

Hughes, K., Moore, D., & Bailey, T. (1999, November). *Work-based learning and academic skills.* New York, NY: Institute on Education and the Economy.

Idorenyin, J. & Pitts, V. (2005, July). High expectations: A "how" of achieving equitable mathematics classrooms. *Negro Educational Review, 56*(2–3), 127–134.

Kardos, S., and Johnson, S. M. (2007). On their own and presumed expert: New teachers' experiences with their colleagues. *Teachers College Record, 109*(9), 2083–2106.

Kaufman, P., Bradby, D., & Teitelbaum, P. (2002). *"High Schools That Work" and whole school reform: Raising academic achievement of vocational completers through the reform of school practice.* Berkeley, CA: MPR Associates.

Kline, E., Kuklis, R., & Zmuda, A. (2004). *Transforming schools: Creating a culture of continuous improvement.* Alexandria, VA: ASCD.

Lapan, R., Gysbers, N., & Petroski, G. (2001, Summer). Helping seventh graders be safe and successful: A statewide study of the impact of comprehensive guidance and counseling programs. *Journal of Counseling and Development, 79*(3), 320–330.

Lapan, R., Gysbers, N., & Sun, Y. (1997, March-April). The impact of more fully implemented guidance programs on the school experiences of high school students. *Journal of Counseling and Development, 75*(4), 292–302.

Lee, V. E., Smith, J. B., & Croninger, R. G. (1995). *Understanding high school restructuring effects on the equitable distribution of learning mathematics and science.* Madison, WI: Center on Organization and Restructuring of Schools.

Lewis, M. V., & Kosine, N. R. (with Overman, L.). (2008). *What will be the impact of programs of study? A preliminary assessment based on similar previous initiatives, state plans for implementation, and career development theory.* Louisville, KY: National Research Center for Career and Technical Education, University of Louisville.

Luecking, R., & Fabian, E. S. (2000). Paid internships and employment success for youth in transition. *Career Development for Exceptional Individuals, 23*(2), 205–221.

Luna, G., & Fowler, M. (2011). Evaluation of achieving a college education plus: A credit-based transition program. *Community College Journal of Research and Practice, 35*(9), 673–688.

Marks, H. (2000). Student engagement in instructional activity: Patterns in elementary, middle school and high school years. *American Educational Research Journal, 37*(1), 153–184.

McCombs, B., & Miller, L. (2009). *The school leader's guide to learner centered education: From complexity to simplicity.* Thousand Oaks, CA: Corwin Press.

McDonough, P. (1997). *How social class and school structure opportunity.* Albany, NY: SUNY Press.

McDonough, P. (2004). Counseling matters: Knowledge, assistance, and organizational commitment in college preparation. In William G. Tierney, Zoe B. Corwin & Julia Colyar (Eds.). *Preparing for College: Nine Elements for Effective Outreach* (pp. 69–88). Albany, NY: SUNY Press.

McPartland, J., & Schneider, B. (1996). Opportunities to learn and student diversity: Prospects and pitfalls of a common core curriculum. *Sociology of Education, 69*, 66–81.

National Research Council. (2003). *Engaging schools: Fostering high school students' motivation to learn.* Washington, D.C.: The National Academies Press.

Oakes, J. (1989, June). What educational indicators? The case for assessing the school context

Educational Evaluation and Policy Analysis, 11(2), 188–189.

Penuel, B., Korbak, C., Yarnall, L., & Pacpaco, R. (2001). *Silicon Valley Challenge 2000: Year 5 Multimedia Project report.* Menlo Park, CA: SRI International.

Plank, S., & Jordan, W. (2001). Effects of information, guidance and actions on post-secondary destinations: A study of talent lost. *American Educational Research Journal, 38*(4), 947–979.

Rutter, M., Maughan, B., Mortimer, P., & Ouston, J. (1979). *Fifteen thousand hours: Secondary schools and their effects on children.* London: Open Books.

Smith, M. L., & Shepard, L. (Eds.). (1989). *Flunking grades: Research and policies on retention.* New York: Falmer Press.

SREB. (2002). *HSTW technical assistance guide for team members: Improving the reading, mathematics and science competencies of career/technical students.* Atlanta, GA: Author.

SREB. (2003). *Literacy across the curriculum: Setting and implementing goals for grades six through 12.* Atlanta, GA: Author.

The SREB Commission for Educational Quality. (1985). *Ten recommendations for improving secondary vocational education.* Atlanta, GA: SREB.

Wonacott, M. (2002). The impact of work-based learning on students. ERIC Clearinghouse on Adult, Careers, and Vocational Education—ERIC Digest. Columbus, OH: ERIC.

Young, J., & Cline, F. (2009). *A concurrent validity study of the 2008 HSTW assessment scores.* Princeton, NJ: Educational Testing Service.

Young, J. W., Cline, F., & Educational Testing Service. (2009). *A concurrent validity study of the 2008 "HSTW" assessment scores.* Princeton, NJ: Educational Testing Service.

Index

Adams, J.E., 19
Adelman, C., 216
Allaire, Y., 76, 78, 80
Allen, T.D., 174
Allensworth, E., 51
American Association of School Administrators, 147
American Institutes for Research, 149
Anderson, S., 1, 2, 13, 47, 169, 201
Arcaira, E., 201
Argyris, C., 75
Association for Supervision and Curriculum Development, 128

Bailey, T., 216, 217
Baker, G.A., 21
Balfanz, R., 220
Barnett, B., 56, 60, 63
Barnett, K., 2
Barth, R., 47, 49, 53, 54, 55, 71
Begley, P., 50
Bell, L., 47, 50
Bernhardt, V., 139

Berry, J., 148
Betts, J.R., 17
Beyer, J.M., 75
Bickman, L., 71
Blasé, J., 51
Bliss, J.R., 76
Bloom, B., 219
Bloom, G., 205
Boaler, Jo, 216
Bolam, R., 47
Bolman, L., 78
Bosker, R., 47, 71, 72
Bossert, S., 1, 47, 49, 51, 52, 71, 72, 76
Bottoms, G., 228
Bouchner, J.E., 21
Bowers, A., 51
Bowring-Carr, C., 47
Boy, N.H.O., 21
Boyer, E.L., 21
Bragg, D., 217
Bridges, E., 47, 48, 49, 51, 62
Brookover, W.B., 17
Brown, T., 76

INDEX

Browne-Ferrigno, T., 56
Bryk, A., 18, 19, 51, 62
Burns, J.M., 19
Burt, W., 107
Butty, J., 21

Camburn, E., 18
Carriere, R.A., 18
Carson, B., 3
Castagna, C.L., 205
Castellano, M., 51
Celio, M.B., 107
Chan, Y.C., 50
Characteristics of Successful Schools, 142
Cheng, Y.C., 50
Cizek. G.J., 37
Cline, F., 226
Codding, J., 127
Cohen, E., 51
Collaboration, Leadership, & Accountability for Student Success Assessment, 141
Colley, D.A., 217
Conley, D.T., 19, 20
Connors, R., 2
Cooley, V.E., 139, 146
Copland, M., 51, 138, 139, 149
Cotton, K., 128, 214
Cousins, B., 50
Crandal, D.W., 21
Cravens, X., 3, 13, 14, 56, 59
Creemers, B.P.M., 72
Croft, J., 140
Croninger, R.G., 18, 78, 221
Cuban, L., 49, 54, 55, 62
Cubillo, L., 47

Daly, A.J., 138
Darling-Hammond, L., 216, 218
Data-informed decision making, 6—9, 107–8, 129
  confirmatory factor analysis, 123
  discrimination analysis, 124
  guidebook for school improvement, 137–38, 145–66
  higher-order factor structure, 124
  literature review of, 108–112
  methodology of researching, 115–17
  reliability analysis, 125–26
  rise of, 138–39
  role of, 139–40
  scale analysis, 124–25
Datnow, A., 51, 147
Davies, B., 47
Davis, K., 71
Day, C., 47, 50
Deal, T.E., 49, 54, 55, 78
Desimone, L.M., 33
Donaldson, G.A., 53
Downing, S., 24
Driscoll, M.E., 18
DuBois, D., 174
Duck, G.A., 18
DuFour, Richard, 218
Duke, K., 47, 59
Dunn, A., 59
Dwyer, D., 1, 47, 49, 56

Eaker, R., 218
Earl, L., 139
Easton, J., 51
Eberts, R.W., 50
Eby, L.T., 174
Edmonds, R., 21, 49, 214
Effective Principal, Effective School, 48, 51
Ehrich, L., 56
Eisman, J., 21
Elliott, S.N., 3, 13, 14, 25, 56, 59
Ellison, L., 47
Elmore, R.F., 19, 127
Erickson, D., 49
Eubanks, E.E., 21
Evans, S.C., 174

Fabian, E.S., 217
Far West Lab, 56
Feldman, J.A., 82
Firestone, W.A., 76
Firsirotu, M., 76, 78, 80

Flessa, J., 53
Fowler, M., 216
Frederiksen, J.R., 21
Friedlander, D., 216, 218
Fullan, M., 20, 87
Fuller, B., 83
Furnham, A., 29
Futernick, Ken, 218

Garibaldi, A.M., 21
Gauthier, W., 50
Germinario, V., 18, 21
Goddard, R., 218
Goddard, Y., 218
Goldman, P., 19
Goldring, E., 3, 13, 14, 17, 20, 21, 25, 56, 59, 60, 63
Gomez, M.O., 73, 77, 79, 81, 83, 84, 87
Grobman, H., 48
Grogger, J., 17
Gronn, P., 89
Gross, N., 47
Grubb, W.N., 53
Guarino, Cassandra, 218
Gysbers, N., 215, 219

Haladyna, T.M., 24
Hall, G., 71
Hallinger, P., 2, 17, 47, 49, 52, 53, 56, 57, 58, 72, 76, 80, 83, 84
   assessment practices, 71
   democratic leadership, 78
   educational leadership, 169
   enhancing student achievement, 1, 13
   instructional leadership, 21, 48, 63
   role groups, 59
   school improvement, 51
   student learning, 73
   VAL-ED, 15
Handbook on Restructuring and Substantial School Improvement, 141
Hannum, J.W., 75, 82
Hansford, B., 56
Hansot, E., 48

Harris, A., 47
Harvey, J., 107
Hausman, C., 20, 21
Heck, R.H., 2, 17, 47, 50, 53, 72, 73, 75, 76, 79, 82, 83, 84, 87, 89, 90
   administration, 80
   democratic leadership, 78
   educational leadership, 169
   enhancing student achievement, 1, 81
   learning-centered leadership, 21
   organizational cultures, 77
   school improvement, 51
   student learning, 74
   teacher attitudes, 88
   VAL-ED, 15
Henderson, A.T., 19
Herrington, C., 51, 62
Herriot, R., 47, 48
Hertzog., L., 220
high-impact strategies, 107–8, 116–17, 129
High Schools That Work (HSTW), 10, 211, 222–24, 226–27
   accelerating student performance, 221–22
   context of, 212
   development process, 212–13
   evaluation findings for, 224–26
   resources for, 227–28
   school improvement model, 213
   ten key practices of, 214–21
   tools of, 211
Hofstede, G., 73, 75, 78, 79, 81, 82, 83
Holt, C.R., 76
Hong, S., 115
Honig, M., 51
Hopkins, D., 47
Hord, S., 71
Horng, E.L., 55
Howe, W., 50, 59
Hoy, W.K., 67, 76, 81, 82
Hughes, K., 216, 217
Hunter Foundation, 50

Idorenyin, J., 214
Ingersoll, R., 78, 81

instructional leadership, 47–51, 62–63, 171–73
  assessing the practice of, 55–57
  barriers to, 53–55
  conceptual framework of, 51–53
  using data to strengthen, 59–62

Jamison, D., 217
Jantzi, D., 20, 47, 72, 87
Johnson, Susan Moore, 218
Jones, P., 50
Jordan, W., 219

Kardos, Susan, 218
Karp, M., 216
Katz, S., 139
Kim, Y.M., 50
Kingston, S., 1
Kirby, B., 148
Kirby, P., 20
Kirst, M.W., 19
Kline, E., 221
Knapp, M.S., 17, 21, 51, 138, 139, 149
Kosine, N.R., 215
Krug, F., 50, 59
Krüger, M., 47, 50, 51, 71
Kruse, S., 18
Kuklis, R., 221
Kuperminc, G.P., 83
Kyriakides, L., 72, 89

Lambert, L., 47, 53, 63
Lapan, R., 215, 219
LaPoint, V., 21
Larsen, T.J., 71
Larson, T., 50
Latham, G., 57, 59
Leading for Learning, 142, 145
leadership and organizational processes, 71–73
  conceptual model of, 73–83
  future direction of, 89–90
  integrating results of research, 87–89
  survey instrument of, 90–103

Leadership Issue Groups, 178
Leadership Performance Planning Worksheet (LPPW), 3, 9–10, 169–70
  additional applications of, 192–95
  design and development of, 178–82
  early career principals and, 170–71, 195
  facilitating leadership development, 188–91
  instructional leadership and, 171–73
  mentoring and coaching process, 174–76
  national testing of, 182–88
  network of users, 192–95
  performance of school leaders, 176–77
  purposeful use of, 173–74
  sample pages from, 197–200
  test results, 184–88, 191–92
Learning Point Associates, 42, 147
Lee, G., 1, 47, 50
Lee, M.S., 55
Lee, V.E., 18, 78, 221
Leithwood, K., 2, 17, 20, 47, 49, 50, 51, 52, 72, 76, 78, 85, 87, 89
  educational leadership, 169
  effective pedagogy, 18
  enhancing student achievement, 1, 13, 81, 88
  instructional leadership, 48, 201
  organizational culture, 19
  student performance, 21, 71
  VAL-ED, 15
Leitner, D., 50, 59
Lemus, N., 76
Levine, D.U., 21
Lewis, M.V., 215
Lezotte, L.W., 17
Lieberman, K.A., 83
Lipman, J., 48
Little, J.W., 18
Lloyd, C., 47, 71
Long, C., 56, 60, 63
Loucks, S.F., 21
Louis, K.S., 1, 2, 13, 18, 51, 76, 169, 201
Luecking, R., 217
Lumsden, L., 76

INDEX | 239

Luna, G., 216
Luppescu, S., 51

MacBeath, J., 50
MacCallum, R.C., 115
MacIver, D., 220
MacQueen, A.H., 18
Manasse, A.L., 20
Mapp, K.L., 19
March, J.G., 54, 62
Marcoulides, G., 50, 71, 72, 73, 75, 76, 79, 82, 84, 87, 89, 90
   administration, 80
   organizational cultures, 77
   teacher attitudes, 88
Marks, H., 18, 51, 53, 219
Marshall, K., 54, 55, 62
Marx, G.E., 146
Marzano, R., 1, 2, 7, 13, 20, 21, 112, 115, 122
   framework and instrument development, 116–17, 118–21, 126–27
   leadership, 107
   school curriculum, 18
Mascall, B., 47, 85, 87
Mason, S., 147
Mattis, M.C., 175
Maxwell, L.A., 42
May, H., 51, 71
McCombs, B., 219
McCormick, J., 2
McDonough, P., 219, 220
McNulty, B.A., 1, 13, 107
McPartland, J., 215, 220
Medley, A., 222
Mercer, S., 59
Mesa, R.P., 50
Meyers, C.V., 15
Michigan School Improvement Framework, 8, 140–48
   comparison to other models, 143–45
   definition, 140
   development by research institutes, 142–43
   state education agencies and, 140–42

Miles, M.B., 18, 83
Miller, G., 48
Miller, J., 50
Miller, L., 219
Miller, R., 51
Mintang, L.D., 175
Mitman, A., 49, 50, 51, 52, 53
Moir, E.R., 205
Monpas-Huber, J., 138, 149
Montgomery, D.J., 19, 21, 49
Moore, D., 217
Moore, Q., 59
Moriyama, K., 71, 72, 73, 90
Mortimer, P., 72, 83
Mulford, B., 51
Mullin, P.L., 21
Murphy, J., 3, 13, 14, 15, 17, 18, 22, 25, 47, 49, 51, 52, 56, 57
   evaluation of teachers, 59
   instructional leadership, 21
   professional behavior, 20
   role groups, 59
Murphy, Joseph, 207
Muth, R., 56

National Research Council, 18
Nettles, S., 51, 62
Newmann, F.M., 2, 17, 18
Ng, T., 174
No Child Left Behind, 107, 138, 140
NYC Leadership Academy, 169, 171

Oakes, J., 220
O'Day, K., 50, 59
Ogawa, R., 76
Ogden, E.H., 18, 21
Opdenakker, M., 51, 72, 73
Organization of the School and Teacher Satisfaction with Their Work Environment, 5
   organizational cultures, 75–77
Owens, R.G., 80, 82

Packer, A., 72

Papanastasiou, C., 73
Park, V., 147
Patten, S., 72
patterns of practice, 141
Penuel, B., 216
Pérez-González, J.C., 29
Petersen, J.L., 138
Petrides, K.V., 29
Petroski, G., 219
Phillips, I., 228
Pickett, W., 76
Pitts, V., 214
Plank, S., 219
Plecki, M., 51
Polikoff, M.S., 25
Pomfret, A., 20
Poovatanikul, V., 50
Porter, A., 3, 13, 14, 16, 25, 56
Portin, B., 51
Principal Instructional Management Rating Scale (PIMRS), 4–5, 57–59
  conceptual framework, 52
principals/principalship
  characteristics of, 130
  evaluation of, 1
  importance of, 1
  student achievement and, 1–2
  teacher efficacy and, 2
  tools for improving, 3
Printy, S.M., 48, 51, 53, 63
Proctor, P., 50
Purkey, S.C., 17, 21, 49, 52

Race to the Top (RTTT), 108, 127
Ratchaneeladdajit, R., 50
Reeves, D., 127
Reeves, P., 107
Reynolds, D., 72
Robinson, V., 47, 51, 71
Rodriguez, M.C., 24
Rosenholtz, S.J., 18
Roueche, J.E., 21
Rowan, B, 1, 47, 49
Rowe, K., 47, 71

Rutter, M., 214
Rutter, R.A., 2

Saffold, G.S., 75
Sammons, P., 47
Saxl, E.R., 83
Scheerens, J., 72
Schein, E.H., 73, 75, 76, 78, 81
Schmidt, W., 21
Schmoker, M., 127, 139
Schneider, B., 19, 215
School Administration Manager Process (SAM), 10, 201–3
  history of, 203
  NPIS scale and sustainability, 208
  results of, 206–8
  tools of, 204–6
Seashore, L.K., 169
Sebring, P., 51
Senge, P.M., 127
Shaver, A.V., 19
Shaw, A., 220
Shen, J., 7, 8, 139, 146, 147
Shepard, L., 220
Shoemaker, A., 50
Silins, H., 51
Silva, J., 51, 55, 62
Sinclair, B., 201
Sirinides, P., 71
Sleegers, P., 50
Smith, J.B., 18, 221
Smith, M.L., 220
Smith, M.S., 2, 17, 21, 49, 53
Smith, R.M., 76
Southern Regional Education Board, 211, 212
Southworth, G., 50
Spillane, J.P., 47, 51, 53, 63
Spiro, J., 175
Stack, C., 147
Stager, M., 50
Stalling, J., 10
Stiggins, R., 59
Stone, J.A., 50

INDEX | 241

Strauss, T., 47
Stringfield, S., 20
Stuary, J., 48
Sun, Y., 215
Supovitz, J., 51, 71, 76
Sweetland, S., 76
Swinnerton, J.A., 138, 139, 149

Taraseina, P., 50
Tarter, C.J., 76
Tashakkori, A., 76
Taylor, D.L., 76
Taylor, F.W., 10
Teaching for Learning, 150
Teddlie, C., 20, 72
Tennent, L., 56
Thomas, V., 21
Thompson, D., 21
Thompson, J., 78, 80
Trice, H.M., 75
Tschannen-Moran, M., 75, 218
Tucker, M., 127
Turnbull, B., 201, 203, 207
Tyack, D., 48

Uhls, H., 48

Van Damme, J., 51, 72, 73
Vanderbilt Assessment of Leadership Education (VAL-ED), 3–4, 13–15, 40–42, 206
  assessment, 29–30, 35–38, 39
  core components of, 17–19
  instrument development, 25–26
  ISLLC alignment and, 21–24
  key processes, 19–21
  leadership behavior and, 33–34
  national trial of, 26–28
  pilot testing, 25–26
  principal's report on, 34–35
  professional growth from, 39–40
  reliability, 24–25
  respondents to, 30–32
  short form of, 28–29
  theoretical framework, 15–17
  validity, 24–25, 29
Villani, S., 175
Villanova, R., 50
Volk, J.F., 75

Wahlstrom, K.L., 1, 2, 13, 51, 169, 201
Walker, A., 56, 63
Walker, J., 202
Walls, R.T., 19
Warren, B., 205
Waters, T., 1, 13, 107
Weil, M., 50, 51, 52, 53
Wellisch, J.B., 18
Westat and Policy Studies Associates, 19
Wexley, K., 57, 59
Whale, D., 146
What Works in Schools, 126, 128
White, G., 51
Widaman, K.F., 115
Wiley, S., 51
Wimpelberg, R., 20
Witziers, B., 47, 50, 71
Wohlstetter, P., 147
Wonacott, M., 217
Wongtrakool, P., 50

York-Barr, J., 47
Yoshida, R., 51
Young, J.W., 226

Zhang, S., 115
Zmuda, A., 221